MW00624268

THE WAGNER GROUP

THE WAGNER GROUP

INSIDE RUSSIA'S MERCENARY ARMY

JACK MARGOLIN

REAKTION BOOKS

For K.

Published by Reaktion Books Ltd
Unit 32, Waterside
44–48 Wharf Road
London N1 7UX, UK
www.reaktionbooks.co.uk

First published 2024
Copyright © Jack Margolin 2024

Printed and bound in Great Britain by Bell & Bain, Glasgow

A catalogue record for this book is available from the British Library

ISBN 978 1 78914 957 9

CONTENTS

Introduction *7*

PART ONE: A PREHISTORY OF VIOLENCE

1 Atrocity Exhibition *12*
2 Sous Chef *24*
3 Origins *41*

PART TWO: FREELANCERS

4 Ukraine, 2014–15: The First Campaigns *64*
5 Syria: Blood and Treasure *80*
6 Sudan and the CAR: The Next Frontier *98*
7 Libya: Blueprint for Contemporary War *126*
8 The Sahel: Crisis and Opportunity *139*
9 Pillage *161*

PART THREE: BLOWBACK

10 Cry Havoc *178*
11 The Meat Grinder *198*
12 Mutiny *235*
13 The End and the Beginning *263*

REFERENCES *295*
ACKNOWLEDGEMENTS *318*
INDEX *319*

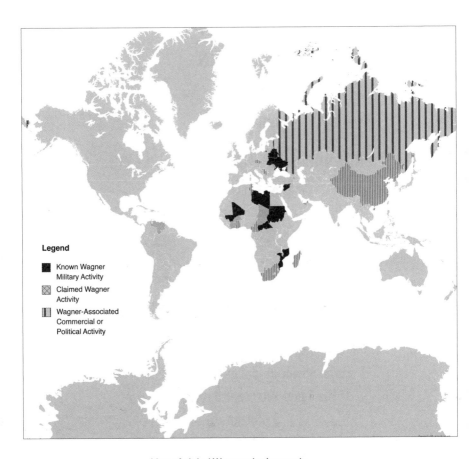

Map of global Wagner deployments.

Introduction

I encountered the Russian mercenaries in Sudan. It was the middle of the day, a scorcher in the dead of summer, and I was in the capital, Khartoum, standing in the Afra Shopping Mall. I was there to buy a local SIM card to dodge international charges. As I sipped ginger-infused coffee to stave off jet lag, the sound of a conversation in Russian echoed across the hall. I looked up. The mercenaries wore fatigues and trainers and joked with one another. Merchants and shoppers watched them curiously, but the uniformed men didn't seem to mind.

It was 2021 and the situation in Sudan was tenuous. I was there with a non-profit assisting the new government in developing corporate transparency after decades of rampant corruption. Two years earlier, street protests had led the military to turn against the dictator who had ruled the country for thirty years. Now, an uneasy alliance of the army, paramilitaries and hopeful civilian reformers ran the country.

No one knew quite what to make of the mercenaries or whose side they were on. They had worked for the old regime, roaming the streets of the capital in armoured cars. Now, they were reportedly training the country's most dreaded paramilitaries, who had been leading players in the genocide in Darfur. They also mined gold just a few hundred kilometres to the north. I had been following them since 2018, poring over their leaked documents and corporate records, and talking to the journalists investigating them. I was keenly aware of their reach. They looked unassuming here in their dirty shoes and worn-out camouflage, but they had thousands of men fighting in the neighbouring Central African Republic and Libya, and a continent away in Syria.

A small cast of their most experienced men ran the operation from Syria to Libya, while a mercurial oligarch held the reins of the finance and vast corporate infrastructure. Both had visited Khartoum in the year prior to my arrival – a respected veteran of the Chechen war known as 'Ratibor' and a bald catering magnate named Evgeniy Prigozhin.

They achieved international notoriety in 2022 as they entered Russia's war in Ukraine, now tens of thousands strong. Ratibor and Prigozhin were both there. Their organization, called the Wagner Group, forced Western governments and militaries to wonder if the age of mercenary warfare had returned. Many conjectured that they were powerful enough to threaten President Vladimir Putin himself.

Two months later, they marched on Moscow. Their convoy met the might of the Russian military, shooting down planes and helicopters over Russian cities. It seemed there was no way back from the brink. Against all odds, Putin and the mercenaries struck a backroom deal. Their agreement – standing down in exchange for amnesty – held for a month until Putin spectacularly reneged, assassinating Prigozhin by downing his private jet.

The story of Wagner, with its myriad twists and turns, seemed finally over. For Prigozhin it was, yet their fighting men, from scrappy prison recruits to their legendary commanders like Ratibor, were still out there. They still have a role to play in the future of Russia, Africa and the changing face of global conflict.

Analysts and journalists have struggled for years with what to call the Wagner Group. It was in name a private military company, or PMC, but in practice it fought on behalf of the Russian state. Was it truly mercenary? Was it a 'private army', as its figurehead, Prigozhin, claimed? A patriotic movement? Wagner was in fact many things at once – a cultural phenomenon, a corporate network, a criminal enterprise and a military contractor. A creation of Russia's security services, Wagner would grow, like so many clandestine creations, to have a mind of its own, defying neat categorization.

To describe Wagner, many writers tried to find historical parallels. The group has drawn comparisons with mercenaries from the past: Japanese *rōnin*, masterless samurai in feudal Japan who frequently found work as bodyguards or warriors for pay, or German Hessians, soldiers hired out to the British Army during the American Revolution. These examples are romantic, but obscure what makes Wagner singular, and, more importantly, what it must tell us about its many contemporary analogues and the modern global market for force.

The world is in many ways a more peaceful place than it was in the golden age of mercenaries when monarchs were expected to send 'freelancers' to fight their battle for coin. Globalized capital and the liberal global order have made interstate war painful and costly. Paradoxically, both factors have created fertile ground for a new age of mercenaries, proxies and novel takes on old modes of conflict. Wagner, in its campaigns in Europe, the Middle East and Africa, has competed and collaborated with other entrepreneurs of violence, from Syrian mercenaries to American contractors, symbols of this flourishing market in guns for hire. Like Wagner, these organizations use secretive global networks of companies to run their businesses, exploiting the international system of trade and finance. They allow their customers and patrons to avoid the political costs of sending young men and women to fight and die. They offer strongmen, warlords and sometimes even nascent democracies the chance to turn the tide against otherwise impossible odds.

This book does not offer a neat compartmentalization of Wagner, nor does it offer a theory of the case connecting Wagner to a grand conspiracy by Putin and his circle to overturn the global order. It is the story of a group of people, some violent and ambitious, others desperate and opportunistic, as they fight for survival and influence. Using their extensive leaked documentation, first-hand accounts and evidence collected over years by journalists and activists, we can piece together a history that reveals to us not only the evolution of the network known as the Wagner Group, but what it means for the future of politics and war – both for Russia and for the world.

PART ONE
A
PREHISTORY
OF
VIOLENCE

1

ATROCITY EXHIBITION

Image is everything!
Dmitriy 'Wagner' Utkin, Wagner Group commander

The Ukrainian soldiers stand with rifles at the ready, peering through a barricaded window. Gunfire chatters in the distance. The room they occupy was once someone's study and the soldiers have piled sandbags onto the desk to give them cover. Children's toys litter the floor and family pictures hang on the wall. In the next room, two Russian mercenaries are stalking them. They plant an explosive charge against the wall.

An artillery shell hits close, the concussion shaking the room. The Ukrainians shudder. Pictures rattle in their frames and an orthodox icon tumbles to the floor. One of them props his rifle against the wall and returns the icon to its shelf. He is young, clean-shaven, caked in dust and dirt. He crosses himself and returns to his post, picking up his radio.

The explosive charge next door detonates, punching a hole through the wall and knocking the Ukrainians off their feet. The Russians fire at them in bursts through the wallpaper. They enter, rifles first, and take positions facing the hallway. One after another, a line of Russian mercenaries enters the apartment. There are more Ukrainian soldiers deeper inside, and they pursue them into the building.

The last of the mercenaries clambers through the room. He notices the same icon, again knocked to the ground, and returns it to the shelf, crossing himself. He moves to the exit, but something catches his leg. One of the two Ukrainians is alive. He tackles the mercenary to the ground and tries to overpower him, but the Russian bashes him with his rifle and pushes him onto his back. They grapple on the floor. The Russian pulls the magazine from his rifle and swings at the Ukrainian's face. He bludgeons him until he releases his grip. The Russian backs away, gasping for air, slotting the magazine back into his weapon. He shoots the collapsed soldier dead.

This scene was written by a Russian mercenary and shot on location in a city that his forces had captured just months earlier. The writer, Aleksey 'Terek' Nagin, had fought among the very buildings where the drama takes place. He was himself killed by Ukrainian forces a month after it was released.

'Terek' was fighting in Ukraine as part of the secretive Wagner Group, a Russian private military company with operations not just in Ukraine, but across Africa and the Middle East. He and his compatriots had shored up the regimes of authoritarian clients in Sudan, Mali, Libya and Syria. Terek was serving in one small corner of a much larger commercial and geopolitical conquest, but his own legend – from the film that he wrote to the memorials in his honour – would outlive him.

More broadly, Terek was part of a mercenary renaissance. Wherever the Wagner Group went, it fought against or alongside other mercenaries, be they Syrians, Libyans, Sudanese or even Americans, Australians and Brits. Wagner was in good company, but it attained greater notoriety than any of its fellow travellers.

Its clandestine nature contributed to this public fascination. Prior to 2022, the leaders of the group denied its very existence. Russia disavowed any reports of Wagner's operations, calling the people involved Russian 'instructors', or even 'tourists'. Evgeniy Prigozhin, a Russian businessman believed to be the man behind Wagner's vast corporate network, vehemently denied any involvement with the group. He even sued foreign media outlets that claimed he was linked to it.

Wagner and its leadership came into the light as Russia invaded Ukraine. Prigozhin, a now-infamous former criminal, restaurateur and catering magnate, went from years of denying an association with Wagner to claiming it was his invention. The group flaunted their symbols on battlefields in Ukraine, bragged about their exploits in Africa and publicly lobbied the Russian government for better treatment. Vladimir Putin thanked them for their efforts to seize Ukrainian cities.

Before 2022, Wagner fighters whose images ended up online were investigated and disciplined by the group's internal security service. Russia, and by extension Wagner, had vivid memories of how 'selfie soldiers', service members posting pictures of themselves in eastern Ukraine in 2014 and 2015, had made a farce of their denials of involvement in the war. Reams of records maintained by Wagner document their internal investigations and the penalties for unauthorized phone calls and social media use that might expose their 'business trips'. But within the last three years, individual fighters have given interviews to state media, the group has proudly displayed its name on the side of its office building in St Petersburg, and Wagner has bought up billboards advertising throughout Russia.

Like many others, I was surprised by each step that the Wagner Group took out of the shadows. It had long seemed that one of the key advantages the group provided to Russia was deniability – whether its members were in Ukraine, Syria or Sudan, or the Central African Republic (CAR), both the Russian government and Prigozhin could always shrug off accusations that they were behind Wagner. They denied Wagner even existed. This was particularly useful as the group left reports of widespread human rights abuses in its wake.

While anyone sensible could see how thin these denials were, the Russian government persisted. Much like Russia's support for pro-Kremlin separatist militants in eastern Ukraine in 2014, the lack of overt state control of Wagner allowed Russia to skirt international responsibility for its activities, to avoid criticism at home over Russian men dying in foreign wars, and to maintain involvement in international negotiations over the very countries ravaged by its mercenaries.

With Russia's invasion of Ukraine, the Wagner Group's and the Russian government's attitude towards the public image of the mercenary army was changing. Wagner had become a powerful global brand, one of the most recognizable military enterprises in the world and a symbol of Russia's international influence.[1] Western media and policy responses contributed to the mythos surrounding Wagner, describing it as a shadowy, powerful arm of the Kremlin, fighting secretly around the world.

Wagner's leadership decided it was time to lean in. They had much to gain – stature in Russia, recruitment opportunities and new business in Africa. Putin's vertical of power (the terminology used to describe Putin's style of absolute governance) rewarded patriotic businesspeople who deployed their financial and corporate resources to serve the state. If they could make Wagner a visible part of the Russian war effort, they stood to gain wealth, influence and security. The Russian state allowed it, even when Prigozhin used Wagner's reputation to lobby publicly and aggressively against the Russian defence establishment. Russia would continue to allow it until Wagner shook the foundations of Putin's political system. And even when Prigozhin was gone, the myth and image of Wagner would live on.

This chapter addresses the 'face' of Wagner: how it presents itself to the world and how its fighters think and talk about themselves. It is an important part of the Wagner phenomenon that is not only a military, commercial and political engine, but a social network and a brand. This facade stretches over all the other aspects of the group's operations, informing its relationships with Russian and foreign elites, as well as competition with Western adversaries.

It is woven into the history of Wagner documented in this book, a recurring theme of the power of their image and central myths that has coloured its fighters' exploits from Ukraine to Mali.

Wagner's directors and the Russian state media ecosystem both saw that Wagner could be used to tell any number of stories. It could represent Russia's cunning and effective repartee to the West. It could represent a humanitarian mission, extending support to the peoples of the developing world, plagued by insurgency and forgotten by the West. Most of all, it could be what Russian propaganda desperately needed: something new.

The 'Orchestra'

All of this publicity was a far cry from the communities I observed forming over the last nine years. They had started from small beginnings, distinguishable from other Russia-backed militants mostly in their obscurity. Their communities grew around core themes of valorization of their service, sacrifice to Russia and consequent grievance at their lack of official recognition. They established language and innuendo that served to differentiate the in-group of fighters and aficionados from out-groups and embraced fascist and esoteric symbolism that connected them to a lineage of warrior cultures. Eventually, they began merchandising these symbols and the Wagner brand for profit.

When Wagner first appeared as a battlefield rumour in Ukraine in 2014, it was discussed by Russian military bloggers as just one of many irregular units fighting the Ukrainians at that time. Other Russian fighters had their own online communities on Russian social networking sites like Vkontakte (VK) and Telegram, where they shared their perspectives on the war and circulated memes and images. These ranged from repeating Russian government propaganda to more craven expressions of white nationalism, Soviet nostalgia and other common ideological tendencies.

Wagner was a subject within this discourse, but not an active participant. The group's own online subcultures did not start to appear until later, as Wagner entered Syria to support dictator Bashar al Assad in his war against a range of rebels, Islamist insurgents and his own people.

In 2017 and 2018, images of Russian fighters in Syria began to appear on Telegram and VK. These were not part of the detachments of the regular Russian military in Syria, but something else. They were referred to jokingly as 'tourists', 'archaeologists' and most prolifically as 'musicians' performing in the 'orchestra'.

'Orchestra' was an in-joke for Wagner itself and a reference to its alleged namesake, a fighter named Dmitry Utkin who had taken his call sign from German composer Richard Wagner. Utkin reportedly adopted this nom de guerre out of his 'affinity for Third Reich imagery', a generous characterization for a man sporting an ss tattoo. He wasn't alone in his tastes: members of the ultra-nationalist paramilitary group Rusich appeared alongside Wagner in Syria, posing for photographs at the ancient city of Palmyra, arms raised in a Nazi *heil*.

Rusich's own symbols, a blend of fascist and neo-pagan imagery, coincided with the esoteric belief system espoused by Utkin and other Wagner commanders. Runes and symbols like the *kolovrat*, the black sun, the *valknut* and an array of Nordic runes appeared as watermarks on images of Wagner fighters in Syria, on the patches they wore and painted on the sides of their vehicles. This was not entirely unique to Wagner. Elite *spetsnaz* detachments of Russia's Federal Security Services, the FSB, also liked to sport runes celebrating a 'might makes right' ethos.[2] But for Wagner it became a core part of the group's identity as both a social network and a social movement.

This duality of in-jokes and fascist imagery grew as a series of anonymous accounts carved out a niche as gathering points for Wagner fighters and admirers alike. They referred to Syria as 'SARatov', a play on the Russian abbreviation for Syrian Arab Republic and a Russian town, or simply as 'Mars', in reference to its desert landscape. They repurposed common memes to make jokes about Wagner in Syria. A slew of 'military correspondents' and bloggers, generally working for pro-Russian outlets, saw the appeal of this growing movement and hitched themselves to it. For their part, Wagner seemed happy to allow this – the propagandists knew enough to refer to Wagner only in winking double entendre.

The group itself was also clearly investing in its culture and identity. In early 2018, images appeared of a monument erected in Syria, depicting a soldier protecting a child. Its inscriptions in Russian and in Arabic read 'For Russian volunteers, martyred to liberate the Russian oil fields from ISIS.' An identical monument appeared in Ukrainian territory occupied by Russia. Both monuments featured Wagner's black-and-red crest.

While these cultural signifiers were being developed and popularized, Wagner was waging war. Most of the details of its operations were not yet known, though grisly rumours circulated. In November 2019, they came to life. A video was uploaded across a variety of social media networks that showed a group of Russian men torturing and killing a Syrian national. This was an extended version of another clip that had appeared online in 2017 showing the same incident. But now there was enough evidence within the video to identify the men involved and to confirm that they were in Syria under Wagner's banner. The victim, a Syrian army deserter named Muhammed Taha Ismail al-Abdallah, is shown being tortured by Wagner fighters with knives, entrenching tools and a sledgehammer. They beheaded him and burned his body. His family later held a funeral in secret.

The episode became a major turning point in Wagner's public image. Internal Wagner files show that the fighters involved were interrogated and polygraphed, but only the man who recorded the incident was punished. The commander who ordered the torture and execution was not disciplined. Most telling of all, the sledgehammer became one of Wagner's most recognizable images. Fighters circulated it in memes; it appeared on T-shirts, hats and patches; and eventually Prigozhin himself would hand out Wagner-engraved sledgehammers to his allies and champions – a symbol of the group's brutality.

Merchandising and Mainstreaming

The growing social network of Wagner fighters was grasping for symbols and language to give meaning to the members' experiences. The Russian state denied the group's existence, yet Wagner fighters had seen many of their compatriots die on distant battlefields. They were looked down on by the Russian military, even as they themselves felt they were more effective and professional. They couldn't even talk about their feats. Now thousands strong, they sought an identity that could give form to what they saw as service and sacrifice.

The Wagner Group had no 'official' branding beyond its black-and-red crest and the seals and logos of the numerous front companies that provided its finance and logistics, and they couldn't sport those in public. The community of current and former fighters and admirers stepped in and provided this branding. There was a ready market for these products, and patches sold by vendors with names like 'Reverse Side of the Medal' and 'Soldier of Fortune' appeared on fighters in Syria, CAR and beyond, oblique references to the presence of Wagner. They invariably featured a grinning skull.

When these same symbols appeared on the uniforms of Wagner's local allies, it was in many ways a return to form. The most recognizable 'symbol' of Wagner, a skull in crosshairs, was in fact lifted from the Syrian 'ISIS Hunters' unit, a small detachment within Syria's 5th Army Corps that was formed with Russian oversight and trained by Wagner. In 2021 the same imagery appeared in the CAR, in garish T-shirts worn by CAR gendarmerie and CAR Armed Forces (FACA) trained by Russian 'instructors', and as patches sported by FACA soldiers on patrol and during parades. Pro-Wagner Telegram gleefully shared these images as signs of Wagner and Russia's influence in the country.

As the merchandisers formed YouTube talk shows and popular social media channels, pro-Wagner music even appeared. Rapper Akim Apachev, a propagandist who reported from the Donbas, published songs celebrating Wagner that became popular on TikTok, usually interspersed with footage of Wagner soldiers in combat and clips from the killing of Ismail. His most popular song mixes Wagner lingo, Russian euphemisms and a celebration of Wagner's spreading footprint:

Summer and crossbows
Wagner will pull up
Somewhere, where the coins jingle
The 'they aren't there' are dancing
I was in the discotheque in Tripoli, 'Ride of the Valkyries'
I danced in Benghazi, in the Donbas, in Palmyra

Wagner as a social movement was becoming more overt and proving itself more attractive to young Russians than the tired language of propagandists. Wagner's culture was more organic than the attempts at pro-Putin youth movements and provided an edginess to Russia's military image. Even as Russian spokespeople denied knowledge of Wagner – they were 'volunteers' or 'instructors' or 'Russians on vacation' – they knew how transparent these denials were. Russian officials' statements were a declaration that even if the world knew that they were behind Wagner, there was nothing anyone could do to stop them.

The Wagner Cinematic Universe

Meanwhile, Prigozhin was working on mythologizing the many projects he had undertaken for the benefit of Russia's foreign influence. In 2019 a 'sociologist' named Maksim Shugalei, who had worked for political-influence organizations linked to Prigozhin, was arrested in Libya along with his interpreter. Shugalei was undertaking a convoluted effort by Prigozhin to establish bridgeheads among powers rivalling the UN-recognized government in Tripoli. A secret meeting with one of the sons of Muammar El-Gaddafi landed Shugalei in hot water with Libyan authorities and eventually in Libya's notorious Mitiga prison.

As part of the campaign by Prigozhin-linked outfits to free Shugalei and his interpreter, a disinformation outfit called the Foundation for the Defence of National Values ran an advertisement in the *Washington Post*. Online networks launched campaigns asserting Shugalei's innocence, and a company named Aurum LLC produced a film dramatizing the events of his imprisonment. The movie, released in 2020, is a swashbuckling adventure through the streets and deserts of Libya. It follows hard-nosed Shugalei as he investigates a web of corruption and terrorism within Libya's government, all orchestrated by the United States. The real Shugalei was eventually freed, paving the way for two sequels.

The production company behind the Shugalei drama, Aurum, was just getting started. Between 2020 and 2022 it produced eight movies, all of them dramatizing the exploits of the Wagner Group or Prigozhin's disinformation operations. Among them were not only Terek's movie, titled *The Best in Hell*, but *Tourist*, about Russian mercenaries in the CAR; *Granit*, about their adventures in Mozambique; *Sunlight*, about the war in Ukraine in 2014; and *16th*, about Russian interference in the 2016 U.S. presidential election.

Many of these movies were tied together by common characters that form a 'Wagner cinematic universe'. These were stand-ins for real-life figures, Wagner commanders who generally stayed out of the public eye. A thuggish-looking bald warrior, referred to as 'Sedmoy' or 'Seventh', is a stand-in for the famous Dmitry Utkin, Wagner's namesake. A character with the call sign 'Sedoy' or 'Grey-Haired' shares that name with the real-life Andrey Troshev, who was awarded the title Hero of Russia for his role in Wagner's capture of Palmyra in 2016. A soldier named 'Pamir' features in many of these films, his name from one of the men who tortured and killed Ismail in Syria. Many of the extras in the background of the films were actual Wagner fighters.

Stranger than Fiction

Apart from the merchandisers, most of the Wagnerites dutifully remained quiet about their experiences. The enterprise maintained a veil of secrecy despite the movies, books by veterans, leaks of their documentation and extensive media reporting of their crimes. Their field commanders kept their silence most effectively avoiding the limelight save for a photo of four of them standing with Putin at a Kremlin reception in 2017. Of these four, Utkin was not seen in public for years. Troshev stayed under the radar except for an embarrassing episode where he was carted off to a Russian hospital with alcohol poisoning, his pockets stuffed with thousands of dollars and maps of Syria. The other Wagner men who had been photographed with Putin had similarly hazy backgrounds and low profiles. Aleksandr Kuznetsov, or 'Ratibor', cropped up in rumours around Africa and was spoken of with reverence in Wagner communities online. Andrey Bogatov, a lantern-jawed veteran who lost an arm in Syria, left little trail beyond his Hero of Russia recognition and a parking ticket.

There was a firm barrier between the 'face' of Wagner – its propaganda, its merchandise and its mythos – and the actual machinery of the enterprise, the web of hundreds of companies, call signs, debt transfers, commercial contracts and command structure that formed its foundation. In 2022 those worlds collided. The Wagner Group's flag began to appear in photographs across Ukraine. Its 'symbol', the grinning skull in crosshairs lifted from ISIS Hunters, appeared on the chest rigs of Russian fighters in Popasna, then in Lysychansk. In the brutal, grinding battle for the town of Bakhmut in eastern Ukraine the many symbols of Wagner were ubiquitous: the signature skull, Nordic runes, white nationalist iconography, violins and its most gruesome calling card, the sledgehammer. In April 2023, it was Wagner that planted its own black flag in the rubble of the Bakhmut administration building alongside the Russian flag, documented in a night-vision video featuring Prigozhin himself.

Wagner as a social network and movement, both organic and vaunted through its propaganda, is only half the story. It can show us how Wagner wants to be seen, how its fighters make sense of their career as 'freelancers' and how this benefits a Russian state looking to drum up support at home and sow fear abroad. But to understand what Wagner is as an enterprise and its links to the Russian state, we need to trace its lineage and its adaptations over time. From there, we can see the full network of networks that comprise the group. It is just one of the many fish in Russia's authoritarian pond, where elites seek to serve the state for fortune and favour, but it is unique in its chosen export: violence.

The following chapters trace Wagner's history. We will chart Wagner from its early days in Ukraine as a small unit of professional fighters to its sprawling, ad hoc corporate infrastructure that it uses to mine diamonds in Central Africa, pump propaganda across social media and wage war against Ukraine. To understand how Wagner reached such heights in the Russian political sphere and the international imagination, we have to unravel the story of its most infamous protagonist, Evgeniy Prigozhin.

2

SOUS CHEF

The real truth always sounds improbable, do you know that?
To make truth sound probable you must always mix
in some falsehood with it.
Fyodor Dostoyevsky, *Demons* (1872)[1]

Rich and ostentatious food was arrayed on the white tablecloth: duck liver pâté and black caviar. Through the broad windows of the vessel, the sun set on the Neva. They passed the facade of the Hermitage, and the tall, golden cathedral spire of the Peter and Paul Fortress. The proprietor, a man in a suit that disguised his paunch, hung back, smiling as his guests talked and dined. A photographer shot a picture of the occasion as President George Bush regaled his audience with a story and Putin laughed.

It was 2002. Bush was taken with Putin, then still only three years into his time as president. Putin was nonetheless intent on making an impression on the American president and his wife as they visited his hometown of St Petersburg, Russia's second city. His staff spared no expense in arranging a dinner at one of its most renowned restaurants, New Island, with a floating dining room that offered a great view of the 'Venice of the North'. It served a menu that sought to cater to its exceptional clientele of kings, princes and presidents.

New Island's proprietor was a bald, jowly man. In his early forties, he looked the part of the chef, presenting President Bush with an expensive vintage port. Mostly, he hovered in the background, beaming, as photographers captured Bush and Putin dining. He had been building his restaurant business for the last ten years from humble beginnings and had every reason to be proud of his status as President Putin's go-to table in St Petersburg, serving the American president.

His name was Evgeniy Prigozhin, a St Petersburg native who had already come fantastically far in the new Russia. He had gone from petty crook, to convict, to successful businessman. In the years to come, he would go further still. He would corner a lucrative market for corrupt contracts, create a global disinformation network that would sow doubt in the U.S. presidential elections and become the patron of a mercenary army that would challenge Western powers from Syria to Ukraine. By 2023 he would become one of Russia's most recognizable nationalist figures, threatening the foundations of Russia's political system.

Despite all of this, Prigozhin never quite penetrated the inner circle in Putin's Russia. Others had Putin's trust, not only to carry out his wishes, but to influence his view of the world. These individuals often, but not always, come from the same world as Putin. Some, such as Security Council secretary Nikolai Patrushev, are from the security services, the Soviet KGB or GRU, and cut their teeth as spooks in the 1970s and '80s. Others hail from Putin's hometown of St Petersburg and proved themselves through effective service to Putin during his ascendancy, such as Rosneft CEO Igor Sechin. Still others, like Minister of Defence Sergey Shoigu, have demonstrated their professionalism, political acumen and ideological adherence to Putin's view of Russia's past and future. Prigozhin might have been from St Petersburg, but he was neither a former spy, a savvy political operative nor one of the original gang. He was trusted to prepare the notoriously paranoid president's food, but he was still an outsider.

Why, then, was Prigozhin allowed to direct a mercenary army, officially illegal in Russia? How did he attain such stature, not just in Russia, but in the Western imagination? The answer was a matter of Prigozhin's luck, ruthlessness and determination; Putin's international ambitions and indecision; and the Russian political system of rewards for greed, violence and initiative.

Convict

Twenty-two years earlier, on 20 March 1980, a cold night in Leningrad, Prigozhin left the Ocean restaurant with three friends. Both Prigozhin and at least one of his friends had already been convicted of robbery and had spent the last several weeks holding up citizens across the city – they were looking for trouble.

They spotted a young woman walking alone, and Prigozhin suggested to his friends that they mug her. They followed her down Matrosa Zheleznyaka Street, near the site where the Russian poet Aleksandr Pushkin had been fatally wounded in a duel 150 years earlier. They passed apartment blocks and train tracks. They were probably drunk. Prigozhin and another young man approached the woman and asked her for a cigarette. As she opened her purse, Prigozhin sprang on her, grabbing her by the throat and dragging her off the road. His friend waved a knife in her face. Prigozhin throttled the woman until she was unconscious, and his friend began working her boots from her feet. Prigozhin removed her gold earrings, and the young men fled the scene, shoes and jewellery in hand.

This concluded a month-long spree of petty crimes by Prigozhin and his band of misfits. They broke into apartments to steal radios and pens and posed as black-market salesmen of blue jeans and other Western goods to defraud and rob victims. In the end, they were caught, and Prigozhin was sentenced to thirteen years in a labour colony in 1981.

Just a few years earlier, Prigozhin had been studying in an athletics-focused boarding school in Leningrad alongside future Olympians. According to his own version of events, he had ambitions of becoming a professional cross-country skier. But now he was to serve more than a decade in the Soviet Union's notoriously harsh prison system. For most, this would portend a bleak future in and out of the penitentiary system, punctuated by stints of poverty in between. But Prigozhin was a survivor.

We know very little of Prigozhin's time in prison. As he told it, he routinely broke the rules of his prison colony and served extensive time in solitary confinement, where he began to read voraciously. He changed his behaviour, took up vocational courses and asked to be transferred to a labour colony where he would harvest timber – an extremely difficult way to pass his sentence, but one that would bring in some money. We do know that he was pardoned early and released on 21 March 1990, amid the Soviet Union's slow-motion disintegration. A little less than two years later, the USSR was no more.

Prigozhin had gone into prison when the Soviet Union was under Brezhnev's lethargic leadership. While he served his sentence, the USSR had seen three other leaders: Andropov, Chernenko and finally Gorbachev. He emerged into a Russia that was very different from the one he had known, a Russia with an uncertain future. Some saw the opportunity of perestroika and glasnost, the possibility of democracy, prosperity and reform. Others saw Russia and the other Soviet republics teetering on the edge of chaos.

As it turned out, Russia was in for a bit of both, depending on where you sat. In the mercenary 1990s, a few made their fortunes at the expense of the many and lawlessness reigned. Prigozhin was one of those few poised to seize the moment.

Cook

Prigozhin had been raised by his stepfather, Samuil Zharkoy, and his mother, Violetta Prigozhina. Zharkoy was supportive, a ski instructor who had tutored Prigozhin in the sport before he fell afoul of the law. When Prigozhin was released from prison nearly ten years to the day from his sentencing, Zharkoy was there to help him get on his feet.

Prigozhin enrolled in pharmaceutical college right out of prison but never finished his studies. Instead, he got married and went into business. Along with his stepfather, he opened a chain of hot-dog stalls in his hometown, recently rechristened St Petersburg. Prigozhin claimed that their bootstrapped operation was first to the punch, making their mustard 'right in my apartment' and paying off local thugs for protection, and earning $1,000 a month, a substantial sum at that time. The roubles piled up, such that his mother 'struggled to keep count'.[2]

As with so many parts of Prigozhin's story we have to take his word on the hot dog stand: The sole source for this version of events is Prigozhin himself. Hot dogs or not, Prigozhin was in the food business. Consequently, he was likely paying protection rackets to beneficiaries that included the notorious Malyshev crime syndicate, who along with the Tambov syndicate held an iron grip on the city in the 1990s. Malyshev and Tambov initially comprised 'gangster athletes', young men who had been channelled into careers in competitive sports by the Soviet system, but who now found themselves without prospects. In the lawless 1990s, both organizations grew into international criminal syndicates. It was nearly impossible to run a business in St Petersburg without crossing paths with them.

As Malyshev and Tambov consolidated their influence in the city and started to legitimize their business, Putin was also climbing the political ranks in St Petersburg. Documents in a Spanish warrant for members of the group detail connections between the groups and Putin's associates.[3] In Putin's telling, it would be around this time that he and Prigozhin first became acquainted.

Within a year of Prigozhin beginning his new business, a classmate from his boarding school named Boris Spektor called on him with an opportunity. Spektor was involved in the casino business in St Petersburg, an industry rife with organized crime. Prigozhin entered the gambling industry with Spektor and his business partners Igor Gorbenko and Mikhail Mirilashvili, who had founded the first casino in St Petersburg, Conti.[4]

By 1991 Putin was chairman of St Petersburg's Supervisory Council for Casinos and Gambling Businesses and sat at the head of the council that awarded casino licences. It is likely here that Putin first encountered Prigozhin. Putin had established a company called Neva-Shans through the St Petersburg Committee on External Relations, which he led, essentially a government gambling concern that would hold stakes in casinos in the city, rein in their lawlessness and direct a percentage of proceeds to social programmes.[5] Prigozhin's business partner Gorbenko became the director of Neva-Shans, an organization that Karen Dawisha, an authority on crime in Russia under Putin, described as a hotbed of graft and organized crime, enriching both the mob and security elites.[6]

Spektor and Prigozhin expanded beyond the casino industry. Spektor brokered an arrangement between Prigozhin and Kirill Ziminov, who ran a successful chain of supermarkets under the Contrast brand. Prigozhin took control of finances in exchange for 15 per cent of shares in the enterprise. This opened a new world of connections that launched Prigozhin from ex-con to casino boss to restaurant magnate.

In 1995 he opened his own bar, Wine Club. A year later, Ziminov gave him the opportunity to take over a property in St Petersburg's famous Kunstkamera, a historic building erected under Peter the Great that faced the grand Winter Palace across the Neva. Here, Prigozhin opened the up-scale Old Customs House with an investment of more than U.S.$250,000, which was reportedly paid off in five months. The Old Customs House became a fixture in St Petersburg's elite dining establishments almost immediately, and Prigozhin was able to open a string of additional restaurants across the city.

The real jewel in Prigozhin's culinary crown was yet to come. Ziminov and Prigozhin were inspired by Paris's waterfront eateries along the Seine and saw a perfect opportunity to mimic them on the banks of St Petersburg's rivers and canals. They hunted down a rusting vessel that hosted a disco, purchased it for U.S.$50,000 and invested nearly half a million in remodelling it.

When they opened a restaurant named New Island aboard the vessel in 1998, it was a sensation. It served conspicuously expensive dishes, including Russian staples like caviar on bliny and status symbols like king crab, and included an entire menu for truffles. Putin chose it as his venue of choice for hosting foreign leaders. Prigozhin made an impression on him when he insisted on serving these guests himself, including then U.S. president Bush. He mingled with Putin's entourage and befriended his head of security, Viktor Zolotov, future head of Russia's National Guard. He was affable and funny. One former associate described him as the 'royal jester' at such events, but he was better known in Russia as 'Putin's chef'.

Prigozhin's real business acumen has always been in leveraging his connections and knowing how to scale his businesses. New Island gave him prestige and connections, but it was not the basis of a business empire on its own. Both he and Ziminov wanted to start something that could grow further. With this growth in mind, Prigozhin created Blin!Donalt's, a play on *bliny* (the word for a Russian pancake) and McDonalds. As the name suggested, it advertised traditional Russian fare at affordable prices. However, the enterprise was dogged by inconsistent quality and had to compete against chains with similar concepts, like Teremok, which served rubbery bliny with names like 'E-Mail' that sandwiched American-style fast-food toppings into mass-produced facsimiles of the Russian culinary staple.

It wasn't a complete loss. Prigozhin and Ziminov had started a catering company to serve their fast-food products called Concord. Ziminov used his connections to St Petersburg's vice governor to establish Concord's role as the go-to contractor for city events.

At this time, Prigozhin's relationships with the cadre that had established him were souring. Mikhail Mirilashvili, the Israeli-

Georgian entrepreneur who was partnered with Spektor and Gorbenko, feuded with Prigozhin and Ziminov and tried to persuade Prigozhin to give him the Old Customs House. This feud was cut short when Mirilashvili was arrested for kidnapping in 2001: Russian authorities found that, after an organized-crime group mistakenly abducted Mirilashvili's father for ransom, Mirilashvili had members of the security services arrest members of the group and hand them over to him at his company's offices. The men who had been handed over to Mirilashvili were tortured and executed, and the men who kidnapped Mirilashvili's father were found dead soon after. Such were Prigozhin's circles in St Petersburg.

After nearly two successful decades in the restaurant business, Prigozhin said he decide to expand on an 'industrial scale'. It was 2010, and Putin had ascended from the St Petersburg governor's office to the role of president and then shuffled to become prime minister when he reached his term limit. Dmitry Medvedev was president, but it was widely acknowledged that Putin was still in charge. In the intervening years, Putin had fully consolidated the economic balance – no longer were the renegade oligarchs running the country. The biggest show in town was the state, and those wanting to make their fortune needed to hitch themselves to the Kremlin.

The most successful of this generation were those who got in close with Putin. Prigozhin went to deputy head of the Presidential Administration Aleksandr Beglov – a man who would later become his sworn enemy – with a concept for a series of culinary factories, supplying school meals. Beglov brought the news to Medvedev, who brought it to Putin. The project was evidently greenlit and Prigozhin constructed a series of factories under the moniker Concord. From Concord's offices, he would build the foundation for his empire.

Concord

By 2012 Concord was already modestly successful. Prigozhin had shifted his school catering business from St Petersburg to focus on Moscow. In some quarters, parents complained about the quality of the food, but generally business was good. Concord companies served around four hundred schools in Moscow and had started diversifying to supply the Ministry of Emergency Situations.

Prigozhin was growing his business effectively, but he had greater ambitions. His real breakthrough came with another opening in the market, a consequence of the outsourcing of Ministry of Defence food supply in 2010. Minister of Defence Anatoliy Serdyukov was undertaking bold reforms at the time in an effort to rapidly modernize the Russian military. This included privatizing military catering. The contracts went to an array of smaller suppliers and a conglomerate called RBE Group, but Prigozhin had his eyes on this prize. In a then rare interview with the St Petersburg magazine *Gorod 812*, in 2011, he told a journalist, 'We have plans – the army. That's half a million people. The police – Two million.'

Within just one year, he would come to control more than 90 per cent of the military's catering contracts, which was worth more than 90 billion roubles, or nearly u.s.$2.9 billion at December 2012 exchange rates. These contracts went not just to Concord, but to an array of companies, some owned by Prigozhin; some owned by his second wife, Lyubov; others only tied to him through obscure corporate structures, shared phone numbers or overlapping addresses. We do not know exactly how Prigozhin brokered this coup – most signs point to a conspiracy involving the directors of the state-owned military supplier Voentorg – but we do know its result. Prigozhin became a major player while building a vast and secretive corporate infrastructure that would prove pivotal as he expanded into new markets.

Why would Prigozhin have spread these contracts across such a confusing universe of companies? Part of the answer was deniability. It looked less conspicuous if the MOD restructured its catering supply to a range of new companies rather than signing it away to one entity with the stroke of a pen. The other was to defend himself from business rivals and angry parents.

From 2012 on, there was a growing tide of complaints from his school and military customers about the quality of the Concord Group's product. The Russian investigative media outlet Project found that from 2011 to 2019, 711 lawsuits were filed against Prigozhin's firms with total claims of 900 million roubles. Students found worms and plastic bags in their food. Cadets at an aviation academy found cockroaches in their porridge and human hair in their bread. Across Russia, military academies and schools reported cases where dozens of people who had eaten food from Concord companies were poisoned with salmonella, dysentery and other diseases. Some even had to be hospitalized.

Despite this, the Concord companies kept their contracts, defended by their confusing corporate structure and their friends in high places. Concord even expanded its business into construction of military bases and other services for the military and the Russian Ministry of Emergency Situations. Russian investigative journalists exposed schemes by which recently created companies, who had none of the necessary licences required for working with the military, and whose founders had no business experience, all won lucrative tenders – and all applied using the same IP address as Prigozhin's Concord Management and Consulting. Prigozhin became the single largest private player in the Russian military contracting world between 2011 and 2016 according to the late Russian opposition politician and political prisoner Aleksey Navalny.

Prigozhin's rise coincided with another revolution in Russian politics. With a creative interpretation of the Russian constitution, Putin reassumed the presidency in 2012 amid protests in Moscow.

He blamed the protests on Western interference, a vast conspiracy to challenge Russia's sovereignty and its rightful influence over its neighbouring states. The system in many ways became Putin, eschewing the semblance of democracy in favour of a nationalist quest to recover Russia's place as a great power. Russia accelerated down a more authoritarian course with greater ambitions to challenge the West.

In turn, the Kremlin leaned harder on the businessmen who had made their fortunes thanks to the blessings of Putin's political system. The Kremlin needed these entrepreneurs, who could cow the opposition at home and establish Russian influence abroad in ways that the state could not or would not. Putin had taken Russia's runaway capitalism and tamed it with the power of the state. The private actors who were now beholden to Putin could perform favours for the Kremlin at a lower political cost, faster and with a veneer of deniability.

This was particularly useful when Russia's policy seemed to struggle in execution. Time and again, Putin set the direction of the wind, but doddered when it came to following through on decisive foreign policy. The most successful oligarchs took the hint. They raised their sails and rode these winds to serve the Kremlin's interest around the world, funding propaganda efforts, building foreign companies that established economic influence, and competing with the West in every sphere they could. Against this backdrop, Prigozhin set out to prove his usefulness, guaranteeing that he would continue to benefit from favouritism. Others might have larger fortunes or closer relationships with Putin, but he was determined to prove he would go farther than any of them to support Russia's challenge to the world order.

Conspiracy

When I was studying in St Petersburg in the spring of 2015, the Farm had already been in business for nearly two years. While I ascended the cavernous escalators at the Chernyshevskaya metro station on my way to class, another group of young men and women made their commute to a small, modern commercial building to the north of the city. They arrived exactly on time, checked in with security and passed through a turnstile on their way into the office. They split off according to their divisions within the Farm: graphics, unit of social media specialists, special projects. They looked like most young people in the city: hip, frequently tattooed, often wearing clothes bearing English-language slogans.

The group who entered the special-projects office sat down at their desks, activated VPNs to disguise their locations, and began to log in. Their passwords were saved in colour-coded spreadsheets and held the keys to countless identities. There were American frat boys from Boston, gun-toting conservative moms from Texas, Americans from every conceivable racial and political background. Some of them performed a more familiar role, operating Russian and Ukrainian accounts. The Farm's employees started posting, guided by a set of instructions from their editors, keen to hit their daily quotas lest their pay be docked. They posted Facebook quizzes, linked to music videos and uploaded photographs of puppies. They also posted long screeds about the corruption of the new Presidential Administration in Ukraine, Obama's imperialistic ambitions for America, police killings of Black Americans as well as chemical catastrophes in the American south that had never happened. These were the trolls of 55 Savinsky Street, foot soldiers in Prigozhin's fast-growing project to exploit social media to sow distrust and chaos among Russia's enemies at home and abroad.

The euphemistically named Internet Research Agency (IRA) had been created in July 2013, when Prigozhin had already started dabbling in political-influence operations. He paid agents in 2012 to infiltrate the Russian opposition to capture or invent compromising material that featured in a documentary aired on the Russian NTV network. These agents also carried out Prigozhin's first forays in 'coordinated inauthentic behaviour', a term popularized by Facebook that describes the creation of numerous 'sock puppet' accounts to propagate a specific message. These campaigns and their coordinators would later become commonly known in the West (somewhat inaccurately) as Russian bots, or simply 'trolls'. To the PR-minded Prigozhin, they were a fantastic tool. Russia was awash with spin doctors, so-called 'political technologists' who espoused expertise in the dark arts of social manipulation. Prigozhin began collecting an entourage of these characters, who would form the basis for much of his future service to the Russian state.

The building on Savinsky Street became popularly known as the Troll Farm after it was exposed by a series of investigations by Russian and U.S. investigative journalists from 2013 to 2015. Trusted intermediaries had established these enterprises to keep Prigozhin's fingerprints off the effort. By all accounts, they were extremely unpleasant places to work, with constant surveillance and micromanaging, tendencies in all Prigozhin's future projects. Their output was nonetheless prolific, with hundreds of employees churning out posts and comments around the clock.

This was nothing new in Russia, with similar troll farms operating even prior to Putin's reassumption of the presidency. But the IRA had more ambitious aims than its predecessors, in particular a project codenamed Lakhta that would shake American politics and catapult Prigozhin to international recognition.

According to U.S. Special Counsel Robert Mueller, the primary aim of Lakhta was to 'provoke and amplify political and social discord in the United States'. It achieved this in cyberspace through the fundamental tactics of the IRA, with countless accounts masquerading as Americans from a range of backgrounds. But the IRA also conducted campaigns in real life, organizing election rallies in favour of then candidate Donald Trump in the United States.

These events were sparsely attended, but the later revelation that a mysterious Russian oligarch – who very much looked the part of the Bond villain with his jowls and bald dome – had organized political rallies in the United States set off a partisan feedback loop that consumed the American news cycle. The IRA's efforts mixed in the public imagination with the more consequential Russian efforts to harm the campaign of Hillary Clinton and bolster Trump, including the hacking of Democratic Party institutions by units affiliated with Russia's military intelligence service. Prigozhin and a line-up of his companies and IRA associates were indicted by the U.S. Department of Justice in 2018, charged with 'conspiracy to defraud the United States', and the FBI issued a bounty for information leading to his arrest.

While it is unlikely that Prigozhin's IRA swung the election for Trump or had any significant impact on the political beliefs of Americans more generally, it undoubtedly won him international notoriety. He had embarrassed the Americans at no small personal expense. He had proven that he was loyal, useful and more than willing to get his hands dirty to make the Kremlin's opponents look bad, whether they were in Washington or just around the corner in Moscow.

He himself had found just how much he stood to gain by making trouble in the info-space. It didn't matter if he really had the power to tank the entire American political system, or sow discord in Ukraine, or split the Russian opposition. What mattered was that his targets were afraid that he might. This had the direct result of making them less trusting of each other and making everyone more dubious of anything they learned online by, in the words of Trump's former chief strategist Steve Bannon, 'flooding the zone with shit'.[7]

The Kremlin noticed. Few other businesspeople in Russia could claim to have caused the Americans so much alarm and create so much fear among the Russian political opposition. Prigozhin's spectacular success in winning contracts with the Russian military was no doubt closely linked with this patriotic service. He and his family benefited tremendously: their palatial estates outside St Petersburg were captured in drone footage by Navalny's organization, including helipads, basketball courts and giant garages for his collection of Audis, Range Rovers and BMWs. He built another mansion along the Black Sea coast, not far from Putin's secret estate. None of this wealth blunted Prigozhin's ambition. He wanted more than wealth; he aspired to power and influence.

Crusade

Prigozhin liked to characterize himself as 'two handshakes away' from Putin, but he never really managed to close this distance. The double-edged sword of Prigozhin's success as the patron of so many criminal, ruthless or simply risky projects was that he proved his usefulness but only so long as he was outside the inner court. The more he succeeded, the more he was kept at arm's length. Prigozhin lacked personal access to Putin and had no official role within the state that he could use to influence policy. What he did have was a sprawling and secretive corporate infrastructure, connections in the Ministry of Defence and a willingness to undertake the kind of unsavoury work that other Russian businessmen of his stature avoided.

Different Russian elites have taken on different 'portfolios' for the Russian state, accepting risk in the form of sanctions, asset seizures and reputational harm to push Russian policy objectives. They are rewarded with security and favourable access to rents.[8] It is tempting to think of it as a simple displacement of the mob protection rackets that ruled Russia in the 1990s, but the Russian state is able to offer at least as much carrot as stick in encouraging this behaviour. The incentives are such that some entrepreneurs will advocate for taking on portfolios or pursue them independently in the hopes of later being rewarded.

Sometimes this is through soft-power initiatives. Billionaire Roman Abramovich served as governor of the remote far eastern region of Chukotka in the early 2000s. Hardly a glamorous post, he did his part by investing a substantial sum of his personal fortune in the region, before representing Russia positively in his international business and as owner of London's Chelsea Football Club. For others it is financial. Gennady Timchenko has acted as patron for significant international financial interests in Switzerland and elsewhere, offshoring wealth tied to Putin. For still others, it is a question of political influence: businessman and politician Aleksandr Babakov collaborated with Timchenko and another businessman, Roman Popov, to orchestrate illicit business with Iran and the furnishing of a loan to far-right French politician Marine Le Pen.[9] Still others, like Oleg Deripaska and Alisher Usmanov, maintained favour by undertaking risky sanction evasion ventures that allowed the Russian state to continue to access international capital. These endeavours run from illicit to illegal, and the businesspeople involved rely on intimidation and even murder to keep them secret. Prigozhin would compete with these men, many of whom had greater influence and wealth, by finding his own niche. His commodity of choice was force.

In 2014 the people of Ukraine overthrew their president, the corrupt autocrat Viktor Yanukovich, after he submitted to Russian pressure to reject an agreement with the EU that would have paved the way for his country's integration with Western Europe. Russia began an unorthodox and undeclared war against Ukraine and its new Western-oriented government. Their goal was not to conquer Ukraine, but to scuttle its hopes of joining Western institutions like the EU and, most of all, NATO. First there were troops without insignia, a wave of 'little green men'. Orchestrated by the Russian security services working hand in hand with paramilitaries and Russian businessmen, they first took Crimea. Then they began to move in eastern Ukraine.

Paramilitaries and Russian security agencies worked with local criminal elements to seize control of the cities of the Donbas, Donetsk and Luhansk, which declared themselves independent territories loyal to Russia. The newly formed government in Kyiv was overwhelmed by the Russian annexation, but the Russians too were unprepared for the momentum of their own 'hybrid' war against Ukraine. Taking Crimea was relatively bloodless and popular at home, but Russians were not willing to see their sons die for a war in the Donbas. The Russian state was similarly unwillingly to bankroll the breakaway republics that were taking shape. What had by most accounts been an attempt to shoulder Ukraine with a costly and destabilizing internal conflict was now producing actors with their own agency in Ukraine, paramilitary leaders who demanded that Russia follow through and annex the eastern regions of Donetsk and Luhansk.

The Kremlin worked hard to maintain its veil of deniability and to wrest control from the most radical separatist leaders. It claimed that this was a civil war, and while Russia supported the right to statehood of the self-declared 'Donetsk People's Republic' and 'Luhansk People's Republic', there were no troops officially dispatched to Ukraine. The Russian security services needed more experienced men to stabilize the chaos, maintain the pressure on Ukraine and keep a lid on the increasingly brazen leaders of pro-Russian armed groups in eastern Ukraine. They set on an idea: the concept of a mercenary, deniable force that they had been experimenting with for more than a decade. And they had a willing manager – one willing enough to pitch himself for the role: Evgeniy Prigozhin.

3

ORIGINS

I don't think of myself as a mercenary or non-mercenary.
I represent, firstly, Russia – my own country.
Aleksandr Tsarikov, contractor for Moran Security,
Slavonic Corps and the Wagner Group[1]

The Iraqi guards waved them through the checkpoints, and the Russians hurtled off in their white minivan. A man in the back with a buzzcut smoked a cigar. Another hung partway out of the open door of the van, cradling a Kalashnikov. Vadim Gusev sat in the front on the radio, wearing a black T-shirt and a bulletproof vest, calling out warnings about other vehicles on the road. A submachine gun sat on the console next to him.

The minivan fell in line with the convoy of freight trucks they escorted. They were bound for an electrical station in Basra, Iraq, and they would have to cross the better part of the country to get there. In Basra, a team of Russian specialists was working to repair the power plant destroyed in the Iraq War. They were employed by a company that was a subsidiary of Russia's state-owned arms manufacturer, Rostec, one of the few companies with the appetite for risk necessary to take part in the often lucrative work of restoring the country's war-torn infrastructure. Gusev and his men were there to help handle that risk. They protected the equipment bound for Basra from militants before handing it over to another group of armed Russians at the plant. Those men had shaved heads and wore wraparound sunglasses that led locals to mistake them for Americans. Their commander, Sergey Epishkin, wore a T-shirt like Gusev, a rifle slung across his chest.

Gusev and Epishkin were not soldiers, but contractors. They were directors of different Russian private military and security companies or PMSCS, sent to Iraq to defend the interests of Russian companies. Their encounter took place in the early 2010s, nearly ten years after the American invasion of Iraq, but the persistent instability created by the global War on Terror created a new market for companies selling force and deterrence.

Gusev and Epishkin were leaders of an emerging wave of Russian companies in this industry. Their enterprises would lay the groundwork for a new phenomenon: the contemporary Russian PMSC. Like many other PMSCS flourishing at the time, Russian PMSCS would blend a centuries-long legacy of mercenaryism with the modern features of a globalized criminal network. They would at once serve the Russian state while shielding it from blowback. It would be neither a national army nor a private company, but something in between.

Russian PMSCS are a product of an effort by Russian security services to imitate the types of security company they saw propagating in the West. Russia has spent the last three decades watching global conflicts, borrowing the ideas it saw employed by state and non-state actors, and experimenting with them in practice. Its security services have a uniquely strong grasp on the use of complex corporate structures to generate off-book cash and undermine their adversaries. They have exploited the interconnected global system of trade and finance, using dark money and shell companies to great effect.

This didn't happen by accident, nor was it a conspiracy: it was the result of years of trial and error by entrepreneurs close to Russian security services. Its outcome would herald the arrival of a new period of twenty-first-century mercenary warfare.

The Past Is Prologue

Mercenaries are as old as commerce itself. For most of the history of warfare, wars were fought between hired soldiers rather than national armies, whether they were called condottieri, landsknechts or *Freikorps*, or later privateers, Hessians and, in the contemporary world, contractors.[2] It is no surprise, then, that historians of mercenaryism refer to hired guns as the 'second-oldest profession'. In this sense, Russian use of mercenaries is a return to form.

People are uncomfortable with the word 'mercenary'. In popular culture, this is because of the negative connotations of 'soldiers for hire', killing for money rather than for allegiance to a country or idea. In law and diplomacy, this discomfort is because of the challenge of defining a mercenary in modern conflict, where private companies play an integral part. Countries around the world, from the United States to China, rely on PMSCs, legally distinct from mercenaries. They conduct a myriad of tasks, both at the 'tail' end of military operations – rear-echelon tasks like feeding soldiers and moving them from point A to point B – and the 'tooth' end, that is, lethal operations that range from guarding sites for companies or countries all the way to engaging in front-line combat.[3]

Mercenaries, on the other hand, are subject to a set of definitions that are both specific and contested. International laws and regulations governing PMSCs and mercenaries tend to agree that they must be motivated by private gain, must be paid significantly more than the armed forces engaged in the conflict, must not be a national of one of the parties to the conflict or a member of their armed forces and must have not been sent in an official capacity by another state. Hence the French Foreign Legion does not fit because they are sent on official duty. Blackwater, Dyncorp and the litany of other Western firms evade the definition as well, often through intentional structuring of their corporate vehicles, contracts and staff. Very seldom does a company or individual neatly fit the description of a mercenary as laid out by the Geneva Conventions, the Montreux Document (an international agreement governing private military activity) or any other domestic or international regulations governing mercenaries. As we will see, this applies to Russia's constitutional prohibition on mercenaries as well.

Most of the companies referred to as 'mercenary' by the media and in the public imagination are in fact PMSCs. For the purposes of this book, I use the term 'PMSC' when referring to a company or organization that fits within the corporate definition, the shorter 'PMC' or 'private military company' in reference to Russian organizations that use the Russian equivalent of that acronym, and 'mercenary' to describe fighters employed by such a company who engage in combat operations outside a national military. This fraught taxonomy becomes murkier still when the line between 'state' and 'company' is blurred, as they are so often with PMSCs.

The Rise of Modern Mercenaries

Mercenaries change with the times. Prior to the primacy of the nation state model, they were the norm in warfare. They survived the genesis of the modern state by moving into more specific roles and buttressing national armies. They have supported colonial conquest and allowed former imperial powers to continue their adventurism even after relinquishing their colonial possessions. In the Cold War, they found they fit well within the rubric of proxy warfare, where great powers sought to support smaller states and armed groups at war with their adversaries. Now they have continued not just to survive but to flourish in the post-Cold War era, where civil wars, insurgencies and low-intensity conflicts have endured beyond the grand struggle of capitalism and communism.

This evolution accelerated tremendously during the second half of the twentieth century, when the term 'PMSC' came into fashion. The PMSCs' immediate predecessors, mercenaries in the truest sense, played an active role in postcolonial conflict throughout the post-war period. British mercenary 'Mad' Mike Hoare was hired by Congolese prime minister Moïse Tshombe to fight in Katanga and to put down Congo's Simba Rebellion before failing to stage a coup in the Seychelles. His exploits inspired the 1978 action film *The Wild Geese*, starring Richard Burton and directed by Andrew V. McLaglen. French mercenary Bob Denard also fought in the Congo, commanding *les affreux* ('the awful ones'), and subsequently in conflicts across Africa, attempting to overthrow the government of the Comoros four times (most of these men harboured ambitions of taking over island nations, though they failed at least as often as they succeeded). Mostly, they were engaged to support the interests of Western governments in their former colonial possessions in Africa. They were competent, deniable forces that allowed European powers to continue to influence power relations in Africa, Latin America and Asia in an ostensibly post-colonial world.

As the collapse of the colonial international order created a market for force, so too did the end of the Cold War. Proxies found themselves without patrons and companies found themselves with a new power to shape world affairs. Armed conflict persisted and the free market for force flourished.

A series of enterprises created in the late 1980s and early 1990s formed the blueprint for the modern PMSC, perhaps none of them more so than South Africa's Executive Outcomes. Executive Outcomes, or EO as it was frequently known, was created by Eeben Barlow, a charismatic veteran of both South Africa's apartheid-era special forces and the shadowy Civil Cooperation Bureau, which ran clandestine operations from sanctions evasion to assassination. Barlow had a keen understanding of working by, with and through irregular forces and how to use complex corporate structures to avoid scrutiny. This allowed his operation to magnify the impact of their local allies, leverage their local partners' knowledge to inform their tactics and operations, and maintain a long reach using flexible, secretive companies around the world.

Barlow channelled his frustration with the corruption and inefficiency of South Africa's security and intelligence services into EO, a company that provided services ranging from training and strategy consulting to direct combat support. Unlike the more ad hoc mercenary companies that preceded it, EO ran as a truly independent enterprise that often operated counter to the policy of South Africa itself.

EO was also uniquely successful in changing the course of conflicts across Africa, establishing itself through its involvement in Angola and Sierra Leone. EO's first major contract demonstrated the blend of state and private interests, as they recovered equipment belonging to Heritage Oil & Gas in Angola in 1993. While they sought to recover equipment belonging to a UK firm, they were officially brought in by Angolan state-owned Sonangol, and fought against UNITA rebels that challenged the Angolan government. Their success led to Angola contracting EO to train its armed forces and support their counterinsurgency, driving a series of victories that led UNITA to sue for peace.

In 1995 EO was contracted by the government of Sierra Leone to fight the Revolutionary United Front, or RUF, a rebel group notorious for its brutality. The RUF, known internationally for its practice of amputating the limbs of civilians, menaced the government in the capital, Freetown, and was a source of horrific suffering and poverty across the country. EO was to drive back the RUF and retake a series of diamond fields that constituted a key revenue source for the rebel group and its main backer, Liberian dictator Charles Taylor. EO succeeded in turning the tide, allowing Sierra Leone to hold democratic elections in 1996.

These efforts weren't cheap, but they cost less than a UN peacekeeping mission, and were arguably more effective – at least in the short term. Under pressure by the United States and UN, who were uncomfortable with the role of private forces in determining political outcomes, EO left both countries. In both Angola and Sierra Leone, wars resumed. As then under-secretary general for peace-keeping Kofi Annan would say in 1994 when the UN weighed using PMSCs to respond to the Rwandan genocide, 'the world may not be ready to privatize peace.'[4]

South Africa took a more aggressive tactic against EO in 1998, banning 'mercenary activities' and leading the company to dissolve. Barlow and the other veterans of EO would go on to lead a series of other ventures in Africa and beyond, but their real impact would come through the new generation of PMSCs that they inspired. None of these imitators quite achieved EO's impact or notoriety. The most successful parts of its model were widely copied, particularly the use of complex corporate structures to facilitate sometimes illicit trade and finance and the use of airpower, from helicopter gunships to retrofitted civilian planes, to counter insurgent forces. Barlow himself identifies that other PMSCs failed largely because of hubris: they didn't live among their local partners, building trust and cultural understanding, and they failed to grasp the local dynamics that fuelled conflict. Most saw EO's well-trained men, their arms and equipment and their operational success, but failed to appreciate the aspects of their effectiveness that were based on their practices off the battlefield. The most successful favoured a less risky model than EO's, focusing on guarding people, transport or locations. A tenacious few remained in the business of direct combat operations.

Cambrian Explosion

The attack on the World Trade Center and the Pentagon began both the global War on Terror and a global revolution in PMSCs. From 1999 to 2008 the U.S. Department of Defense's contract obligations nearly quadrupled. Fighting a prolonged series of counterinsurgencies around the world was difficult and expensive for the

United States and its allies, and these campaigns were possible in small part thanks to the private sector. Feeding, supplying, housing and transporting the u.s. military was a colossal mission, and titan firms like Brown & Root and MPRI stepped in to fill the gap. Growing and developing local forces in countries like Afghanistan and Iraq demanded experienced instructors and strategists, a role filled by companies like DynCorp. Finally, the USA needed its assets and people protected in these often hostile environments, a service furnished by companies like Blackwater.

This turn to the private sector was driven by concerns over cost, efficiency and politics. PMSCs were often cheaper to leverage and freed the limited numbers of enlisted soldiers from rear-echelon roles, allowing the USA to field more of its men and women in combat roles. There was less public scrutiny over deploying contractors rather than enlisted soldiers and the deaths of contractors were less politically sensitive at home – the American public held to the age-old belief that contractors knew what they were signing up for and that their role as 'employees' differentiated them from soldiers in both life and death. As a result, the ratio of contractors to u.s. military personnel in Iraq and Afghanistan tilted precipitously towards the contractors, until they were roughly equal in Iraq, and contractors were twice as numerous as u.s. military personnel in Afghanistan. Contactors shielded the American public from battlefield losses: in 2010, towards the end of the War on Terror, there were more contractors than soldiers killed in both Iraq and Afghanistan.

This helped to resolve problems around cost and casualties, but it created new ones as well. When PMSCs commit human-rights abuses, it creates a double bind for policymakers. In 2007 Blackwater contractors evacuating u.s. embassy personnel opened fire into a crowd of civilians in Nisour Square, Baghdad. Seventeen civilians died and another twenty were wounded. The Nisour Square massacre led to public outcry and four Blackwater employees were later convicted by u.s. courts, one for murder and the other three for manslaughter. All four were later pardoned by u.s. President Donald Trump.

The reputation of Blackwater was soiled by the atrocity, leading the United States to pull Blackwater out of Iraq, launch investigations into the conduct of the PMSC and pass a new law regulating PMSCs. The incident strained relations between the United States and the new government in Iraq – but it also allowed the United States to control the damage. The United States could shift blame to Blackwater, limit its responsibility to a mea culpa of insufficient oversight, drop Blackwater's Iraq contract and move forward with repairing relations. It stands to reason that this would have been more challenging if u.s. service members ha been behind the massacre.

As Sean McFate points out in his *The Modern Mercenary* (2014), this is not always the case. u.s. Marines of Kilo Company killed 26 unarmed civilians, including children and the elderly, in Haditha, Iraq, in 2005 as part of a spree of retribution for a roadside bomb. The squad leader was court-martialled but acquitted and charges against all the other perpetrators were dropped. Blackwater is infamous; Kilo Company is not. While PMSCs allow their employers to evade responsibility, they are also often subject to far greater public scrutiny for their abuses than regular militaries, largely thanks to the public distaste of PMSCs as mercenaries or 'dogs of war', a perception that can lead us to underappreciate the abuses of regular militaries. For states engaging in particularly indiscriminate warfare, this can be a blessing – if the world blames your PMSCs, it may reflect badly on you, but it can shield your national military from condemnation or even prosecution. The ability to charge commanders for war crimes relies on the ability of prosecutors to establish their command and control over offending units and it is easy enough to claim that PMSCs that have committed crimes did so on their own initiative.

The War on Terror coincided with a growing industry of maritime security companies that specialized in deterring piracy off the coast of Somalia. These waters host a critical shipping route from the Red Sea to the Indian Ocean and abundant fishing stocks. Local entrepreneurs engaged in hostage taking at sea built a profitable cottage industry in the early and mid-2000s. An array of private security companies, including PMSCs with business in Iraq and Afghanistan, offered their services to protect vessels navigating these treacherous seas. Both in this maritime security market and in Iraq and Afghanistan, a set of Eastern European PMSCs was taking root. At face value, they appeared conventional, barely distinguishable from the enormous number of American, British and South African enterprises appearing in the security market. Among this cast of entrepreneurs and veterans of the Russians security services entering the private sector, the roots of the Wagner Group took shape.

From Cossacks to Contractors

Russian PMSCs like to trace their roots back to a legacy of Russian mercenaryism. Like the rest of Europe, Russia has a long history of soldiers for hire, perhaps none more recognizable than the Cossacks. Originating in Ukraine and southern Russia, they were a diverse people organized along military lines into groups called hosts that offered their military services to local authorities in exchange for wealth and autonomy.

Cossacks from both Ukraine and modern-day Russia – like the Zaporizhzhian Cossacks from the lands around the Dnieper river and the Don Cossacks from modern-day south Russia – fought fiercely for independence for much of their history, but also forged alliances of convenience with neighbouring empires: the Ottomans and particularly the Russians. The Don Cossacks led some of the most legendary revolts in Russian imperial history, including the

Bulavin Rebellion and Pugachev's Rebellion, the latter threatening the Crown and proclaiming an end to serfdom before it was crushed by the empire. When they served the state, motivated by resources, security or just coercion, they played important roles in conflicts from the Crimean and Napoleonic Wars all the way to the First World War. They were trusted with the safety of the very heart of the empire: His Imperial Majesty's Convoy was an elite guard of the tsar formed from Terek and Kuban Cossacks that lasted from around 1811 to 1917. It is also the namesake of the Russian PMC Convoy based out of the occupied territory of Crimea.

After the Bolsheviks seized power, the Cossacks were generally perceived as counter-revolutionary, a bit too invested in their own independence and historically friendly with the tsar. Some even fought the Soviet Union. Cossack units allied with the Whites in the Russian Civil War, and units like the XV SS Cossack Cavalry Corps fought alongside the Nazi Waffen-SS in the Second World War. As a result, they were first repressed and then co-opted by the state.

With the collapse of the Soviet Union, there was a revival of Cossack traditions, many of which were again captured by the state; Cossack organizations have played roles in Russia's wars of conquest from Georgia to Ukraine in the last twenty years. Security companies like Convoy and volunteer units like Severo-Slavyanskaya Stanitsa embraced the symbols and ethos of the Cossack martial lifestyle, exchanging the defiant autonomy of the original Cossack hosts for service to capital and the Kremlin.

However, the true roots of Russia's private military industry are economic, not cultural. Its growth began with the disruption of the security state and the fast money and violence of the 1990s. With the state gutted, lawlessness reigned, whether it be criminal organizations in Russian cities or secessionist movements on the periphery. The titanic wealth of Russia's strategic enterprises, amassed through breakneck privatization, was protected by force. Companies like Gazprom fielded formidably armed security detachments to defend their interests in the volatile north Caucasus, and across Russia a private-security industry bloomed to protect enterprises from theft, racketeering and raiding.

Elite soldiers of the Russian Federal Security Service (the FSB), the Main Directorate of Military Intelligence (the GRU) and airborne forces (the VDV) sensed opportunity that far surpassed their options in anaemic military and security services. Some of them struck out to create their own companies. They registered firms that borrowed their names from infamous *spetsnaz* special operations units, like Alfa and Vympel, who had participated in operations ranging from overthrowing the Afghan government in 1979 to the rescue of Soviet diplomats held by Hezbollah in Beirut in 1985. Through the 1990s and early 2000s, the Russian private military industry grew organically but with regular interaction with Russia's security services. Veterans maintained contact with their military and intelligence communities, and the security services for their part wanted to keep tabs on the market for force. It paid to know what these groups of armed and experienced men were up to and who their customers were.

These new companies found significant pools of talent to draw from. The Soviet Afghan War and the First and Second Chechen Wars created generations of young men with combat experience who found little in the way of prospects back home. In the 1990s they were excellent candidates for organized-crime enforcers, with Afghan veterans hired as 'torpedoes' – contract killers – by mob groups across Russia. They created their own veterans' organizations that served as social networks for men with combat experience who could help each other find work, prime communities for private security companies to draw from.

Russian PMSCs took on jobs in demining and securing people, places and assets from West Africa to Iraq to Sri Lanka. While many veterans of the Russian services took better-paying work with foreign PMSCs if they could, the domestic industry did well owing to a close relationship with major Russian companies and state-owned enterprises. Men like Gusev and Epishkin, described at this beginning of this chapter, created some of the most prominent companies – Antiterror Orel (or 'Eagle') and Moran Security. These companies and their competitors, like RSB Group, Redut-Antiterror and Tigr Top-Rent, contracted with energy enterprises like Gazprom and major Russian shipping firms. Where Russia's industry went in the developing world, these firms followed. All of them aggressively touted their adherence to Russian law, particularly Article 359 of the Criminal Code of the Russian Federation, which outlaws mercenaryism. But like most such laws, 'mercenaries' are subject to a very specific set of definitions that most such firms managed to evade.

The first signs that these firms might be taking on less than savoury business, even in the murky world of PMSCs, began in the 2010s. As Russia's politics became more repressive, as its foreign policy became more revanchist, and while Prigozhin and other businessmen turned to increasingly illicit means of helping the Kremlin, the Russian private military industry was no different. There was money to be made and favour to be won.

Privateers

Gusev braced himself against the gunwales of the vessel, swaying with the waves of the Red Sea. With his unkempt greying hair and beige collared shirt, he looked less martial than he had in Iraq. He gazed out at the horizon. 'My grandmother always told me, "Grandson, everything is nonsense, the most important is that there is no war – that children don't see a war in our country."' The journalist interviewing him started to ask a question: 'She said that, but it turns out that here you are, doing . . .' Gusev talked over him. 'The more we do this, our presence and what we're doing here, in the Indian Ocean – in these hot zones, in the role of protecting our people – the more they'll respect us. And they'll think before they come and poke at us in Russia.'[5]

He was far from Iraq. He was speaking to Russian television aboard a nondescript blue vessel in some of the most dangerous waters in the world, near the coast of Somalia. He was by now the deputy director of Moran Security, one of Russia's larger private security companies.

The boat itself, the *Myre Seadiver*, was in the Red Sea to defend Moran's clients from pirates. The *Seadiver* was a 50-metre-long (164 ft) standby safety vessel, something like an overgrown tugboat: it wasn't much to look at. But it was host to a group of armed men with combat experience who posed a real threat to would-be attackers. They were modern-day privateers with the right to use violence to protect Russian shipping interests from being stolen or held for ransom.

In October 2012, shortly after that interview was shot, the same vessel was flying under a Cook Island flag off the coast of Nigeria. After it called in at the port of Lagos, the Nigerian Navy stopped the vessel to find a wealth of undeclared arms onboard: AKM rifles and Benelli shotguns and 8,000 rounds of ammunition. The men aboard, Gusev's men, were Russian, and claimed they were sailing from Madagascar to Guinea. The contractors and crew were held in Lagos for months before being released with the intervention of the Russian Foreign Ministry. They were then transported to the embassy, but Moran claimed that Nigerian authorities would not allow them to leave the country.

Gusev's public stance was clear:

We would like the President of Russia to approve the conduct of a special operation to free Russian citizens who are now on the territory of the Embassy. We are ready for this; we have everything necessary for this. We have spent many years in Nigeria, we know what their military and police are like, their weapons and training. We can do it. There are certain forces behind us, and we are ready to independently, as a private company, or jointly with the state, carry out this operation to free the hostages in Nigeria.[6]

Gusev never got the opportunity to kick off a mercenary showdown with the Nigerian government. The men of the *Myre Seadiver* were eventually returned home without incident.

Nigerian authorities might have been wrong about Gusev's men trafficking the undeclared weapons on board, but Moran did have connections to the arms-smuggling world. While Moran operated the *Myre Seadiver*, the vessel was owned and managed by Russian company Westberg Limited, which was part of complex corporate network spanning from Belize to St Petersburg. Westberg also owned the MV *Chariot*, a hulking red rust bucket with a rap sheet. The *Chariot* was detained by Cypriot authorities in January 2012, on its way to Syria from St Petersburg carrying 35 to 60 tonnes of explosives.[7] Cypriot authorities released the vessel after its crew assured them that it wouldn't travel to Syria. It promptly turned off its location transponder and sailed to the Syrian port of Tartus, home to a Russian naval base. No one can say what happened to the explosives after that. Before that incident, the *Chariot* had carried grenades, rockets, mortars and bombs from Egypt to the Democratic Republic of Congo in 2011.[8] Moran's clients also included a company that featured two former directors of Beluga Shipping, which had helped Pakistan's notorious nuclear technology trafficker A. Q. Khan ship centrifuges to Libya. That client itself had moved missiles to Myanmar and tanks to South Sudan.

Through these connections, Moran was part of a network of companies referred to as the 'Syrian Express', or the 'Odesa Network' due to its large presence in Odesa in Ukraine and the neighbouring port of Oktyabrsk. The Syrian Express owned and operated vessels that moved Russian arms and equipment to Syria, years before Russia began overt military involvement there in 2015. This was a massive and clandestine arms-trafficking operation that used ostensibly private companies at a scale seldom before seen. Their effort was crucial to laying the groundwork for Russia's largest foreign intervention since the collapse of the Soviet Union. Leadership of these companies was tied back to top figures in Russia's government. Moran was a small player but had an important role: protect the illegal arms that Russia was sending to its allies abroad. Don't let the Kremlin get caught.

The Syrian Express was a shining example of Russia's new public–private partnerships, where ostensibly private enterprises were mobilized to do the Kremlin's dirty work. They were cheap, fast and deniable, letting the Russian state export arms to its allies while offsetting the risks of sanctions and interdiction. So what if a company was caught? Its owners could spin up three more in its place, using complex offshore structures, and transfer their vessels to this new set of firms. It was a profitable arrangement for anyone with boats, capital and few scruples about arming a dictator like Syria's Bashar al Assad. PMCs like Moran shouldered into this opportunity alongside bigger fish, ambitious and connected businessmen like Evgeniy Prigozhin.

Turkish Delight

Prigozhin's involvement in the Syrian Express was rumoured, but unconfirmed. If he was part of Russia's effort to use commercial vessels to support the Syrian government's war effort, it would demonstrate that his role in Russia's arms trafficking and support to Russia's authoritarian allies extended beyond the Wagner Group. It would also show another degree of overlap between the Russian PMCs like Moran involved in the Express and Prigozhin himself at a seminal moment in Russia's use of private networks for geopolitical ends.

In reviewing Prigozhin's correspondence leaked in 2023, I noticed an undated letter ostensibly sent by Prigozhin to the Ministry of Defence. In the letter, he asked Defence Minister Sergey Shoigu for a favour:

> Dear Sergey Kuzhugetovich!
> In September 2015, the President of the Russian Federation issued a secret directive to the Ministry of Defence accepting eight cargo ships as a gift. The acquisition of these ships was carried out by Russian companies exclusively for the needs of the Russian Ministry of Defence.
>
> I ask you to consider contacting the Chairman of the Government of the Russian Federation regarding the issue of signing a decree on the exemption from customs payments in respect to ships transferred to the Ministry of Defence.
>
> E. Prigozhin

According to this message, Prigozhin was out a fair bit of money on account of the help he had recently provided to the Ministry: he had just acquired civilian vessels from Turkey. Now he was looking to get an exemption for the customs fees he was being charged to import them.

To verify the letter, I turned to Russian customs records. There I found that in October 2015, a Russian company named Main Line LLC imported a 111-metre-long (364 ft) cargo vessel named *Dadali* from Turkey. Main Line LLC was not well known and would not have raised suspicion among the Turkish sellers. It was generally only familiar to Russian journalists who had identified it as one of the hundreds of companies that Prigozhin had created to accept government contracts in catering and construction in the 2010s.

The *Dadali*'s activity after it was purchased by Prigozhin showed that this was not a simple purchase of a commercial ship.

Within a month of arriving in the Russian port of Novorossiysk, the Turkish vessel was rechristened *Vologda 50* and sent on its first voyage by its new owner, the Russian Ministry of Defence. Bloggers noticed the vessel transiting the Bosporus and tracked it to Syria. The former commercial cargo vessel began its new life as part of the Syrian Express.

Moran Security and Prigozhin's shared involvement in the Syrian Express was representative of how the Russian security services leveraged private actors to do their dirty work. It shows how Prigozhin's collaboration with the Russian defence establishment extended beyond his mercenary enterprises. These networks had other links: by 2015, when Main Line LLC bought the *Dadali* for the Russian military, Prigozhin had several former Moran men in his employ and had entered the PMC market himself. Prigozhin and Moran's stories intersect with a series of events two years earlier, the product of an ill-fated plan by Moran's directors that marked a transition of Russian PMCs from armed security to soldiers in foreign wars.

Wild Geese

In the winter of 2012–13, while Moran's men were still held in Nigeria, the company's directors were onto something new, a bigger venture that the Russian FSB had co-signed. Through the Federal Security Service (FSB) they had cover and the opportunity to expand to new frontiers of business, this time in Syria.

Calls went out to the network of Moran employees and their associates, to veterans of the VDV and the *spetsnaz*: $5,000 a month to protect energy facilities, $200 if you are wounded, $40,000 for your family if you are killed. In all, more than 250 men volunteered, many of them veterans and Kuban Cossacks.

Candidates spoke with the head of Moran, an FSB colonel in reserve and the company's self-professed 'representative of the special services', the aptly named Vyacheslav Kalashnikov.[9] According to Kalashnikov, he had concerns about the security services' attitude towards the operation and met his associates in the FSB to discuss it. At first, they were apprehensive and advised against the deal. But then came a change of heart – not only did they approve of the Syrian job, but they introduced Kalashnikov to the representative of the Syrian end of the deal, a certain Yusef Jabar.

To Kalashnikov, it appeared that the FSB had passed Gusev the deal with the Syrians. While Kalashnikov would later express his misgivings and try to distance Moran from the debacle, Moran's fingerprints were all over it. Boris Chikin, Moran's deputy director; Kalashnikov, the head of Moran; Gusev, its deputy CEO; Ilya Shabanov, head of Moran's operations department; and Evgeniy Sidorov, head of Moran's personnel department – all were involved. New recruits signed a contract with a Hong Kong-registered company called Slavonic Corps. Its director was a man named Sergey Kramskoy – another member of Moran.

Many of these men had backgrounds in the security services and *spetsnaz*, like Sidorov, who served with the 45th VDV Spetsnaz. This was also true of the men they recruited, like Dmitry Utkin, a former captain within the 2nd Separate Guards Spetsnaz Brigade. Others were drawn from Moran, such as Vladimir Titov, or Cossack organizations, such as Sergey Degtyarev. Slavonic Corps' men had served in places such as Afghanistan, Chechnya, Dagestan and aboard Moran's vessels. For some of them, like the men named here, their time with Slavonic Corps would set them on the path for a long mercenary career.

The FSB had advised Gusev and company not to send all their men aboard one plane, so they split them up and flew them into the port city of Latakia. At first, everything went to plan. The fighters of Slavonic Corps were only supposed to protect oil facilities. The weather was nice in Latakia. When they noticed that their rifles and tanks were from the 1960s, some raised their eyebrows. A few men protested to management when their Syrian hosts started welding metal plates to trucks for armour. When they approached Gusev, he asked them, 'Did you come to fight or guard? If you came to guard – you'll be on a permanent housekeeping detail.'[10] Then they went on their first trip into the desert.

Their convoy, a hodgepodge of trucks, welded metal and spray-painted camo, wound along dirt roads. The Russians travelled with the Syrians but were distinguishable in their gear and bearing. The men of Slavonic Corps favoured a look that was common to contractors – they wore fatigues in variants of the popular beige and olive 'desert tricolour' originally designed by the u.s. military in Operation Desert Storm. They wore chest rigs and sunglasses. The Syrians, on the other hand, wore what was available. Like the makeshift armoured vehicles, they were working with what they had.

It wasn't long before the expedition went sideways. A Syrian helicopter buzzed low over the convoy, showboating. Its rotors tangled in power lines, and it came crashing to earth, injuring a Slavonic Corps fighter in the process. When his compatriots returned to their airfield base to treat him, Gusev was arguing with the Syrians. It sounded like it had to do with money.

Two days later, on 17 October 2013, they were called back into the field to defend pro-Assad militias against an assault in Homs. They arrived at their positions and came under fire. Thousands of insurgents descended on the Russian mercenaries, trapping them in a pincer movement. They saw that the fight was hopeless – they were vastly outnumbered. The men of Slavonic Corps beat a retreat, shooting their way out. They took few losses given the odds, blessed by a fortunately timed storm.

In the chaotic withdrawal, one fighter lost his belongings. Shortly thereafter, the Islamic State began posting photographs of them online, claiming that they had killed a Russian mercenary. Among the items they posted was a contract with Slavonic Corps.

Back at the airfield, Vadim and his Syrian customers were screaming at each other again over payment. Their disagreement had escalated and was made all the worse by the disastrous encounter with the Islamic State nears Homs. Gusev had had enough. By the end of the month, the fighters had climbed aboard planes bound for Moscow – their contracts were for five months, but Slavonic Corps's fight was already over.

When they landed in Russia, men in black uniforms stormed the planes. The fighters, including Utkin, Titov and Degtyarev, were interviewed but released. Gusev and Sidorov, on the other hand, were not. Ultimately, they were tried and convicted under Russia's law against mercenaries. A wave of media attention hit not just Slavonic Corps, but Moran.

Gusev and Sidorov both served time for their crimes. It was a warning, not so much to those who would engage in mercenary activity, but to those who would embarrass the state in the process. It also smacked of an inter-service squabble. Did someone in the FSB sign off on Slavonic Corps's doomed mission, incurring the ire of another department, or maybe another service entirely? Or was a key part of Slavonic Corps's arrangement with the security services a tacit acknowledgement that their protection was contingent on their success and discretion? Most likely, Gusev's and Sidorov's sentencing was some combination of both factors, an effort to clean up a mess that had been endorsed by the security services and now was proving a nuisance.

When Gusev got out, he chose a different lifestyle and registered a dairy farm in St Petersburg – but not before making some mysterious trips to the Ukrainian border with members of other Russian PMCs.[11] Sidorov would return to the mercenary life, founding a company called Redut Security, based in Kubinka, near his legally recorded address, and right alongside the base of the 45th VDV Spetsnaz. Redut would, in the years to come, emerge as one of the largest Russian mercenary enterprises, tightly bound up with the GRU.

Slavonic Corps may have failed in its mission, but it heralded a new age in Russian PMSCs. If the wild 1990s and their attendant security companies were the first revolution, and the global War on Terror and its myriad opportunities for private force the second, then Slavonic Corps marked the arrival of the third revolution for contemporary Russian PMCs. For many of Slavonic Corps's fighters, their mercenary lives were just beginning. New enterprises would look to poach them. Among those being scouted were Titov, Degtyarev and that former *spetsnaz* captain named Dmitriy Utkin, call sign Wagner.

PART TWO
FREELANCERS

4

UKRAINE, 2014–15: THE FIRST CAMPAIGNS

I, like many other businessmen, travelled to the training grounds
where the Cossacks were gathering, and tried to spend money on
getting a group together that would go and protect the 'Russians'.
Evgeniy Prigozhin on Wagner's history, September 2022

The Luhansk Airport was a husk of twisted metal and concrete rubble, but it still had a working runway. Ukrainian soldiers held fiercely to what was left. They were besieged on all sides by Moscow-backed separatists of the self-declared 'Luhansk People's Republic' (LNR) who had mined the surrounding fields. They had no way out, no path of retreat. They knew that surrender might mean torture or death.

It was June 2014, and this little airport was a key foothold for Kyiv in resisting the Russian push to consolidate control of eastern Ukraine. Without delivery of arms, ammunition and soldiers by air, the men inside were totally cut off. They were already exhausted and hungry and couldn't hold off the surrounding forces much longer. Kyiv undertook a daring operation to resupply their men.

After midnight on 14 June, two hulking Il-76 transport planes flew towards the airfield with their lights and radios off. Aboard the first were soldiers, nine pilots and three Soviet-era infantry fighting vehicles – key reinforcements for the soldiers holding the airport. The pilot kept his navigation equipment turned off until the last possible moment. Making an approach like this, without navigation and in the dark, was incredibly dangerous, but it was preferable to alerting the enemy below.

Pro-Russian militants massed around the airport. They comprised locals opposed to the Kyiv government who were armed by the Russian security services. They had been drafted into or volunteered for militias organized by the new local authorities, often criminal figures with connections to Russia who put them in a position to seize power in the chaos. Among them were also Russian volunteers: patriots, Soviet nostalgists, neo-fascists and thrill seekers who had come to Ukraine for adventure or because they had no options left.

Distinct from the amalgam of Russian volunteers was a relatively small unit led by more experienced veterans. They had seen action in Chechnya and Afghanistan, and some had won state awards for their service. A few of them talked about a recent 'business trip' to Syria. They included Andrey Lebedev, a forty-year-old man of military bearing, and Andrey Guralev, a 24-year-old fighter from a large family in eastern Siberia. Both men belonged to an anti-aircraft unit and carried Igla shoulder-mounted air defence systems, long cylinders that fired infrared homing missiles. Lebedev had served in Slavonic Corps, and he was now in Ukraine with some of his former colleagues. Their commander was Dmitry Utkin.

At some point, Utkin had given their unit the order to shoot down Ukrainian aircraft landing at the airport. The Il-76 descended in the darkness; there were no lights in the decimated airport. As the plane came closer and closer to the earth the pilot finally flipped on its instruments to allow him to line up for final approach, exposing its location.

We don't know whether Lebedev or Guralev fired the missile that struck the plane, but we know that it was hit by one of their Iglas and came under a barrage of machine gun fire from the ground. The plane crashed to earth 2 kilometres (1 mi.) from the runway at 00:51, killing everyone aboard. A month and a half later, the Ukrainians were driven out of the airport by Lebedev and Guralev's fellow soldiers, many of them mercenaries.

Command in the First Campaigns: The Birth of the Wagner Officer Corps

There are multiple competing versions of Wagner's genesis. None of them are entirely satisfying. Some, like that of Russia analyst Michael Kofman, hold that it was an invention of Russia's Presidential Administration, tying it closely to Putin. Others, like the seasoned Russian investigative journalists Irina Borogan and Andrei Soldatov, believe it was created originally by the GRU itself, and even identified a GRU department dedicated to monitoring Russian PMSCs. Some Russian journalists hold that the influential South African PMSC Executive Outcomes detailed in Chapter Three directly inspired the GRU after its creator, Eeben Barlow, visited the St Petersburg International Economic Forum in 2010 – though it should be said that Russia's PMSC industry was already in full swing at that time.

Prigozhin claimed that it was his own creation. While his disinformation networks were broad, he himself had no military experience. He enjoyed good relationships with parts of the Ministry of Defence and security services but was by no means popular. According to investigators with the Dossier Centre, a London-based investigative organization run by exiled Russian businessman Mikhail Khodorkovsky, the Ministry had considered other possible 'patrons' or 'curators' for armed groups before settling on Prigozhin. But Prigozhin's version of events, which distances Wagner's genesis from the Ministry and the GRU, serves them just fine.

Most likely, the reality is somewhere between these versions. A source close to the Russian Ministry of Defence whom I corresponded with in autumn 2023 indicated that Prigozhin may have sought a role in the war in Ukraine by engaging with Putin indirectly, through the Presidential Administration, much as he had broached his concept for Concord's catering venture. The GRU was introduced to this arrangement and, somewhere along the line,

Prigozhin was put in contact with Utkin. A third man was introduced to the group, a former colonel named Andrey Troshev, who would appear to act mainly as interlocutor with security services. This mythical initial meeting is also the subject of conjecture, with some claiming that the meeting between Prigozhin and Utkin was arranged by the GRU, or Putin's former bodyguard Aleksey Dyumin.[1]

In hindsight, it is easy to divine a grand plot in the combination of Utkin and Prigozhin, but it is likely that whoever brokered the first contact between these men never envisioned what it would lead to. Utkin was not especially distinguished at this stage in his career and the nameless force that he and Prigozhin were inaugurating was only around two hundred strong at the start. Its scale was hardly unique among paramilitary organizations in Russia in 2014. It may have been that Utkin was simply available, connected and qualified by virtue of his *spetsnaz* career and recent Slavonic Corps experience.

Wagner's internal history documents the group's creation on 1 May 2014. On that day, Prigozhin and Utkin allegedly formed the organization, signing a document that bound them to expectations as 'director' and 'commander'. Prigozhin would provide arms, finances, guarantees for casualties and defence from prosecution, and 'would not go against the Russian people'. Utkin would organize the men, train them, 'eliminate' deserters, enforce sobriety among the troops and not 'go against VVP [Putin]'.[2] This document, photographed in Prigozhin's home, is impossible to verify, but comports with the documented early history of Wagner.

Wagner's true authors remain obscure, but the most compelling evidence points to its original creation by the Russian state with Prigozhin as a volunteering patron and steward. He was, after all, both a proven patriotic businessman and a practised evader of sanctions.

Just as, on a much smaller scale, Moran Security's officers were engaged by the FSB to support Russia's allies in Syria in 2013,

Wagner was likely a 'portfolio' of activities that Prigozhin lobbied to take on sometime in 2014. While at first it did not identify as a 'PMC', Wagner was a continuation of the experiment conducted by Russia's security services, principally the GRU, in an effort to field a deniable, agile force that could support proxies, conduct clandestine operations and generally challenge Russia's foes in ways that would thwart their superior economic and military power. For that, they needed a 'curator' to provide some level of off-book finance, facilitate recruitment and create a healthy level of legitimacy for the operation as a truly private enterprise.

And so, once ink was put to paper, a group of men from St Petersburg gathered to train at a small camp in Veseloye, a town in southern Russia. They grew to around two hundred men and were deployed to Ukraine. After their first successes in Luhansk, the mercenaries were relocated to Molkino, a town in Krasnodar, Russia. They were placed in a camp that they shared with the 10th Separate Spetsnaz Brigade of Russia's military intelligence, the GRU (Officially the 'GU', or Main Directorate).

They shared more than just real estate. A leaked document from 2015 records the arms transferred from Russian military units to Wagner over six months, from December 2014 to June 2015. This includes hundreds of rifles, ammunition, mortars and self-propelled howitzers, all transferred from a military unit identified as '35555'. This unit, which belongs to the 78th Intelligence Centre of the GRU, is based near Rostov-on-Don, and part of the Southern Military District, where Wagner would maintain close ties throughout its existence. The Southern Military District, just one of Russia's regional military headquarters, would foster and supply Wagner for the next nine years, before being the site of key scenes in the organization's growth, and later its betrayal and quest for retribution.

All of that was yet to come. Wagner was at this point a modestly sized, if well-outfitted, crew thanks to the GRU. The security services helped Wagner in other ways: the passports issued to Wagner's men tied them to years of GRU clandestine operations around the world. As first reported by Ukrainian intelligence, verified by Bellingcat and confirmed by this author in leaked Wagner documentation, many Wagner fighters who deployed to Ukraine – and later to Syria and Africa – had internal Russian passports issued by Central Migration Office Unit 770-001, which also issued sequentially numbered passports to GRU undercover officers. Others who had received passports from this office included the agents who poisoned former Russian intelligence officer Sergey Skripal in the United Kingdom in 2018.[3]

Wagner's first iteration referred to itself as a 'Company Tactical Group' or 'RTG' organized around Reconnaissance–Assault Companies (RShRS), which would later be shortened to Assault Detachments (shOs). In this early period, there were only a few such units, each of around one hundred men, supported by units specializing in tanks, armoured vehicles, artillery, snipers and so on. The leaders of these units and their direct subordinates would become some of the most significant figures in Wagner in years to come.

They came from a variety of walks of life but embodied the common characteristics of Wagner's officer corps: many had served in other PMCs, whether Slavonic Corps or Moran or others like RSB, including Titov, Degtyarev and Utkin himself. Some had served in the *spetsnaz*, several even coming directly from the 10th Spetsnaz Brigade that Wagner shared their Molkino base with. Nearly all were veterans who had seen combat. Many of them had left their military careers in disgrace after being charged with crimes ranging from embezzlement to robbery.

Utkin himself, variously referred to at that time as the 'battalion commander' or 'regiment commander' of Wagner, with oversight over the RShRS, had had a relatively successful military career, entered the reserves and joined Moran before Slavonic Corps and Wagner. He was generally respected by his men, particularly as the myth of Wagner took on a life of its own with Utkin at the centre.

The commander of Wagner's 1st RShR, a man named Aleksandr Kuznetsov, whom we met as 'Ratibor' in the first chapter, had also served in the *spetsnaz* before being convicted of kidnapping and robbery, released just a year before he joined Wagner. In the years to come, he would become one of Wagner's most storied figures, recognized within the organization as a uniquely talented commander. Ratibor has an almost esoteric approach to warfare. He claims to 'feel the battlefield', and to start each day with the intuitive knowledge of how many men he will lose, where his enemy is located and whether he will be victorious. He professes to preferring to fight under the full moon.[4]

I spoke with Marat Gabidullin, one of the men who served under Ratibor. I asked him about Wagner and other Russian PMCs. He expressed disdain for some of Wagner's commanders, men whose corruption, incompetence and cruelty he has documented in his memoirs. But his tone changed when the topic turned to Ratibor. 'As for Ratibor,' he explained, 'at the tactical and operational level, he was always perceived as a military genius.' Ratibor is not the only commander that Gabidullin expresses respect for in his writing, but he stands out on the page and in our conversation.

> When people like Ratibor command in battle, then in the end, after the battle, you seem to have a feeling that compared to the rest of the detachments you had an easier task. But when you look back and analyse things you realize – it wasn't easy. You were just organized and had great leadership and command.

Both Utkin and Ratibor were alleged in Russian media and by former Wagner fighters to have been *rodnovery*, adherents to the old Slavic neo-pagan faith.[5] This strain of belief, frequently xenophobic and nativist, accounts for some of the tendencies in Wagner's imagery and legend, and its alliances with other militant groups. Utkin blended this belief with Nazism. He was tattooed with an ss symbol, a Nazi eagle, and liked to sign documents with 'ss', giving respect to Prigozhin by concluding messages with 'Heil Petrovich', Sergey Petrovich being the pseudonym of Prigozhin.[6]

Other fighters who joined the organization in 2014 did not fit this mould. Oleg Simunyak, a Serbian who lived in Ukraine, had years of experience fighting in the Balkans with Russian volunteer units before going mainstream to work in explosive ordnance disposal with American and Balkan firms, publishing several books on the topic. He then joined Wagner to lead its sapper unit.

Other militias and 'volunteers' illicitly bankrolled by the security services offered many of the same benefits as Wagner, but the key distinction was in the control that Russia held over the Wagner Group. These other paramilitary fighters were wayward and wilful. Wagner could be directed. They proved their unique utility in 2014 not just as fighters, but as custodians of Russia's other proxy forces.

Cleaning House

The downing of Ukraine's Il-76 in June 2014 and the subsequent capture of Luhansk Airport were the Wagner Group's first major successes. They were not announced in the media and it was not until years later that Ukraine's intelligence services identified Wagner's involvement. We can now corroborate Ukrainian intelligence claims with Wagner's own leaked internal reports.

When the plane was shot down, the group was referred to simply as 'Wagner', and there was scarcely anyone who knew what or who Wagner was. Russian fighters began murmuring about a mysterious 'Wagner' online in later months. But they weren't discussing the Luhansk Airport, which the Russian-backed separatists continued to claim credit for – they were discussing the killing of one of their own, a militia leader named Aleksandr 'Batman' Bednov.

Bednov was a tired-eyed militia leader who had worked in the dreaded OMON riot police of the USSR, then the Ministry of Internal Affairs of the newly independent Ukraine, and finally in a series of private security roles. After the Maidan Revolution overthrew Viktor Yanukovych, he joined a group of pro-Russian activists and found a new lease of life as an enforcer for the LNR. The 'Rapid Response Group Batman' patrolled Luhansk, where local authorities would later accuse him of torture and theft.

There were many men like Bednov who saw opportunity in the aftermath of Russia's annexation of Crimea. They rose from unremarkable roles in private industry, organized crime and local administration (often all three) to 'official' positions in unrecognized states, and led groups of armed men, free to visit violence on whomever they wished. Battalions with names like Ghost, Sparta and Somalia were armed by Russian security services and funded by patriotic Russian oligarchs, and played an important role in battles with the Ukrainian military.

They suited Russia's purposes at the beginning of the war, giving Russia deniability, preventing Ukraine from retaking its territory and allowing the Kremlin to outsource some of the violence in Ukraine. They fought alongside Russian soldiers – whose presence Moscow denied – in places like Ilovaisk. But the type of people who would emerge as leaders in the chaos of eastern Ukraine were also unlikely to follow orders, especially if they were being told to stand down. Already by 2015, they were a thorn in the side of the self-declared local authorities and the Russian security services. Russia was looking for a way to destabilize Ukraine in the long run without having to continue to pour money into the troublesome war in the Donbas. Crimea had been a popular, quick conquest for domestic audiences, but the war in the Donbas was costly in terms of both money and lives, and the Russian people were less enthusiastic about their country being launched into a quagmire for 'states' that Russia did not even recognize. These militia leaders challenged the local power brokers over any negotiations with Kyiv. Eventually, they began to outlive their usefulness.

Bednov was travelling in a convoy on New Year's Day 2015 when his car was attacked with machine guns, RGPs and thermobaric rockets. Officials of the LNR said that he had refused to comply with an arrest order. Some fighters accused the head of the LNR, Igor Plotnitsky, of having Bednov killed for insubordination. On the blog of Boris Rozhin, a pro-Russian blogger who goes by the name 'Colonel Cassad', the first mention of Wagner appeared: 'According to Batman's people, the execution was carried out by a PMC of a certain "Wagner", who is retired military/vacationer from the Russian federation.'

Reporting began to appear in Russian media accusing 'PMC Wagner' of orchestrating the execution not only of Bednov, but of other militia leaders. Wagner Group internal documents dated to 2016 also detail these activities. Wagner's internal history documents their work in this period of early 2015 as subduing 'illegal gangs' and 'Cossack formations' in eastern Ukraine. The memoirs of former Wagner fighter Marat Gabidullin also detail Wagner's role and reputation in eastern Ukraine in 2015: 'As for the fighters of the Army of the Luhansk Republic, we did not have any problems with them. They knew right away that we mercenaries were there to keep an eye on them, and they kept in line. They knew all too well what we were capable of.'[7]

In addition to Batman, Wagner variously claimed or was rumoured to have been involved in the killing of militia leaders like Aleksey Mozgovoy and the arrest or disbanding of units like Odesa and those under Cossack *ataman* Sergey Kosogorov. All these units and their commanders had crossed the leadership of the self-declared republics and were engaged in raiding and pillaging. They compromised Moscow's push towards a favourable negotiated settlement that would prevent Ukraine's westward integration and give Russia control through the people's republics. The deniable forces cultivated and armed by Russia now demanded a new, deniable force to manage them.

Branching Out

By their own accounts, Wagner's numbers in Ukraine in the spring and summer of 2015 grew to more than seven hundred men. Their retrospective documents and descriptions of Wagner's history by Prigozhin do not yet refer to Wagner as a 'PMC' at this stage but as a 'BTG', or a 'battalion tactical group'. BTGs are combined-arms units within the Russian military, increasingly emphasized within Russia's military reforms of the early 2000s to improve readiness. While it is unusual to define this unofficial structure within such doctrinal terms, it makes more sense considering Wagner's roles and direct command by Russia's military, and military intelligence, at the time. Wagner's mission expanded to become an engine for sabotage and attacks behind enemy lines and to reinforce Russia's proxies in key battles against Ukrainian forces.

Many saw Dmitry Utkin, the tall, severe, former *spetsnaz* officer, as the commander of Wagner. He was, after all, its alleged namesake. Wagner's principals, people like Prigozhin, would tell you that Utkin was its overall commander and had been since the early days in Ukraine. This version of events fits Wagner's story as a private enterprise, established by Prigozhin, and overseen by a retired officer. A preponderance of documentary evidence shows that this was not the case.

From the beginning, Wagner was under the command of Russia's military. Russian passenger records identified by the investigative non-profit organization Bellingcat, as well as phone intercepts published by Ukraine's military intelligence, document close coordination between Dmitry Utkin and Russian military intelligence. In February 2015 Utkin spoke on the phone with Oleg Ivannikov, a senior officer in Russia's GRU. Utkin reported to Ivannikov on the ceasefire at the time and frustration with trigger-happy militias: 'The process of negotiations, as I understand, has stalled due to the fact that our motherfuckers continue to pepper them with fire.' Ivannikov responded, sounding tired: 'Well, I hope it's not ours out there. These Cossacks are uncontrollable. I think we'll sort it out now. Okay, I understand you. Good luck. If you are here, call me, and we must meet.'[8]

Ivannikov served as a 'handler' of LNR political leadership in 2014 and 'coordinated and supervised the military activities of Russian militants, pro-Russian separatists and "private army" contingents from the Wagner group', according to Bellingcat.[9] He also played a key role in the transfer of weapons, including Buk air defence systems like the one that shot down Malaysia Airlines flight MH17 in July 2014.

This was not Utkin's only contact with the Russian military at this time. He spoke on multiple occasions with Major General Evgeniy Nikiforov, who then served as chief of staff of Russia's 58th Western Army. Utkin and Nikiforov coordinated the transfer of men and equipment and Wagner's combat operations. Utkin was not the man calling the shots. He was reporting to the GRU and to military brass. As Wagner's role transitioned from cleaning up the blowback of separatist militias to being a fearsome force in their own right, these relationships were key.

Debaltseve

Utkin was on the phone again on 14 February 2015. It was the day before the Minsk II ceasefire was to enter effect, a key step in Russia's effort to secure a favourable settlement in Ukraine. He was at his wit's end, shouting into the phone at Andrey 'Sedoy' Troshev, now Wagner's managing director: 'Yeah, for now I'm just standing, standing, standing. Because, well, if I'm honest, I'm pretty fucked out here, [Andrey] Nikolayevich. I haven't fucking slept in several days; I'm starting to lose it."[10]

Utkin had a growing number of casualties among his men. He had just lost two tanks. He was commanding men amid one of the most decisive battles of the war, and his numbers were suffering: 'Nikolayevich, get me out of here. My own fucking guys are going to shoot me soon.' 'Well,' came the dry response from the other end of the line, 'we're trying, we're trying.'

Debaltseve occupied a pocket between the Donetsk People's Republic (DNR) and LNR-controlled territory in eastern Ukraine and holds a strategically valuable railway junction. Ukrainian forces recaptured the city from Russian-backed separatist control in summer 2014, and held it fiercely through early 2015. By late 2014, the first Minsk Agreement and its tenuous ceasefire had completely collapsed and, in January, the Battle of Debaltseve began in earnest. Five thousand Ukrainian forces would be assaulted by a force more than twice their number. Russian-backed separatists, supported and equipped by Russian forces in Ukraine, showered the area with artillery, and sought to cut off the Ukrainian supply line along the M3 highway, dubbed the 'road of life'.

Even with the advantage of numbers, the fight was not an easy one. More than two hundred Wagner fighters (five hundred according to Wagner's telling) would participate, in close coordination with the Russian military.

Prigozhin would later say that the Ukrainians abandoned their positions and didn't truly try to resist, but the recordings of Utkin from the time, and the documentation of losses within Wagner Group internal records, say differently. Ukrainian intelligence reports that at least 21 Wagner fighters died in the fighting, and Wagner records document memorials or medals for at least fifteen men. Eleven of these are recorded as dying on the same day: 28 January 2015.

On 25 January Wagner forces reinforced a separatist attack on a Ukrainian position defending the M3 highway, their lifeline to Debaltseve. The Ukrainian forces repelled the attack. Three days later, Wagner forces made another attempt on the position. According to Ukrainians defending the location, they only had about twenty men, a fact unknown to the attackers. The Ukrainians killed eleven Wagner fighters and destroyed two of their tanks and three of their armoured vehicles.

If those losses weren't bad enough, two of those armoured vehicles were KAMAZ-43269 'Dozors', at the time only used by Russia. If the Ukrainians recovered them, it would be proof that Russian troops were fighting in Ukraine, right at the moment when Russia was seeking to push for advantageous terms in the Minsk II negotiations. Utkin learned about the lost vehicles in February. He called a man named Sergey Kovalov, the deputy company commander of Wagner's 1st Reconnaissance and Assault Company, one of the units engaged at Debaltseve.

'Serega! Let's resolve these issues as they appear. The most important thing for me right now is to get our fucking destroyed Dozors out of that fucking field, so that nothing of ours is left behind.'

'But the most important thing is to get our people out of there –'

'We'll pull them out and the people, definitely – fuck – We'll pull them here and then we'll figure it out – we could, fuck, fucking saw them in half, the Dozors, and shove them into some Ural or Kamaz [trucks]. Understand?'

The deputy commander tried to explain that he understood, but Utkin talked over him. 'How many do we have, three fucking destroyed machines on the field?'

A cowed Sergey answers, 'Two . . .'

'Two . . . Two fucking Dozors . . .'[11]

In the end, it didn't matter. There was ample evidence of the involvement of regular Russian units. Ukrainian soldiers captured a hard drive that documented Wagner fighters around Debaltseve, including their effort to recover their precious armoured vehicles.

The second ceasefire came into effect on the day after Utkin made his call begging to be pulled out. The pro-Russian forces ignored the ceasefire and pushed on. With the advantage of numbers and the reinforcement of Russian weapons, equipment and forces, they forced the Ukrainians to withdraw three days later.

Wagner's battlefield casualties in Ukraine – upwards of eighty men being killed or wounded – and Utkin's panic at key moments at Debaltseve do not tell the story of a well-organized or formidable fighting force. But Wagner was nonetheless able to claim victory at Debaltseve and continued its campaign in eastern Ukraine through the rest of 2015. The group would ultimately be honoured with monuments in Luhansk, dedicated to the Russian 'volunteers', but bearing Wagner's signature black crest.

The Brain Trust

Wagner was coalescing around a core group of commanders who would come to lead its assault detachments, the basis of the fighting element of the group. Many of these men served in Ukraine and many of them were injured at Debaltseve. Utkin himself was wounded lightly, while future Wagner leaders like Boris Nizhevenok, call sign 'Zombie', were severely injured but recovered. Wagner continued its 'third campaign' across eastern Ukraine. They engaged in sabotage and harassment operations behind enemy lines, while others guarded enemy positions and generally sought to maintain order among the militias. At least six of their men were killed in these operations.

Wagner was just one of many actors in Ukraine in 2014 and 2015, variously serving the interests of the Russian state and themselves. They distinguished themselves as a deniable force to manage proxies. In this regard, it was nothing new – Russia, the Soviet Union and indeed their adversaries in the Cold War had used clandestine action, 'instructors' and specialized forces to work with proxies around the world, whether it was the Soviet Union in Cuba, Angola and Mozambique, or the CIA across Latin America, in Afghanistan and in Vietnam. Using experienced fighters to 'advise' insurgent forces against an adversary is nothing new.

What was unique about Wagner, what made its forces so successful in the eyes of Russian security elites, was that they sat between proxy and legitimate. They were more deniable than regular Russian forces dispatched to Ukraine, but subject to greater control than wayward volunteer movements and local militias. The 'little green men' in unmarked uniforms that invaded Crimea were well and good, but not a ruse that could be kept up forever – you couldn't keep an informal military unit in the field for extended periods of time without oversight and logistics that exposed them, regardless of whether they wore patches.

Over time, the men who fought in Ukraine in 2014 and 2015 formed the core of Wagner's human capital, a brain trust of men who had seen combat and had experience in a variety of different services. The structure that they developed and the tactics that they employed allowed Wagner to move fast and overwhelm enemies even when they enjoyed superior numbers and home advantage. They were the backbone of the first 'Wagner', a military force built for combined-arms assault.

A deniable force was a good thing. A deniable force on a leash was even better. It staffed itself, managed its own discipline and could rein in proxies. The only dent in its status as a 'PMC' was that it didn't seem to be terribly good at making money. That was about to change.

5

SYRIA: BLOOD AND TREASURE

The Russian army's achievements in Syria were largely because of the mercenaries' sacrifices. That fact is completely ignored by the military establishment and not known to the wider public.
Marat 'Ded' Gabidullin, former Wagner mercenary[1]

Wagner veterans talk and write more about Syria than about anywhere else. They call it Peski, SARatov, Banistan, Mars. They write about the ancient city of Palmyra and the hills around Latakia, and they talk about the desert. They write about camaraderie and the terror of being under mortar fire. They talk about horrible leaders and great soldiers. In the stories that Wagnerites tell, Syria is where they achieved greatness. In both battles of Palmyra, they proved their worth. At the Battle of Khasham, hammered by American airpower, they were double-crossed. In Syria, the seeds of grievance were planted that would flower into an abortive mutiny nine years later.

Some of these things are true. But Syria is also where they learned to make money and began referring to themselves as a 'PMC', and where the group earned its other apt internal title, 'the Company'. While Wagner was in Syria to support Assad on behalf of Russia, many of its operations were guided by profit motives.

The Fourth and Fifth Campaigns

Wagner first appeared in Syria in late September 2015, shortly after Russia began to deploy soldiers to the country. The Ministry of Defence launched a 'special operation' on 30 September. A decision had been made at the top that Prigozhin's band would reinforce them.

As with Wagner's founding, there is little reliable information on how Wagner took this critical next step after Ukraine. It almost certainly required approval at the heights of the government, either as a result of Prigozhin's continued advocacy for himself and his organization or at the suggestion of its GRU handlers. According to the same source close to Russia's Defence Ministry with whom I corresponded in autumn 2023, few know how the arrangement came about, but it was likely the result of Prigozhin arguing his case. 'Presumably, this was at the initiative of Prigozhin, who was looking for a use for the Wagner Group after he was asked to leave the Donbas,' they suggest. 'Of course, only Putin could make such a decision.'

Prigozhin's value proposition was clear: by entering Syria, Wagner could take on dangerous missions on the ground that would reinforce the conventional Russian presence and airpower in support of Assad, while guaranteeing that any losses would be easier to hide. Wagner would allow Russia to be more aggressive at lower cost.

Numbering nearly 1,500 men, Wagner's first Syrian missions were in Latakia and Homs, locations familiar to the veterans of the Slavonic Corps. They conducted reconnaissance missions and trained local forces such as the Syrian Army's Tiger Forces and pro-Assad private militia the Desert Hawks. While Wagner's activities were shrouded in secrecy and discretion was one of its selling points for Russia, Wagner nonetheless found it difficult to hide its losses. In October, sources in Russia began reporting that at least eight Wagner fighters had been killed in Syria.[2] Wagner's own documentation of losses, which formed the basis of investigations by Russian journalists, records eight deaths on 19 October at a temporary dislocation point in Syria. This may have been the same incident memorialized by Marat Gabidullin in his literary account of his experiences, where a Wagner site was hit by a guided projectile:

> There was no sound of approach – just an explosion in the tent itself: matter torn to shreds, scattered beds, dead and wounded fighters ... The mutilated bodies of fighters still breathing and showing signs of life with open wounds and entrails spilling out lay intermingled with the disfigured corpses of those who had not even woken up, turned into dead meat.[3]

Russia's military command, together with Wagner, was startled by the event, and pulled out an unknown number of fighters on 20 October. They would return just a few months later, in January 2016.

This 'fourth campaign', as Wagner calls it, was small compared to what was to come. Wagner's numbers in Syria swelled in 2016 as they were flown from their base at Molkino aboard military cargo aircraft. The fighters supported Syrian forces together with Russian airpower in taking towns near Latakia. Together, they succeeded in taking important locations like Salma from rebel forces, putting the wind in the sails of Assad's campaign.

In the process, Wagner restructured its forces around the new enemy being faced. They adapted from their previous 'BTG' approach to one founded on assault detachments, mobile units able to stage quick attacks that were covered by fire support that could take out enemy vehicles or soften fortified positions. As Gabidullin explained to me in an interview in July 2022, 'when they created the Assault Detachments in Syria, the enemy was very mobile and agile.'

Through January and February, Wagner fighters rolled through the hills in Ural and GAZ trucks, travelling with Syrian units to clear towns and strategic heights. They fought with machine guns, automatic grenade launchers, anti-tank guided missiles and sniper rifles. They rested between battles, drank coffee and engaged in infighting over perceived slights and accusations of incompetence.

Then they entered Palmyra. The March 2016 Palmyra offensive was an effort by Syria and Russia to recapture territory near the ancient city famous for the pillars of its Great Colonnade, from the Islamic State. Palmyra had been a cultural and trade capital that changed hands between empires over millennia. The city's ancient ruins would enter Wagner's mythology, memorialized in photographs of armour-clad fighters posing in front of columns in the Syrian desert.

The offensive began with heavy air strikes by the Russian Aerospace Forces on 9 March. Rockets and artillery rained down on the area, softening ISIS defences for a ground assault. The Syrian and Russian forces attempted to surround the city, attacking from multiple flanks to drive ISIS out of their fortifications. Wagner fighters began pressing the ground assault west of Palmyra and made their way to a series of key heights along the Jabal al Qa'id ridge. Wagner was complementing Russian air strikes as shock troops, throwing themselves at ISIS positions to prepare the ground for the primary effort of pro-Assad troops.

The trenches and craters from rockets and artillery are still visible in satellite images. Wagner and the Tiger Forces pushed through the heights to hills known only by numbers, by 15 March reaching a point just a few kilometres south of Palmyra itself. The Syrian military, its allied militias like Hezbollah, Russian Special Forces (SSO) and Aerospace Forces all fought alongside Wagner. This, predictably, made for challenging coordination, and more than once friendly fire from Russian forces claimed the lives of Syrian fighters. But this mixed bag of units gave the Syrian coalition superior numbers. As the battle entered its second week, Assad's assembly of militants and mercenaries gained the advantage over ISIS. They made their way into Palmyra and the city of Tadmur, where house-to-house fighting and ISIS car bombs levelled buildings. By 27 March, after a gruelling two weeks and four days, Palmyra was captured.

To Wagner's forces, it felt that they had made a tremendous sacrifice. Some thirty of their men were dead and many more were wounded. Commander of the Fourth Assault Detachment Andrey Bogatov, call sign 'Brodyaga', had lost his left arm near Palmyra in a Russian air strike, but continued to fight. Later, Wagner fighters would say they were used as 'cannon fodder' to weaken ISIS positions and allow the Syrian Army to advance.[4]

The battle had attracted unusual international attention given its setting and scale, but Wagner fighters weren't permitted to take public credit. They saw Russian special-operation forces celebrated for their feats and the Syrians celebrating their victory. The capture of Palmyra held an enormous position in the Wagner mythos, tainted by the sense that they did not receive the credit they were due.

Then, in 2017, they had to do it again.

ISIS had retaken Palmyra in December 2016 and had pushed west towards the T4 airbase where Wagner was now located. ISIS was repelled and the Syrian Army began another grinding offensive in January 2017 that would last for a month and a half. Wagner fighters were carried into Syria on the Syrian airline Cham Wings and Russian military aircraft. They reinforced the Syrian counter-attack, assisting them in capturing not only strategic heights, but the nearby Hayyan and Jihar gas fields. Wagner fighters were at the bleeding edge of the offensive. Dmitriy Utkin, now going by the call sign 'Ninth', led attacks on the Hayyan gas fields, supported by strikes from Russian aircraft. His unit took the strategic heights of Hills 715 and 725, allowing the fields to be captured. Aleksandr 'Ratibor' Kuznetsov led his First Assault Detachment through the familiar ridges southwest of the city, then wrapped around the southern edge to cut off the airport. For their efforts, both men would be made Heroes of the Russian Federation by President Putin, one of the country's highest honours.

According to Prigozhin, he arrived near Palmyra on 2 March to meet Syrian officials who thanked his fighters for their efforts. Somewhere between forty and sixty Wagner fighters were likely killed in the offensive, and despite the honours that survivors and the dead would receive later in the year, the survivors felt that the honour they had earned was again snatched by the Russian Ministry of Defence. In 2023 Ratibor would write, 'We cannot remain silent about our fallen comrades during the liberation of the ancient city ... the role of PMC Wagner in the fight against terrorism was hidden from the public.'[5]

That Wagner fighters were paid more than their regular Russian counterparts in the field didn't seem to compensate for this moral injury – but it was enough to convince Prigozhin to keep his venture going. While Wagner's list of victories grew long and its ranks swelled, the other side of the network was maturing as well. Prigozhin nurtured an enormous criminal bureaucracy of front companies replete with bookkeepers and administration staff that in 2017 would come to transform Wagner into an entirely different animal.

The Firm

Evro Polis LLC was a small, anonymous Russian company registered on 13 July 2016. It had only one employee and no website, and it was registered to the same address as dozens of other companies. This little firm, with an authorized capital of just a few hundred dollars, would become the lynchpin of Wagner's commercial network.

Even as the network of Prigozhin-associated companies behind Wagner grew to nearly four hundred, Evro Polis and his original invention, Concord, would continue to occupy a central position. Their chief accountants were copied in on almost all important correspondence across the network and Evro Polis administrative personnel had oversight over almost all significant contracts.

Evro Polis was the heart behind the financial arteries of Wagner, the key to its ability to pay fighters and engineers, to move men and equipment and to continue prosecuting wars on behalf of Russian state interest.

Evro Polis occupied this role because it was central in Wagner's first profit-generating venture: Syrian oil. In 2017 Evro Polis got a new general director, a retired Ministry of Internal Affairs detective named Oleg Erokhin, who had previously founded a veterans' organization with Wagner's general director, Andrey Troshev. That same year, 'the Company' opened a branch in Damascus, Syria. Most importantly, on 7 January it closed a deal with the Syrian government that would allow it to claim up to 25 per cent of the revenue from oil extracted at sites liberated by Wagner.

Wagner began capturing hydrocarbon sites. While they fought towards Palmyra in 2017, they seized oil and natural-gas facilities. They took the Jihar and al Magr fields. They took al Shaer, Jazal. These fields made up the Hayyan block, which would yield Evro Polis u.s.$162 million in natural-gas revenues alone in 2017. The Company now hired not just soldiers, but engineers and energy professionals. Wagner dispatched specialists from Russia to extinguish the wells set alight by ISIS and restore the energy facilities. By May, Evro Polis had extinguished five oil and gas wells and claimed in a letter to Syria's former minister of presidential palace affairs Mansour Azzam that it had succeeded in securing production of 2 million cubic metres of gas daily.

But there were snags along the way. Much like Slavonic Corps, Evro Polis found that its Syrian partners were not always enthusiastic about holding up their end of the deal. An attempt to create a joint venture with Syria's national oil company fizzled. Syria's Minister of Oil stonewalled the Russian company's attempts to receive payment. Still, enough money came through to justify the creation of still more enterprises in Syria. Prigozhin-linked companies Mercury, Capital and Velada all secured rights to Syrian oil

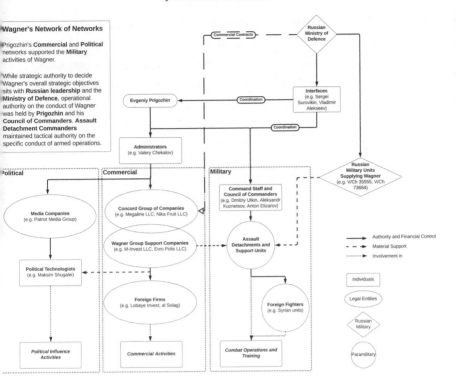

Network map of the companies behind the Wagner Group.

and gas between 2017 and 2021, from onshore blocks to concessions in waters contested by Syria and Lebanon.[6]

These commercial enterprises carried out a range of tasks for the larger network, hiring the specialists to extinguish wells and build facilities, contracting with Russian Ministry of Defence flight units to move Wagner men into Syria and back to Russia, and buying gear like night vision optics for their fighters. They also paid the soldiers themselves, as documented in a library of financial records leaked from the organization. The trail of companies and their intricate systems of payment and management demonstrate how Prigozhin's experience in illicit business set him apart in this realm and allowed Wagner to flourish in ways it never had before.

This was the birth of the 'second' Wagner, a sprawling network of companies born from Prigozhin's earlier illicit endeavours. The 'first' Wagner, the military element, was reliant on this corporate structure. It would also allow Prigozhin to attain new levels of influence in the countries that Wagner operated in, nesting within the business interests of kleptocratic states to foster not just security, but profit incentives. If you were an embattled dictator, Wagner could both protect you and deliver wealth to you and your circle. Insurgents halting your hydrocarbon or mineral business? Wagner could jump-start them both, for a price.

Illicit networks from Hezbollah to drug cartels engage in similar strategic corruption. By using complex financial structures, woven across jurisdictions that allowed them to maintain corporate secrecy, such as the Gulf States, Hong Kong or the UK's overseas territories, they could hide the origin and destination of funds. These funds could be obtained through criminal enterprises (arms, narcotics, corruption) or even legal means and then deployed for criminal ends – arming militias, buying off politicians or acquiring luxury goods for dictators.

This did not mean that Prigozhin was independent. Other leaked Wagner documents record ongoing requisitions from the Ministry of Defence throughout this period, ranging from rifles to tanks. Russia's and Wagner's dual bureaucracies preserved the myriad transfers on paper, enough to equip a small army. Wagner purchased some ammunition itself, but most was sourced from the ministry. Military Unit 7364, based at Khmeimim Air Base, served as the pass-through for a large part of this equipment in Syria. For all the corporate infrastructure and command structure that Wagner had built, they were still the Ministry's animal, benefiting from not just arms and equipment, but intelligence. Wagner worked closely with the GRU's Deputy Chief Vladimir Alekseev to coordinate activities, and in return regularly received the GRU's classified intelligence reports on armed groups in Syria.[7]

The bulk of Wagner's funding continued to be funnelled to the Company through the state budget. In 2023 Prigozhin would shed further light on Wagner's financing. In an open letter to Sergey Shoigu, he claimed that Wagner had reinvested around U.S.$1.7 billion in profits from catering for the military into military ventures in Syria and their later exploits in Africa. Putin himself would also state that the Russian government 'fully financed this group from the federal budget' and that they earned further money from catering contracts.[8] For now, despite the simmering discontent between Russia's powerful cadres in the military and Wagner, the arrangement remained mutually beneficial.

Like much of Wagner, it was once again nothing new – but it was unique in its combination of familiar themes. Wagner mingled an illicit financial network with clandestine assistance to proxies and an ostensibly private military force in the service of the state. Like the companies of the Syrian Express before it, Wagner was a robust state-sponsored illicit network. This approach was the basis of much of Russia's efforts to support fellow pariah states and control its neighbours in Europe through embedding in their markets, whether it meant enriching friendly politicians through sweetheart deals or blackmailing whole economies through Russia's position as an oil and gas producer that could turn off the taps or manipulate prices.[9]

Wagner proved especially adept at wielding this shadowy corporate network in tandem with its military force. Each side could reinforce the other, but without the attendant bureaucracy that hampered the Russian military and security services. Much like the earlier Syrian Express, Wagner's corporate substrata allowed the Kremlin to support its allies despite sanctions, at lower cost and with lower risk. It didn't hurt that the managers of these systems got rich in the process. There are ample opportunities for skimming off the top of a criminal enterprise.

This profit motive made it all the more abhorrent when Wagner engaged in atrocities. Not only were Wagner's fighters able to terrorize civilian populations with impunity; they were making money doing it. Such was the case of the recorded torture and execution of Muhammed Ismail, addressed in Chapter One. His death was particularly cruel and well documented, but it was also a reflection of the bloody reality of Wagner's illicit business: he was killed at the Shaer gas fields, one of the sites that Wagner profited from in its contract with the Syrian government.

This pattern of atrocity overlapping with commercial interests would accompany Wagner in its later campaigns. Excessive violence served as retribution for fallen fighters and as a deterrent to would-be foes, and cemented a grim bond between Wagner's men, through both blackmail and a culture that celebrated these events. Wagner would come to embrace symbols of its most craven violence, from individual perpetrators like Ismail's torturers to the tools they used, like the sledgehammer. It was a threat to foes and, like the infamous tattoos of Soviet criminals in the twentieth century, a symbol of Wagner's place outside the constraints of mainstream society. Wagner was not bound by the same rules as everyone else, whether they were regular Russians or the military. They gave life to the fantasies of violence directed towards Russia's enemies that were the logical conclusion of the narrative of Western conspiracy and the humiliation of Russia espoused by Putin and state media. When the worst manifestations of those vengeful fantasies took shape, even the state felt the need to distance itself from Wagner on the international stage. Yet where the Russian government denied involvement in torture, assassinations and the killing of civilians, Wagner's symbols and lingo would attest, 'Yes, we did it, and they deserved it.'

Sword and Shield

At around noon on 16 June 2019, a convoy of armoured vehicles drove down the highway between the Tuweidan gas fields and al Sukhnah, north of Palmyra. It carried engineers employed by StroyTransGaz or STG, a Russian oil and gas company owned by businessman and Putin ally Gennady Timchenko, accompanied by armed Russians. Several of the guards had been in Syria before with Wagner. Now they had a different employer, a company named Redut Security, known locally as Shield. Redut's legal structure in Russia had been created by Evgeniy Sidorov, one of the protagonists of Slavonic Corps. Redut and Slavonic Corps had a similar mission: protect Syrian oil and gas sites.

The convoy came under heavy machine gun fire from offroad vehicles. It was the type of hit-and-run attack commonly used by militant groups in Syria – the attackers peppered their targets with small-arms fire and sped away. One of Redut's Dozor armoured vehicles peeled off in pursuit with four men aboard. Three of them, under the call signs Kairat, Tanker and Shaiman, were former Wagner fighters. As the car passed the location where the gunfire had come from, an explosive device detonated nearby. Kairat and Shaman were killed, while Tanker was thrown from the vehicle. He was found dead several days later. Shaman's real name was David Honda and he had a family waiting for him in Russia. A colleague returned his remains to them in a zinc coffin, along with an Arabic death certificate that described the cause of his death as 'cerebral haemorrhage as a result of a fragmentation explosion.'[10]

Three days later, Utkin received his own report on the incident, prepared by a Wagner fighter. Wagner was keeping a close eye on Redut, which had poached several of its staff since it appeared in Syria the previous year. Redut's business model was different from Wagner's, since it defended the assets of a much more established Russian company. STG was an energy company that happened to have a PMC attached to it; Wagner was the other way around. As a result, Redut's men typically guarded stationary sites belonging to STG rather than engaging in front-line combat. This was not without risk, as the June 2019 episode demonstrated, but it did mean that a rotation with Redut promised to be less fraught than a deployment with Wagner. They lured a few senior Wagner men to their business, including Marat Gabidullin. Russia's mercenary marketplace was expanding.

Redut was based next to the 45th VDV Spetsnaz base in Kubinka, Russia. It had a tight relationship with the GRU, perhaps even more direct than Wagner's, but its primary beneficiary was the well-known billionaire Timchenko, a long-time friend of Putin's. Russian businessmen like Timchenko had interests in Syria that preceded Wagner's arrival, built on strong connections in the Syrian government and within armed groups on the side of Assad before the war.[11] They, like the Russian security services, appreciated the value that Wagner's toothier take on private security offered for business in Syria. Between the war and sanctions risk, most international energy companies had fled, but having a private army meant that businesses like Timchenko's could use the conflict as an opportunity. The Russian military was closely involved, and Redut's activities were supervised by a body called the Centre for Ensuring Economic Activities of Russian State Companies in Syria, headed by a Russian colonel. Wagner received some of their documentation, either through sources or as favours, enabling them to stay a step ahead of their mercenary competition.

Invested in gas and phosphates, STG ran a business that was likely more profitable than Wagner's in Syria, but it lacked Wagner's battlefield impact. Timchenko and Prigozhin sought different niches according to their stature. Timchenko was already part of Putin's trusted circle and was content to participate in business with a patriotic bent while enriching himself. Prigozhin, meanwhile, needed to prove his value. In 2018 this ambition would lead to Wagner's worst catastrophe to date.

Icarus

While fighting ISIS and the Syrian Democratic Forces (SDF) proved challenging for Wagner, its forces generally benefited from better training and equipment and the support of Russian air power and arms. But in the maelstrom of different interests fighting in Syria, it was just a matter of time before they got into a fight they weren't prepared for.

Wagner had a banner year in 2017. In January, a photograph appeared on social media of Putin alongside four men adorned with military honours. These were familiar faces: Brodyaga, Sedoy, Ratibor and Utkin himself. This image became a symbol of Putin's respect for Wagner and the role of the Russian state in its rise. It was likely taken on the sidelines at the same 9 December 2016 reception for military veterans where Utkin and Troshev appeared in the background of a television broadcast. It was circulated broadly, dissected by journalists and celebrated by Wagnerites.

After victory at Palmyra, Wagner conducted a series of campaigns near the Euphrates river in the Governate of Deir ez-Zor. Its forces pushed towards the city of Deir ez-Zor along with their Syrian partners. The Russian military and the Syrian Army claimed these victories. 'Major triumphs have been achieved in central Syria where the Aleppo province has been fully liberated. Just over the past week the government forces have established control over 1,100 square kilometres [1,300 sq. yd] of territory,' said General Sergey Surovikin, the commander of Russia's forces in Syria.[12] A Wagner ally, Surovikin nonetheless gave no credit to the mercenary forces that were also involved in the campaign.

The campaign brought Wagner to the west bank of the Euphrates. On the other side of the river, the SDF prosecuted their 'al-Jazeera Storm campaign' to dislodge ISIS. The Syrian Army and SDF held an uneasy truce, each focused on the common enemy, ISIS, on either bank of the Euphrates. The United States-led Combined

Joint Task Force – Operation Inherent Resolve provided air support to the SDF in their fight. Both the United States and Russia were keenly aware of the risks of escalation and wanted to prevent their local allies from engaging one another.

There were a few incidents where the line was crossed. In September, Syrian and Russian aircraft and artillery hit SDF forces at the Conoco gas field. Later, Russian bombing killed civilians on the east side of the Euphrates. But the truce held.

On the east bank of the Euphrates, American and SDF forces continued to hold the Conoco gas field. On 7 February 2017 they observed Russian and Syrian forces massing nearby. The SDF's Kurdish forces and their American allies were alarmed – it looked like the pro-Assad forces were going to violate the tenuous agreement with the coalition and attempt to drive the SDF back. Via a deconfliction line, they contacted the Russian Ministry of Defence, who denied the presence of any ground troops in the area.

As night fell, the Russian and Syrian forces began their assault on the SDF. Artillery and mortar rounds punched into the desert, while American troops fired warning shots at the advancing force. Their small-arms fire bounced off the Russian tanks and the coalition force, a few dozen men, was left facing down a five-hundred-strong infantry assault backed by armour and artillery.

It is possible that the Wagnerites didn't realize that the Americans were there. Anonymous American service members also indicate that they may have believed they were protected by air defence systems that would repel American airpower. Either they made a severe miscalculation or were hung out to dry by the Russian military: the USA had full reign of the air domain. MQ-9 Reaper drones, F-16 fighter jets, Apache helicopters and even AC-130 gunships and B-52 bombers appeared in the night sky over Conoco fields, invisible to the Russians with limited night vision.

Survivors describe the confusion. Their accounts all emphasize the sound. The staccato chain guns of Apache helicopters, the pounding of the c-130s' 40-millimetre cannons, the deafening boom of the ordnance dropped from strategic bombers, all mingled with Russian and Syrian tank and artillery fire. Communication was nearly impossible, but the Wagner fighters knew they were fighting for survival. Gabidullin recounts the experience:

> Barely perceptible in the roar of battle, the sound of a rocket approach, an explosion, and the tank, which managed to fire only once, exploded in flames. Another hiss and the position of the mortars was engulfed in a fiery tornado. 'What is it, where is it coming from?' . . . Invisible in the dark sky, attack helicopters raked everything that moved.[13]

Accounts from the American side are mostly restricted to the statements of u.s. military officials and the declassified recordings of the battle. Night vision footage from American gunships captured the moment a Russian T-72 tank was struck. In grainy black and white, the dark outline of the tank stands in relief to the white earth behind it. The frame goes black, then white. The image comes back into focus, revealing heaving clouds of smoke and scorched earth where the tank once stood.[14] The Russian military contacted the United States and sdf and asked them to pause the assault to allow for the Russians to remove their dead and wounded, despite having denied they were there just hours before.

The Battle of Conoco Fields, or the Battle of Khasham as it is also known, left a deep mark on Wagner. The Russians claimed that none of their fighters were present, and the United States claimed a handful of Russian citizens may have died. The circumstances allowed both sides to conveniently de-escalate, but Wagner was left with around eighty dead fighters and a litany of unanswered questions. Did Wagner's leadership or the Russian military order them to attack an American position? Did they know what they would be up against? Why did they allow them to march in unprepared?

Some quietly blamed Prigozhin, but most found the Russian military at fault. Prigozhin would later claim that this was the pivotal moment in the Defence Ministry's betrayal of Wagner, a product of their envy over the success that his men had delivered for Russia.

There are multiple possible explanations for why Wagner and its Syrian allies staged their doomed assault at Khasham. Prigozhin would later claim that the action was coordinated with the Russian Defence Ministry to conquer territory for their Syrian allies.[15] Russian journalists found evidence that Wagner had taken its own initiative to seize oil fields in exchange for money from the Syrians.[16] More evidence supports the latter theory.

In 2018 the *Washington Post* cited unnamed U.S. officials who claimed that Prigozhin had been in touch with Syrian counterparts including Minister of Palace Affairs Mansour Fadlallah Azzam shortly before the attack on Conoco fields. These officials claimed that communication intercepts had documented Azzam guaranteeing Prigozhin that he would be paid if he seized the territory.[17] This claim is at least in part supported by leaked correspondence from a Wagner representative – possibly Prigozhin himself – addressed to Minister Azzam in May 2017. In that letter, the author complains that the Syrian government had not held up its end of the deal regarding Wagner's capture of oil fields or the extinguishing of wells. The letter implores Azzam to intercede with Assad on Evro Polis's behalf to guarantee their payment. 'No funds were received to reimburse the expenses of Evro Polis LLC,' the letter states. 'Meanwhile, Evro Polis LLC's expenses have exceeded $120 million of its own funds.' The letter ends by stating that a copy has been forwarded to the 'Co-Chairman of the Russian–Syrian Commission on Trade, Economic, Scientific, and Technical Cooperation, Dmitriy Rogozin', a man who would later go on to form his own private military enterprise to support Russia's war in Ukraine.

If authentic, this letter suggests that Minister Azzam was a key player in Wagner's financial relationship with the Syrian government and lends credence to the claims reported by the *Washington Post*. It also suggests that Wagner was coordinating this effort with the Russian government – or at the very least telling the Syrians that they were.

If Prigozhin truly felt that Wagner had been wronged by the Russian military at the time, he held his tongue. The Wagner fighters killed were posthumously awarded the Order of Courage by the Russian government. In all, 282 living and dead Wagnerites received this award for their service in the battle. Among those who led Wagner's doomed assault was Aleksander 'Emelya' Emelyanov, leader of the 5th Assault Detachment. He was likely awarded the Hero of Russia, as evidenced by the application for this award recorded in Wagner files. But Emelyanov's career with Wagner was just beginning. The Company was expanding and not just in Syria. There was a new frontier of opportunities to be had in Africa, in terms of both money and Russian influence.

6

SUDAN AND THE CAR: THE NEXT FRONTIER

They will learn the hard way that Mozambique is not Syria.
Eeben Barlow, founder of Executive Outcomes and STTEP International

Sudan had long been a Russian ally. Under thirty years of authoritarian rule by Omar al-Bashir, the country had crushed independence movements in its oil-rich south and the ethnically diverse west, played host to radical Islamists including Osama bin Laden and suppressed a vibrant intellectual tradition. The country was ruled by a cartel that sustained itself through capture of state institutions and industry, and protected itself with a massive security state and a dreaded intelligence apparatus.

Bashir, who came to power in a coup, understood the value of both watering his patronage network and keeping the military in check. He did this through creating a system whereby the military controlled the commanding heights of the economy, and a paramilitary group, called the Rapid Support Forces or RSF, was brought in as an auxiliary force to deter any ambitions of military leadership. The RSF itself was grown out of a smattering of nomadic militias that had terrorized pastoral and agrarian communities in the west of the country. The groups that would comprise the RSF, the Janjaweed, had committed atrocity after atrocity in Darfur and South Kordofan. Bashir gave militant leader Mohamed Hamdan Dagalo, frequently called 'Hemedti', an official role as the head of the RSF, hoping that this would ensure his loyalty. As an indicted war criminal himself, Bashir had little international standing to lose by elevating one of the most recognizable perpetrators of the Darfur genocide to an official position.

Pariah or not, it was not as if Bashir had no allies. The Gulf States and Egypt were key players in North Africa, and Bashir maintained generally positive relations with them into the 2000s. He also had Sudan's strongest political ally and investor in Europe – Russia. Bashir remembered well that Putin opposed UN peacekeeping in Darfur, and Sudan benefited from Russian weapons and investment in key sectors like gold and agriculture. In at least one case, there were Russian nationals working in the pay of the Sudanese military: in 2008 the rebel Justice and Equality Movement shot down an MiG-29 fighter, killing its Russian pilot. Russian media reported that he was an aviation instructor hired by the Sudanese.[1]

Against this backdrop, Russian prime minister Dmitriy Medvedev met Bashir in Sochi, Russia, in November 2017. They discussed commercial and diplomatic projects, and signed agreements on gold mining and mineral exploration. These agreements featured long-standing Russian ventures in Sudan like the Kush for Exploration company, as well as a little-known firm called M Invest. Representing M Invest was a man named Mikhail Potepkin.

Potepkin was a self-proclaimed Russian patriot and had been a leader in a pro-Putin youth group. Before making an unusual pivot to mining in Sudan, he had been co-owner of a tech company. The other co-owner of this tech venture was a woman named Anna Bogacheva, who had previously worked with Prigozhin's IRA – the St Petersburg troll farm.[2] Potepkin had long been in Prigozhin's orbit.

As it turned out, M Invest itself was a Prigozhin project. Its director also directed Prigozhin-linked companies that won contracts with the Ministry of Defence. The company that owned M Invest, called Delta, was directed by an individual who held positions on Prigozhin-linked companies in the Concord network. M Invest founded a company in Sudan known as Meroe Gold, named after the mineral-rich region of the country that was home to the colossal 2,000-year-old pyramids of the Kushite Kingdom.

From the first, it was clear that Meroe Gold was not a normal investor. Aside from concessions for gold extraction, Meroe also won the right to process gold tailings – the leftover materials from gold processing – an industry restricted to local companies under Sudanese law. In 2018 Bashir would even order the Ministry of Minerals to waive the required 30 per cent government owner-ship of mining companies for Meroe. Instead, Meroe and the Sudanese government agreed that the government would take its cut through a military-controlled company called SMT. Meroe was already at work to begin mining: in autumn 2017 Meroe Gold began to import mining equipment from Chinese manufacturers, and vehicles, food and other equipment from Russian companies. Their Russian suppliers, companies such as M Invest, Novolend, Broker Expert, Negotsiant and M Finance, were all connected to Prigozhin's Concord network. They sent Meroe Gold geological equipment in 2017 before later sending trucks and even helicop-ters. As their operations scaled up and video emerged of Russian instructors training Sudanese military forces, it became clear that Meroe, M Invest and the other companies in this network were all part of the Wagner Group.

These Russian firms were supplying other parties in Sudan – companies with names like SMT Engineering and Esnaad Engineering. SMT was part of Sudan's sprawling military–industrial complex, while Esnaad Engineering was directed by Algoney Hamdan Dagalo Mousa, the brother of RSF chief Hemedti. Esnaad imported riot shields, batons and even helicopter engines on behalf of Meroe Gold. Wagner wasn't putting all its eggs in one basket; it played nice with both the military and the RSF.

The foundation of these commercial relationships was a con-tract that Meroe Gold held with another Sudanese company – this one controlled by Sudan's military intelligence – called Aswar Multi-Activities. According to a leaked document obtained by the Dossier Centre, the network agreed to pay Aswar U.S.$100,000 each month to facilitate security, immigration and import activities. M Invest was to pay all taxes and fees on behalf of Aswar and even pay Aswar's staff. M Invest offered Aswar a U.S.$500 bonus for every member of the Russian staff it helped bring into Sudan.[3] Wagner knew exactly which hands to grease for preferential treatment.

Wagner may have been opening the door for still more Russian military exports to Sudan and even the construction of a naval base. While Russia's military exports to the Sudanese Armed Forces (SAF) continued apace, they also expanded to include the RSF. In 2019 another Sudanese company controlled by Hemedti's brother, called GSK, started importing drones from a small company in Russia called Aviatrade. Aviatrade had no real online footprint but exported drones to countries like Venezuela and Mongolia. These trade records hide the brand of drone exported, but their description coincides with that of Russian-made Zala 421-22 surveillance drones.

Meanwhile, Wagner's influence networks spun up in Sudan, creating sock puppet accounts on Facebook that boosted Bashir, smeared the opposition and celebrated Russia's role in Sudan. These posts also argued for some very specific policies, including Sudan's ongoing discussions with Russia about the creation of a Russian naval base at Port Sudan on the Red Sea. These discussions ultimately fizzled against the backdrop of domestic political turmoil, but the spectre of a strategically located Russian naval base raised hackles in Washington and Brussels. Wagner in Syria or Ukraine was one thing, but with their presence in Sudan and a cast of mysterious Russian companies now surfacing in Madagascar, they appeared to be able to establish strongholds far beyond where Russia's military could reach. Wagner was changing Africa, but Africa was also changing Wagner.

Over the Horizon

Wagner's entry into Africa was undertaken in tandem with Russian diplomatic efforts, but as in Syria, it remains unclear whether Wagner was instructed to establish itself on the continent or whether Prigozhin and his allies advocated for this new venture. Given the variety of forms Wagner took in Africa, its commercial enterprises and the level of direct involvement from Prigozhin, it stands to reason that even if this round of expansion was not a result of his initiative, he was at least enthusiastic about it. Wagner would achieve new levels of independence in Africa, engaged as it was on the outskirts of Russia's geopolitical interests. More than in Syria and Ukraine, Wagner had the opportunity to establish itself as a primary agent, becoming the representative of Russian interests in the countries it took hold in. It nonetheless continued to benefit from Russian military arms and logistics. Years later, Prigozhin would fight fiercely to maintain Wagner's foothold in Africa, even against the wishes of Russia's security elites.

As Wagner entered Africa, its operations evolved at a rapid pace. From 2017 onwards, it established security activities, won valuable resource concessions, ran propaganda campaigns and spun up companies from South Africa to Libya. The 'third' Wagner was taking form, drawing on the propagandists and political engineers that Prigozhin had been attracting to his endeavours since 2012. Since 'the Company' was not a single entity, but rather a combination of complementary social and corporate networks, it could appear in any number of guises. Wagner might manifest through its political-interference arm, as journalists, sociologists or election observers with an NGO that was surreptitiously connected to Prigozhin. It could appear in its commercial form, as a private company engaged in resource exploration. In its most impactful deployments, Wagner could leverage its political, commercial and military aspects together to achieve substantial influence, change security dynamics, generate profit and pave the way for security agreements between Russia and developing states.

Western analysts and media scrambled to make sense of this new phenomenon, usually in the context of 'great-power competition' on the continent. This framework has informed u.s. and European policy towards African countries over the past decade, particularly as Western governments seek to counter expanding Chinese influence.[4] As a policy approach, great-power competition casts Western engagement in Africa primarily as a bulwark against Russia's and China's growing influence. In the best cases, it manifests through aid and diplomacy, and in the worst cases, as information operations and coercion.[5] It has elevated Africa in policy discussions but has failed to pay dividends in either the stability of African countries or improved relationships between Western and African governments. The lens of great-power competition has continued to dominate the Western response to Russia in Africa and has time and again actually benefited Wagner.

Humanitarians and journalists identified Wagner's involvement in a monstrous range of human-rights abuses across Africa. Because of a lack of accountability, a ruthless counterinsurgency strategy and the existing patterns of abuse by Wagner's local partners, Wagner fighters took part in summary execution, torture, mass killings, arbitrary detention, rape and pillage in countries including Libya, Mali and the car. Such actions threaten to undo Wagner's short-term security gains as local populations are further alienated.

While much ink has been spilled on Wagner's impact in Africa, less has been written about how networks in Africa have exploited Wagner. In countries such as Sudan or Mozambique, Wagner entered a domain where a cast of characters were already competing with one another for power, resources and legitimacy. In such cases, Wagner was often lacking in knowledge, connections or commitment, and found itself as the subject of history rather than the author. Even in such cases, Wagner proved itself adept at rolling with the punches.

Granit

When Granit, real name Aleksander Bondarenko, was killed in Mozambique on 5 October 2019, it was a turning point. Far from its cinematic portrayal a year later in Prigozhin's eponymous film, Bondarenko's death was representative of the organization's first challenges in finding a foothold in new territory. At that time, Wagner already enjoyed success in places such as Sudan, but in Madagascar its efforts to infiltrate the resource industry and a scheme of heavy-handed political interference were short-lived. Mozambique would prove that Wagner's success depended on its ability to establish ties with local leadership, foster local intelligence and embed itself commercially.

Mozambique was fighting an insurgency in the northern part of the country, primarily against Ansar al-Sunna, a radical Islamist group that had official affiliation with the Islamic State's Central African Province. Though Ansar al-Sunna conducted itself mostly autonomously from the better-known IS, it nonetheless posed a serious problem for Mozambique in a region that felt neglected by the leadership in the south and which held enormous hydrocarbon wealth. As in Syria, partnership with Wagner could allow Mozambique to secure the gas-rich region. Unlike in Syria, Wagner had relatively little knowledge of the local situation, and local security elites were not completely on board with its involvement. They had other options, particularly in the form of South African PMSCs who espoused better knowledge of the country and of the adversary, and who already had relationships with Mozambique's military and intelligence. Nonetheless, Wagner had the benefit of the Russian state assisting its bid and entered the country shortly after President Filipe Nyusi met Putin in August 2019.

As in Syria, travelling by road was often the most dangerous part of a deployment. Granit led a team of seventeen men packed into two Toyota Hiluxes down a dirt road past the village of Limala, in Mocimboa de Praia, northern Mozambique. Their task was to clear the way for Mozambican forces. It was around 5 p.m. when the men noticed smoke rising from houses near their route.

A militant with an RPG and three men with assault rifles stepped into the road and opened fire on the Russians, and a short gunfight ensued. Wagner records of the exchange document more confusion than gallantry. Granit was fatally struck and another soldier, call sign 'Dikiy', took command in the chaos. Shortly after, they were rescued by the arrival of a commander named 'Bes' together with another eight Wagnerites. A few months later, Bes met Dikiy and handed him five state awards from the president of Mozambique, honouring Granit and other the men injured in the battle. More Wagner fighters would be killed or injured in a spate of similar skirmishes in this period, but did not receive state awards.

The South African firms eventually won out and Wagner quietly withdrew. These other PMSCs struggled to fight against the insurgency but did not experience the scale of Wagner's losses thanks to their more risk-averse model and their relationships with the Mozambican armed forces.

Mozambique was not Wagner's only failure on the continent, as we will see. These failures tell us as much as do its successes about Wagner's model, its objectives and what it means for the future of private force. Wagner has demonstrated the limitations of Western aid and security assistance, but also both the opportunities and the failings of its own state-backed 'hybrid' engagements that leverage PMSCs and commerce. Just as Wagner has elevated the public concern about PMSCs in Africa, it has also highlighted the role that PMSCs will play on the continent in the future. Wagner has not overturned the African PMSC market – on the contrary, it has created new opportunities for local PMSCs, and may in the long term lead to a larger role for both African PMSCs and regional security guarantors.

Revolution

Behind the scenes, Wagner's entry into Sudan wasn't so neat either. While Wagner employees, from fighters to geologists, filed into Sudan, the agreements with the government failed to materialize into profitable mining ventures. Rumours circulated that a Sudanese civilian had been shot by Wagner security at an exploration site in March 2018 in a protest over land rights. Internal communications by administrative staff sent to Sudan indicated confusion and fear – it was one thing to pay off the right people; it was another entirely to start a successful business in the complex, patronage-based mining market in Sudan. Balance sheets indicated that Wagner was spending in Sudan, but it wasn't earning, at least not in gold.

The security and political sides of Wagner were doing much better. Staff from the First and Third Assault Detachments were sent to Sudan, where they would be overseen by noted Wagner commanders Zombie and Ratibor, two of the old guard. Their fighters flew in on Russian Ministry of Defence aircraft, principally those of the 223rd and 224th Flight Units, carrying them from Rostov to Syria and then onward to Khartoum. From there, Wagner had set up several locations in Sudan: offices in Khartoum and Bahri to the north, camps at mining blocks and at Port Sudan, and bases at the border with the CAR. The majority of staff were installed at these bases, locations with names like 'Spetsnaz'. Their men were armed, cruising around Khartoum and the provinces in armoured vehicles. Wagner fighters called Sudan 'Solnechnoye', the name of a region of St Petersburg.

In the desert, Wagner trained the RSF. At their 'Spetsnaz' base, below Sudanese and Russian flags, RSF soldiers practised firing mortars. Leaked video recorded by Wagner fighters captures the RSF fighters firing mortar after mortar into the distance, while Russian instructors scold them for their mistakes through an interpreter. In October 2018, Wagner even taught the RSF to parachute. Ratibor and his compatriots loaded dozens of RSF fighters onto transport helicopters and shoved them out over the desert, where they drifted slowly to earth under their canopies. Afterwards, Wagner and the RSF staged an awards ceremony for the men, Russian Airborne-style, in which they earned their wings. In a recording of the event by a member of Wagner, Ratibor beamed as he announced the awards to the massed RSF soldiers.

Back in Khartoum, the commercial and political arms of Wagner were busier still. Mikhail Potepkin, the director of M Invest, was on paper charged with both overseeing Meroe Gold and handling political interference. It took time, but his efforts in both fields would pay off.

Wagner was spinning up its disinformation apparatus across Africa, a series of offices that would take the success of Russia's troll farm, IRA, apply it to local contexts and blend it with far more sweeping recommendations for their hosts. Early in their Sudanese operation, the network looked for regional experts. For analysis on Sudan, they contracted with Nikolai Dobronravin, a professor from St Petersburg who specialized in African politics and energy.[6] M Invest and Evro Polis paid for his flights to the CAR, where he also conducted work for the network. Dobronravin was meanwhile applying for UN positions, eventually winning a spot on the UN Panel of Experts for Sudan tasked with overseeing the UN arms embargo in 2018. The guidance of experts like Dobronravin was folded into planning by 'political technologists' employed by the network, who prepared a series of lofty schemes for Bashir's government to boost his popularity before the 2020 elections. These included recommendations to create controlled opposition parties, suppress dissent through show trials and spread narratives blaming the USA, Israel and the EU for attempting to foment dissent in the country.[7] All of these activities had the explicit aims of supporting Bashir and enhancing Russian influence, as recorded in internal strategy documents.[8]

While it is unclear whether Bashir's government paid much attention to Wagner's political recommendations – Bashir's National Congress Party (NCP) had already employed many of these techniques – the network of political technologists eagerly put them into practice themselves beginning in 2018. From the 'back office' in St Petersburg and their offices in Khartoum, they created websites and fake social media accounts, and hired locals to help them pump out their message. These activities were planned according to a larger media strategy and tracked in colourful spreadsheets reminiscent of the task-tracking documents used by the IRA in its U.S. and European campaigns. Like those campaigns, this activity also relied on the creation of pages that frequently published non-political content to attract readership and frequently re-posted Russian state media.

The approach was not particularly creative and it is unclear what its impact was. If the objective was to generate support for Bashir and defend his hold on power, the plan failed. By December 2018, anti-Bashir sentiment was coming to a head across the country – a direct backlash to his thirty years of authoritarian rule and mismanagement of the Sudanese economy. The ruling party, NCP, withdrew subsidies on essential goods and revalued the Sudanese pound, resulting in a shortage of available cash and a precipitous drop in living standards. While Bashir and Wagner's political technologists might have believed that the Sudanese population was pliant, they proved that they were not. Eight months of nationwide street protests and civil disobedience began, organized by grass-roots 'neighbourhood committees' that served as community rallying points, self-defence organizations and mutual-aid organizations all in one. No amount of Facebook posts could turn off the tap once it was opened.

That didn't stop Wagner's local leadership from trying. Potepkin drew up a plan in late 2018 titled 'Necessary Measures to Counter Protest Activity in the Republic of Sudan'. His recommendations were drawn directly from Russia's own efforts to quash dissent domestically, including staging counterprotests, shutting down sites of protest activities for maintenance, detaining protest leaders and the further use of online disinformation to dupe the opposition.

The political-interference machine was in overdrive looking for ways to prevent Bashir's ouster. In St Petersburg, a man named Petr Bychkov was adding his plans to the playbook. Bychkov, a shaggy-haired, lanky political technologist, had already been in Prigozhin's orbit for some time, overseeing domestic operations in media and disinformation. He was now expanding his role to oversee influence in Africa. Evidently grasping for more creative solutions, Bychkov advised painting protestors as anti-Muslim, blaming the opposition for firebombing mosques and schools and claiming that they carried LGBTQ+ flags at protests. More remarkably still, he recommended the public execution of 'looters' in order to dissuade protestors. Anonymous government sources told Western media that some of these recommendations were implemented, including arresting students in Darfur on counts of fomenting a civil war.[9]

Protestors noticed Eastern European men on the edges of demonstrations in December. The Eastern European men arrived in armoured beige Ural trucks. Occasionally, men with handheld cameras would emerge from the trucks and film the action. But they didn't intervene. Wagner was waiting to see how things would shake out.

The Sudanese security forces, on the other hand, administered a brutal response. This violence did not subside after Bashir was ultimately deposed by the military on 11 April. The new ruling Transitional Military Council (TMC) routinely used violence against protestors to suppress calls for civilian government. The RSF and other organizations in the TMC killed 128 people, raped at least seventy and injured countless more in a massacre on 3 June.

The protestors escalated their civil disobedience and non-violent resistance in response, declaring a general strike. Through July and August, the civilians represented by the Forces of Freedom and Change hammered out a power-sharing agreement with the TMC to create a civilian-led transitional government that came into force on 20 August. Bashir and his other NCP leadership were by now in prison. It was a tenuous peace, but the decades-long rule of Bashir was ended, and the civilians had a real window to achieve a democratic and prosperous future for the country.

Even with the immense change heralded by the revolution, Wagner held on. It had established relationships with the SAF, the RSF and the intelligence services, all of whom still had official roles and bided their time looking for an opportunity to overthrow the new civilian leadership. Wagner's mining ventures and political-interference engine gave the group a strong foothold in Sudan and would become the most mature elements in the country, as they pivoted to focus on whichever pillars offered the greatest return on investment. Meroe Gold began to grow into a profitable venture with cover from Sudanese security elites, while the disinformation arm of Wagner cranked out posts that exalted the RSF and the benefits of Russia's tentative Port Sudan naval base.

These operations were further bolstered by their much larger developing ventures in neighbouring countries. Wagner's numbers in Sudan were now small relative to elsewhere on the continent. In the CAR and Libya, Wagner was in the midst of two wars and was working to sway elections from South Africa to Madagascar.

CAR: Wags the Dog

Nikolai Dobronravin, the future member of the UN's Sudan Panel of Experts who was hired by the Wagner network to consult on Sudan, also consulted for them on the CAR. As part of this arrangement, he made field trips to the CAR, paid for by Evro Polis and M Invest, and at the personal invitation of the CAR's president, Faustin-Archange Touadera. This invitation might have been the result of a 22 August 2017 meeting between Prigozhin and the CAR's ambassador to Russia, as indicated by Prigozhin's personal calendar, leaked to the Dossier Centre. But more than that, it was the result of a per-sistent Russian policy of blocking UN arms embargoes as a matter of principal and of finding regional allies in embattled states.

The CAR certainly fit the bill. One of the ten poorest countries in the world, the CAR is also host to immense natural-resource wealth. A brutal colonial administration under the French, fol-lowed by a series of insurgencies and authoritarian leaders, denied the people of the CAR the prosperity that the minerals, timber and land offered. It is all the more regrettable, then, that the CAR would become best known to many audiences through the activities of the Wagner Group.

I first became acquainted with the CAR when I began investi-gating arms trafficking and corruption. My earlier projects focused on South Sudan and occasionally on the CAR. In both cases, the scale of looting by political elites was astounding. Worse still, many of the most flagrant cases of corruption were actively abetted by companies and individuals in the USA and Europe. Nonetheless, as small, resource-rich countries with underdeveloped economies, they were frequently written off, a tertiary policy priority, until such time as an adversary began investing.

In the CAR, this meant that the government was primarily treated as an aid recipient – its humanitarian catastrophe and its security challenges were intractable problems best left to the UN and other international organizations. So long as it was more profitable for armed groups to raid, to extract rents from controlling territory and to use violence to control resources and smuggling routes, the people of the CAR would live under the threat of violence, and development, both economic and political, would be nearly impossible.

Russia saw this differently – not out of an altruistic desire to do good, or even necessarily wholly as a matter of greed over the CAR's mineral resources, though that too likely played a role. What the CAR presented was an opportunity to establish influence regionally, to assert a role in managing the conflicts in its neighbourhood and to challenge Western influence in Africa. It was an opportunity to act as a great power would, to exploit Western negligence of a scarcely acknowledged, sparsely populated country in order to challenge the status quo in the developing world. Under other circumstances, Russia would have the same obstacles to committing political capital or putting its people in harm's way in the CAR that Western governments grappled with. Russia couldn't simply send its military in to resolve the issue; there was neither political nor financial will for such a move in Moscow. But in Wagner, Russia had a tool that the West did not.

When the CAR's President Touadera was elected in 2016, he inherited a nightmarish security situation, a flagging economy and a UN arms embargo. His government did not help matters with its authoritarian tendencies in quashing dissent. In light of this, Russia's offer to help the CAR by obtaining an exemption from the UN arms embargo was a lifeline. After Prigozhin's alleged meeting with the CAR's ambassador and a fact-finding trip by a group in the pay of Prigozhin's corporate structure in August and September 2017, Touadera met Russian foreign minister Sergey Lavrov in Sochi, Russia.[10] In November, the CAR government officially requested that Russia send five hundred trainers to the country. Russia leaned into pressuring the UN for exemption on its embargo in December, in order to allow transfers of Russian arms and equipment. In January, media and analysts reported on rumours of Wagner's involvement and a more substantial Russian presence, just as the CAR and Russian parties came to agreements on mineral extraction. The promise of men and arms materialized with Moscow's announcement in March 2018 that Russia would send instructors – five military personnel and 170 civilians – to the CAR.[11]

By that time, around two hundred Wagner fighters were already in the country, drawn largely from the First and Third Assault Detachments, the same that staffed positions in Sudan. Over the next three years, their numbers would increase to almost 1,400, based at nearly fifty locations in the CAR.[12]

This timeline of Wagner's entry into the CAR complicates popular views of Wagner's model. Rather than Russia engaging and then directing Wagner to follow, Wagner and the Russian government engaged the CAR and the UN in tandem, suggesting that Wagner was at least as instrumental in opening these opportunities as the Russian government was in providing the official channel for Wagner to deploy. The Russian government's priorities and conditions in the CAR guided Wagner's decision making, while the avenues afforded by Wagner influenced Russia's foreign-policy choices.

Once in the CAR, this unusual relationship continued, now further influenced by the involvement of the CAR government itself and the armed groups that threatened it. Wagner's structure in the CAR mirrored this complexity: mining and commercial activities were carried out by companies that Wagner had created domestically, like Lobaye Invest and Diamville. Their security activities were carried out under the auspices of a local firm that they created called Sewa Security and through an organization that they founded in Russia with the unwieldy title of Officers Union for International Security (OUIS).

Far beyond their security work and training in Sudan, Wagner in the CAR would grow to become a private army, taking on a diversity of tasks and a level of local control that surpassed even that of their campaigns in Syria.

CAR: Capturing the State

Wagner's roles in the CAR would come to encompass the broadest range of their security, political and economic activities to date. Aside from training local forces and providing security for President Touadera, Wagner fought both together with the armed forces of the CAR (FACA) and independently. Its businesses came to include not only mining but the import of alcohol and food and the harvesting and export of timber. Its political technologists ran online disinformation campaigns but also disseminated propaganda through newspapers and radio, filmed movies in the CAR and screened them to audiences in the capital, Bangui. Wagner even took over core government functions in the CAR, including the administration of its airspace and customs, and even the CAR's negotiations with armed groups. This would lead many to see Wagner's relationship with the CAR as simply one of a mercenary army making this African nation into a vassal of Russia. In reality, there were many more actors in the CAR who variously accommodated or exploited Wagner themselves.

Touadera was the most direct beneficiary of Wagner's activities, but he was not the only one. The UN mission in the CAR – MINUSCA – and Rwandan peacekeeping contingents would find that the presence of Russian fighters willing to deploy to the most dangerous missions lightened their load, even where it created challenges to deconfliction or threats to their people. Insurgent groups such as the Coalition of Patriots for Change (CPC) could use the spectre of Wagner to publicly tar the administration in Bangui. Bandits could pose as Russian fighters to improve their freedom of movement and intimidate locals into paying their protection rackets. What was clear was that Wagner had fundamentally changed the nature of politics and conflict in the CAR, but all parties adapted to this new reality.

This complexity also created new dilemmas for Western countries and international organizations. Would they deny aid to the

CAR on the ground that they worked with a sanctioned Russian paramilitary group? Could the MINUSCA contingent carry out its work if it found itself fighting alongside a mercenary army? As was the case historically in the CAR, most parties took the easy way out, trying to avoid rocking the boat or making hard policy choices about what they would and would not tolerate.

Ground Truth

Wagner began testing this tacit neutrality soon after arriving in the country. Russian journalists were eager to investigate Wagner but found it exceedingly difficult to peer behind the corporate infrastructure to understand facts on the ground. Groups such as the Investigation Management Centre, headed by the former editors of the well-known Russian publication *Kommersant* and *Forbes Russia*, considered sending a team to Syria or Africa to investigate Wagner. Journalist Orkhan Dzhemal, director Aleksandr Rastorguev and cameraman Kirill Radchenko – all respected Russian investigative journalists – were hired to investigate Wagner in the countries in which it was active.

Plans moved quickly. The journalists determined that Syria was too risky and, after seeing photographs of a Wagner base in the CAR, began planning a trip. In doing so, they also coordinated with Kirill Romanovskiy, a war correspondent who worked for Prigozhin's media infrastructure. He set them up with a fixer in country.

The journalists arrived in the CAR on 28 July 2018. Unbeknown to the journalists, their driver was in close contact with the CAR gendarmerie from the moment they arrived, using a new phone registered under a false name. The driver spoke with an officer named Emmanuel Kotofio, who had been trained by Wagner instructors at the CAR–Sudan border and would later work as a driver for Russian forces in the CAR. Strangely, Kotofio used a phone that was registered under a false U.S. passport – that passport was also used to register a phone linked to the Whatsapp account of Wagner employee Aleksandr Sotov, who communicated frequently with the head of the Wagner instructors in the CAR and with Valeriy Zakharov, an adviser to Touadera. Kirill Radchenko's fixer, a Dutch UN employee named 'Martin', appears to have been entirely fabricated.

The journalists left Bangui to travel to the town of Bambari, where they were supposed to meet 'Martin' on 30 July. Their travel took them through the town of Sibut, through a FACA base where Wagner fighters were present. From there, they headed north instead of east to Bambari. At some time around 8:45 p.m., all three journalists were killed. Their bodies were scattered outside their vehicle. They had been killed by multiple accurate shots to their centre mass from AK or AKM rifles. Some of the wounds bore powder marks that indicated they were shot at close range.

As soon as the news got out that Russian journalists had been killed in the CAR, the Wagner network, the CAR government and the Russian government began shaping the narrative. The Russians had been killed by bandits or insurgents seeking to rob them – never mind how their driver managed to escape, or that his story kept changing. The details of the court case in the CAR and the later case in Russia were inconsistent and the testimony of key witnesses was different in each. The Russian government announced that the journalists had been killed by militants while travelling in a dangerous part of the country. Petr Bychkov in the St Petersburg 'back office' rallied Wagner's spin doctors to push out this version of events across every platform they could.

Western responses were tepid. The Russian investigation was apathetic, with the victims' belongings left in the hands of the Russian embassy in Bangui rather than returned to Russia. But for those who would investigate Wagner in the CAR, the killings had a chilling effect: if you went looking for what Russia was doing in Africa, you were taking your life in your hands.

The Shape of Wagner in the CAR

The Wagnerites named their location in Bangui 'Bokassa' after infamous Central African dictator and second president of the CAR Jean-Bédel Bokassa, known for his extravagance, corruption and brutality. He was reported to personally take part in the torture and execution of his political rivals.[13] After he was deposed in 1979 in a coup backed by the French, he was accused during his trial of ordering schoolchildren to be executed and of having indulged in cannibalism.[14] From 'Bokassa' and Berengo, Bokassa's decrepit former palace, Wagner organized its campaigns across the country.

By this period, Wagner's command structure had matured into the form it would mostly maintain with minor adaptations. Assault detachments remained the primary unit of command, each consisting of variable numbers of up to three hundred men who could be deployed across multiple theatres but with a single overall commander. These commanders, often the fighters who had been with Wagner since its first campaigns in Ukraine, continued to inform the core of Wagner's tactical edge in combat. They were the learning part of the organization and their competence frequently made or broke the operations of Wagner in the field.

The assault detachment commander was supported by a command staff and directorate. The commander of the assault detachment had direct oversight of a group of units that included platoons of around fifty men, led by platoon commanders, further broken down into assault squads of approximately ten men each. These platoons were backed by support units, including fire support, reconnaissance, armoured groups, artillery, engineers, sniper units, UAV crews and medical groups. These structures were not rigid and were adapted to suit the needs of various deployments. Where components of one or multiple assault detachments were stationed at bases or 'temporary dislocation sites' they were usually referred to by the name of a specific fighter, likely someone with command authority. Their equipment was also adaptable: they might deploy with a group of armoured vehicles, for example, and their armaments varied depending on the forces they were fighting. In the CAR, this mostly meant vehicles like Toyotas and some armoured trucks like Dozors, as well as Wagner's own creation, the 'Chekan' mine-resistant ambush-protected vehicle commonly called the 'Wagner Wagon'.

In the CAR, Wagner mostly carried small arms and light weapons. This was a different war than that in Syria and their armaments were selected accordingly. Most fighters carried AK-style rifles or PKM machine guns, but more senior fighters also carried the more modern AK-103 and rifles favoured by Russian special forces, like the Lobaev Stalingrad. They also carried mortars and anti-tank guided missiles and were supported by air reconnaissance from Russian-made Orlan drones provided by the Ministry of Defence.

Wagner units were based throughout the country by 2019. Beyond Berengo and Bangui in the CAR's southwest, they were in Bria and Bambari to the east; Dekoa, Paoua and Sibut to the north; and Boda and Bouar to the west. Their nearly fifty locations differed in manpower and equipment. At most of these sites, they were deployed with FACA, while at others they were based awkwardly next to MINUSCA. In still others, they deployed entirely independently.

Most international attention focused on a set of more visible characters in Bangui. The main group of instructors that had originally been dispatched to the CAR under the agreement with Russia was overseen by Valeriy Zakharov. International media saw Zakharov, a tall, corpulent man in his fifties, as the 'head of Russian instructors in the CAR', and consequently as the commander of the Wagner fighters. In part, this was true. Zakharov was the official leader of the small contingent of dedicated trainers and he was further connected with Wagner's corporate infrastructure, as he indicated that he was travelling on behalf of Prigozhin's 'M Finance' in his visa documentation. Zakharov was also reported to have a role in negotiating with armed groups in 2018 and 2019. He frequently spoke with international media, leading many to see him as the ringleader.

Zakharov, however, was not ultimately in charge. In Wagner's bureaucracy, his group of instructors was considered distinct from the main body of Wagner fighters in the country, though some of them had previously fought with Wagner or would in the future. Between ill health and tensions between Wagner and the Foreign Ministry in the CAR, Zakharov would eventually leave the country in 2021.

When Zakharov departed the CAR, he left a very young man named Dmitriy Sytiy to take over 'Wagner's non-military activities'.[15] Sytiy and another man named Vitaliy Perfilev would become two of the most recognizable representatives of Wagner in the CAR, since its foot soldiers and commanders kept their faces and their identities hidden. Sytiy, a long-haired thirty-something from St Petersburg who studied in Barcelona and Paris, was snapped up by Prigozhin's business structures due to his language abilities. From his early days as an interpreter, he came to play the role of adviser in the CAR and head of the Russian House cultural centre.[16] Perfilev, the man who would become the most frequent interlocutor with international media, always photographed with his aviator sunglasses, is scarcely documented in available Wagner Group records. He may have been fulfilling a role like Zakharov's, primarily interfacing with local authorities. Despite this, he was regularly identified in international media and sanctions designations as a leader of Wagner in the CAR, where command and authority are seldom what they seem on the surface.

Bellingcat and Russian investigative outlet the Insider found that in other leaked Wagner documentation, a little-known man named Konstantin Pikalov seemed to occupy a unique position in CAR operations. Pikalov, rarely seen without his sunglasses and black baseball cap, kept cropping up in photographs where Russian political interference was taking place. He provided security for two of Russia's chosen candidates for elections in Madagascar before he transferred to the CAR in summer 2018. He previously ran a private detective agency and may have been investigated for money laundering. The UK's later sanctions designation of Pikalov identified him as a leader of Wagner in the CAR, but based on Wagner's documentation and Pikalov's modest background, he was just another guard and instructor. With Wagner, he was looking for an entry into Africa: he owned the Convoy Military Security Company, then just a small private security company connected with a Cossack organization. In time, it would become one of Russia's better-known PMCs.

Information on Wagner's true battlefield commanders in the CAR is scarce, but thanks to leaked documentation we can gain a better understanding of the men behind Wagner's training and military activity in the African country and their backgrounds. Primary command responsibility rotated, but Wagner's main men in the CAR included Zombie, Emelya, Nikolai 'Bes' Budko, Vladimir 'Kitayets' Kitaev and Anton 'Lotos' Elizarov. Wagner's files on troop rotations and locations named a man called 'Pioneer' as the head of the operations department in the country. He would remain elusive until 2023, a key turning point in Wagner's story. The other men could be traced through Wagner's records and public reporting.

Boris 'Zombie' Nizhevenok, whom we met way back in 2014 in Luhansk, was the head of the 3rd Assault Detachment. Units in his detachment would later play an important role in the CAR by pushing insurgent forces all the way to the Cameroonian border in 2021. Aleksander 'Emelya' Emelyanov, one of the commanders who survived the Battle of Khasham, was the head of the 5th Assault Detachment, based at Berengo with authority over the area around Bangui, and which carried out campaigns in Boda. Nikolai 'Bes' Budko, the commander of the 4th Assault Detachment who had rescued Granit's team in Mozambique, also oversaw Berengo with men from the 3rd and 4th Assault Detachments. Bes was one of the men who were issued a passport by the migration office that gave domestic passports to GRU undercover officers.[17]

Vladimir 'Kitayets' Kitaev, later called Iceman, was sent in to lead a combined group of the 5th and 8th Assault Detachments. A brutish-looking military veteran who was missing part of his right ear, he was much trusted by his superiors – he was placed in this role after leadership determined that the 5th Detachment lacked adequate command. Kitayets had been present at the torture and killing of Ismail, and his status may have been connected to his reputation for ruthlessness. He went on to oversee training for the CAR's armed forces. In 2020 he was found to have defrauded company funds, but claimed that he had used the money to provide better living conditions for his subordinates. Unusually, he maintained his position.

Anton 'Lotos' Elizarov was chief of staff and deputy commander of the 6th Assault Detachment. A group named after him would oversee a location in Bambari, near where Wagner is documented to have taken part in the torture and summary execution of civilians. He was listed among the instructors for FACA, alongside Zombie, Bes, Kitayets and other employees of 'the Company'.

Bush War

The civil war in the CAR is fought between a range of insurgent groups, variously divided by religious, ethnic and agrarian or nomadic identities, but primarily motivated by control of key resources.[18] Militant groups are broadly divided into Christian agrarian 'Anti-Balaka' or Muslim nomadic 'Ex-Séléka' categories, a legacy of the CAR Bush War in the early 2000s.[19] In practice, these broad categories failed to capture a more complex reality of organizations and alliance. Militant groups in the CAR were already splintered by the time of Wagner's entry and competing between themselves and with the government for control of territory that would allow them to collect tribute, set up checkpoints and traffic in timber, coffee and minerals. Then, as now, these groups were led by violent entrepreneurs who by 2014 controlled most of the country outside of Bangui. Peacekeeping and peace enforcement missions by the UN and European Union, particularly France, succeeded in safeguarding the capital to allow for peaceful election in 2016, but were unable to turn the tide beyond Bangui.

Before Russia arrived in the CAR, there was already substantial foreign involvement. France was perhaps the most significant player until it withdrew its peacekeeping force in 2016, but other regional players – especially Sudan, Chad and Rwanda – had their fingers on the scale. Wagner displayed canniness in understanding and navigating the complex local and regional dynamics. When Wagner representatives, including Zakharov, worked to negotiate a peace agreement with armed groups in August 2018, they worked with Sudan and conducted the talks in Khartoum, benefiting from Wagner's relationship with Sudanese authorities.[20] These talks ironically pushed the African Union to accelerate its own efforts to broker negotiations in an effort to maintain a consolidated approach, even if the resulting agreement failed to resolve the conflict meaningfully.[21] Throughout these events, Wagner developed relationships outside the government, with rebel leaders such as Ali Darassa of the Union for Peace in the CAR (UPC) and Noureddine Adam of the Popular Front for the Rebirth of the CAR (FPRC).

Elections were scheduled in 2020 and the situation in the CAR was tense. Former president François Bozizé, exiled from the country, announced that he intended to run. Rebel groups declared that they were forming an alliance called the CPC and pre-emptively accused Touadera of rigging the election, claiming that they would take the capital. They began to seize towns near Bangui and cut off the capital's access to the rest of the country. As the rebels pushed through the countryside, they displaced hundreds of thousands of people, committed a slew of atrocities and brought the CAR's already precarious humanitarian and economic situation to the brink.

They weren't prepared for the level of military support that Touadera now enjoyed, however. In videos posted on social media, Wagner troops were visible riding on Toyotas carrying mounted machine guns, clearing settlements near Bangui and fighting insurgents back from the capital. Wagner, along with the FACA, MINUSCA and Rwandan contingents, succeeded in preventing rebels from taking Bangui, and Touadera was announced as the winner of the election on 4 January. Then Wagner started pushing back.

The campaign by Wagner and the FACA that began in 2012 drastically turned the tide in the CAR. The CPC retreated and Wagner and the FACA followed them. Both parties were accused of human rights violations by the UN and independent monitoring organizations, who declared them guilty of actions ranging from summary execution of suspected CPC members to political persecution of the opposition, mass killings of civilians and pillaging from humanitarians.[22] The rebels made life nightmarish for the populations under their control, but for many the return of state control brought no relief. To be sure, a large part of the CAR's citizens preferred the predictability of government control to the chaos of rebel occupation. But for those suspected of collusion with rebels or those merely in the wrong place at the wrong time – particularly Muslims and members of the Fulani ethnic group – the arrival of FACA and Wagner meant more terror, not more security.

Wagner forces mirrored the prejudices and atrocities committed by local forces and brought their own methods of torture to bear through a cadre of 'interrogation experts'. This included methods such as beating, electrocution and mutilation, largely targeting civilians believed to have knowledge of militant activities. Wagner commandeered captives held by local authorities and hooded them, before leading them onto aeroplanes to transport them to its sites for interrogation. They kept prisoners in deep, waterlogged pits.

By their account, all of this was necessary to face an enemy hiding among the civilian population.

Some of Wagner's most senior commanders led the push out from Bangui. According to an internal report from early 2021, Boris 'Zombie' Nizhevenok's 3rd Assault Detachment headed northwest from their base at Berengo, through the towns of Boda, Yaloke and Bouar towards the border with Cameroon. Other than losing a vehicle and acquiring some minor injuries, they proceeded with relative ease. Emelya's 5th Assault Detachment 'periodically occupied' regions in this area, including the town of Boda, the road from Bani to Berengo and the zone to the northeast of Bangui. While the timeline of these units' activities is not certain, between December 2020 and January 2021 there was a series of atrocities attributed to Wagner along this route. This included the massacring of at least twenty civilians, particularly Muslims, in the town of Boyo in mid-December 2020.[23] The UN report on this incident identified the perpetrators as being primarily pro-government militias but documents them travelling aboard Russian Ural trucks.[24] Survivors reported the participation of Russian fighters.

Similarly, internal reports document 'cleaning' operations around Bambari, northeast of Bangui, overseen by a Fedor 'Barin' Lyashchuk, a Belarusian national, and staffed mainly with men of the 7th Assault Detachment. The UN Panel of Experts on the CAR and independent media have documented Wagner fighters and FACA conducting an operation in Bambari on 15–16 February 2021. This included indiscriminate killing of civilians, the targeting of mosques and a gunfight in a hospital. The UN reported that between six and seventeen civilian victims died as a result of Wagner's assault. Images in their reports show the mosque riddled with bullet holes and damage from explosives.

This violence was consistent with the characterization of 'cleaning operations' documented by non-profit the Sentry in their interviews with CAR military sources.[25] In these operations, Wagner forces would seek to drive out militants hidden among the civilian population by deploying terror and indiscriminate violence. The UN confirmed multiple killings in this period, including of unarmed civilians with disabilities in Bodol and Grimari, and the killing of civilians of the predominately Muslim Fulani ethnicity in Ouaka Prefecture.[26] The UN reported that these killings only strengthened insurgent claims that Muslim populations needed their protection and even led to reprisal attacks on civilians believed to have collaborated with Wagner or the FACA, 'perpetuating the cycle of violence across the country'.[27]

This was the ultimate grim irony of Wagner in the CAR: without their presence, militants would have continued to rule the countryside, and the government would have been unable to retake control. No international partner aside from Wagner was willing to take on their primary role in guaranteeing the Touadera government's security. But as long as they were there, atrocities would continue on a greater scale, rebel groups could recruit from their survivors, more arms would be available in the country, and any type of future disarmament or reintegration of militant forces appeared impossible. To make matters worse, Wagner was now using both Syrian and captured local fighters in the CAR.[28] While in Bangui many did see the Russians as saviours, in the countryside the population was faced with an unfamiliar, violent and often indiscriminate force.

With their firepower, tactical acumen and armaments that now included machine-gun-equipped light helicopters, Wagner had fundamentally changed the nature of war in the CAR. Foreign powers had already been present, as had mercenaries, but not in numbers this great and not with this great an impact on the conflict. In many ways, they had made themselves essential not only to the CAR government, but to any international partners who wanted the government in the CAR to survive. Against this backdrop, Wagner's expansion continued, both in depth of control of the CAR and Sudan, and in the fronts it was pushing into in Libya.

7

LIBYA: BLUEPRINT FOR CONTEMPORARY WAR

The world heard Mr Haftar declare he was about to unleash
a new air campaign. That will be Russian mercenary pilots flying
Russian-supplied aircraft to bomb Libyans.
General Stephen Townsend, U.S. Africa Command

A l Jufra Airbase is a sprawling complex in the middle of the Libyan desert. It is 3,810 metres (12,500 ft) of runways, vast concrete aprons and rusting hangers, punctuated by cratered buildings from NATO air strikes a decade ago. Like many of Libya's airbases, Al Jufra is also a graveyard, host to a coterie of abandoned Soviet aircraft. These range from colossal Il-76 transports to angular MiG-25 interceptors. They are parked haphazardly on the cracking asphalt, baking under the sun, or left in the sand, unmoved for decades. But in the spring of 2020, Al Jufra was bustling with life and engines.

Light blue MiG Fulcrums, the modern cousin of the antique MiG-25s, were being towed to metal shelters. They were joined by hulking Sukhoi Fencers, 22.5-metre-long (74 ft) supersonic tactical bombers. Over earth berms at the edges of the runways were Russian Pantsir S1 air defence systems, beige trucks bristling with sensors and missile tubes. Among the aircraft were 150 members of the 6th Assault Detachment, together with Libyan fighters and a group of Syrians. By December, there would be nearly 2,000 Wagner fighters in Libya and almost seven hundred Syrian mercenaries fighting alongside them.

The Syrians were drawn from Wagner's fellow travellers, the ISIS Hunters. One of them, Mahmoud Rami 'Amsterdam' Balut, was bartering with a Libyan soldier for a SIM card for a phone he had found. He and his compatriots did their best to dodge the watchful eye of Wagner's internal security service, which would dock their pay if they were caught with unapproved phones.

Men of the 6th Assault Detachment forced down their over-cooked dinner – the catering was in the charge of 'Briga', a member of the detachment who had been a welder before his time with Wagner. They checked their weapons and prepared for nightly patrols. In rotations, two of them would walk the dusty airfields, smoking while they guarded the hangars and the flight crew's dormitory.

Beyond the Al Jufra base, mercenaries hailing from Russia, Belarus, Ukraine, Syria, Sudan and even the UK were spread across Libya. They fought to support the Libyan National Army (LNA) of Khalifa Haftar, a rebel leader who had taken part in the coup that brought Libyan strongman Muammar Gaddafi to power in 1969. Later, he fought for Gaddafi's government against Chad, then plotted against Gaddafi and defected to the United States. He might have even been recruited by the CIA. In 2011 he was a commander in the forces that overthrew Gaddafi. Over the ensuing decade of civil war, he emerged as one of the most powerful players in the country. By 2020 Haftar's LNA was challenging the UN-recognized Government of National Accord, the GNA, in the capital of Tripoli. He enjoyed a diverse and sometimes contradictory range of foreign support, from Russia to the UAE and even France despite the brutal conduct of his forces.[1]

The Libyan civil war was a showcase for the complex, inter-connected and sometimes paradoxical mode of modern conflict. The Government of National Accord in the west and the House of Representatives, together with Haftar's LNA in the east, fought each other for legitimacy and the commanding heights of the country's resource-rich economy. Their forces included a rotating cast of armed groups and a rogues' gallery of foreign mercenaries. Both sides fought Islamist groups seeking to build a caliphate across North Africa and were supported by an international band of foreign backers who flagrantly violated the UN arms embargo.

As part of that strange set of alliances, Al Jufra was manned by LNA fighters and Russian mercenaries, from guards to experienced pilots. They were protected by Russian air defence systems that had been sold to the UAE, then transferred to Libya, and were now controlled by Wagner. In the months to come, they would face off against Turkey's own Syrian mercenaries and fleets of Turkish drones.

Air Power, Tooth and Tail

When Wagner entered, they brought men, including Syrian foot soldiers, hired on the cheap, and two forms of air power.[2] One was Wagner's fleet of MiG and Sukhoi aircraft. This was among the most advanced set of air capabilities ever fielded by an ostensibly non-state actor – hardware Wagner could hardly be allowed to use without the express approval and support of the Russian state. The other was logistics. Wagner could deploy men and equipment because it was able to both piggyback on the Russian military's heavy airlift and hire its own. Libya revolutionized Wagner's air logistics, as Al Jufra and other bases like Bani Walid, Al Khadim and Sirte became launch pads for Wagner deployments deeper into the continent.

Previously, the Wagner Group had used Syria's Cham Wings airlines and the Russian 223rd and 224th Flight Units under the Ministry of Defence to carry men and equipment on routes from southern Russia to Latakia, then onwards to locations from Sudan to the CAR.[3] Now, they ran a substantial amount of their air operations via bases in Libya. Over the course of 2020, the UN Panel of Experts on Libya documented 505 Russian Air Force flights from Khmeimim Air Base in Syria to bases in western Libya. Cham

Wings, meanwhile, made at least 33 similar flights in the same period, carrying Syrian mercenaries hired by Wagner.

Prigozhin himself was also travelling to Libya, flying there aboard his private jet as early as August 2018. A few months later, he met Haftar in Russia alongside Sergey Shoigu at an official reception. Russian state media's improbable explanation for his presence was that he had organized dinner and took part in the cultural programme of the discussion. Afterwards, Prigozhin's Cayman Islands-registered British Aerospace 125, registration VP-CSP, and his Isle of Man-registered Raytheon Hawker, registration M-VITO, shuttled back and forth between Libya and Moscow – but also to Sudan, the CAR and Syria.[4] Prigozhin was involved in no small level of micromanagement of his enterprises abroad and frequently visited in person, as evidenced by private jet travel, internal communications and a series of photographs that would be leaked years later showing the sixty-year-old businessman posing in a Libyan military uniform.

Wagner's own aircraft, its international facilitators and the Russian military were making hundreds of flights along the route from Latakia to eastern Libya. This was Wagner's primary air line of communication (ALOC), which allowed the network to rotate men and the equipment supplied by the Russian Ministry of Defence and requisitioned by Dmitriy Utkin.[5] It also appeared to Western analysts to be one of Wagner's key weak points: if you could stop the planes, you could hurt Wagner. U.S. officials reportedly engaged African countries, asking them to deny Wagner aircraft overflight privileges or access to air facilities.[6] Sanctions on Wagner personnel, aircraft and related companies were designed to further dissuade foreign countries from allowing them to fly freely. This appears to have done little to slow them down, particularly where they could request overflight privileges through the channels of the Russian military and where local countries saw little to gain by angering Russia.

Wagner also used private charter services. They hired the Russian company Charter Green Light Moscow through familiar front companies like M Invest and M Finance to carry men from Russia to Africa, making it even more difficult to detect them. These companies wouldn't come under sanctions until 2023, five years after Wagner started using them. Even if these companies were sanctioned, Wagner and others were looking further afield to hide their activity, turning to their partner, the UAE.

Allies of Convenience

The veil of deniability for Wagner was already exceedingly thin when Russian media published a video of Prigozhin sitting down with Shoigu and Haftar in November 2018. It was plain to see that Prigozhin was linked to Wagner and, with Wagner flying MiGs and Sukhois in Libya, it was harder still to deny the backing of the Russian state. Like other actors in Libya, Prigozhin and Wagner's leadership appreciated that deniability, no matter how improbable, was still a valuable tool. Libya was still under a UN arms embargo, and it behoved the foreign backers of both sides to disguise their violations of the embargo as they engaged on the international stage.

To support this deniability, Wagner and its embargo runners employed a variety of methods to fly under the radar – sometimes literally. Russian military aircraft and Cham Wings planes flying to Libya from Syria would frequently fly at night, skirting along borders of national airspace in the Mediterranean to avoid reporting their flights to aviation authorities or shirk aviation regulations by reporting their flights as 'non-scheduled' to air traffic controllers. Wagner also began to acquire its own airlift in the form of old Ilyushin aircraft that they would register in the CAR. These planes allowed Wagner to move men and equipment around the region nearly undetected by publicly available flight-tracking data – and without relying on the Russian Ministry of Defence.[7] Wagner also acquired smaller An-28s and L-410s from UAE company Kratol Aviation, which it used in the CAR, Libya and, later, Mali.[8] These were purchased from Kratol by a CAR company called Mining Industries before being registered to the CAR Ministry of Defence but used by Wagner.[9]

The UAE, Russia and others supplying belligerents in Libya's civil war also relied on the UAE's opaque aviation market. They flew the same routes to Libya along air bridges that the UN identified as 'centrally planned'.[10] The UAE has been a haven for illicit airlifts for decades, with little-known companies hiding in the secretive emirates of Abu Dhabi, Dubai or Ras al Khaimah. Notorious Russian arms smuggler Viktor Bout, who spent fourteen years in U.S. prison for his crimes, also frequently used the UAE to register his planes. Since that time, arms traffickers from Russia, Armenia, the USA and South Africa had all used the UAE to register their planes and run their high-risk businesses. One of the core tenets of the arms-trafficking world is that logistics are worth at least as much as the guns themselves, and the UAE remains the premier venue for the infrastructure behind those logistics.

A series of UAE-based networks that had been making flights to conflict zones for decades and identified by multiple UN panels as committing embargo violations reconstituted to avoid detection. They registered planes in Ukraine, Central Asia and Armenia, and flew from locations in the UAE to airbases in Libya and eastern Egypt. Using methods similar to Wagner's to evade detection, they dodged negative reporting and revocation of their licences in the countries in which they registered their planes. If they were caught, they created new companies, transferred their aircraft to them and kept the steady flow of flights into Libya. The UN found that they almost all flew to support Haftar, though Turkey maintained its own web of companies to flout the arms embargo and support the government in Tripoli.[11]

Corporate records and aircraft registrations let us peek behind the web of front companies for aviation firms like FlySky, Europe Air, Deek, ZetAvia and numerous others that flew in support of Haftar. Many of these were identified by the UN, and connect back to UAE-based businessman Jaideep Mirchandani, whom U.S. authorities previously suspected of facilitating the transfer of Russian currency to the Assad regime.[12] While the paymasters for these transfers remain mysterious, we do know their scale and their beneficiaries. These planes made hundreds of flights along the air bridges into Libya, often documented carrying arms, equipment or fighters for Haftar and his allies. Some of them also made stops in the Central African Republic and Rwanda. In at least one case, an Antonov 32B flying in support of Haftar, owned by a UAE company and registered in Tajikistan, flew Wagner fighters out of Bani Walid airbase to Al Jufra.[13]

The UAE and Wagner shared more than just a common ally in Libya; they shared an air bridge and maybe even weapons. In late 2020 the Pentagon released a report that, in passing, suggested that the UAE was co-financing the Wagner Group's Libya operations. Media picked up on the claim and created a furore that threatened a $23-billion U.S. arms deal with the UAE. While the roots of this claim were murky, two facts supported it: the air bridge and the Pantsir air defence systems. Media reports and independent investigations found reason to believe that the UAE had transferred its Russian-made Pantsirs to support Haftar in Libya – and subsequently handed them over to Wagner.[14] This theory becomes more compelling when we look at the large number of Pantsir components shipped to the UAE by Russia during 2019 and 2020, just as the Pantsirs in Libya were taking losses.

Wagner's own leaked records attest to partnership in combat as well. An internal report dated 19 September 2019 claims that Wagner units, drone crews and artillery coordinated with the UAE Air Force to conduct strikes on enemy positions. On 10 September, Wagner's

drones were flying south of Tripoli and noticed pickup trucks carrying enemy fighters. They transmitted the location to the UAE Air
Force, who struck them with their own combat drones. Wagner's
leaked report notes, 'As a result of joint actions with the UAE Air
Force and the use of our artillery, the enemy suffered significant
losses, as a result of which he was forced to abandon certain offensive
plans and go on the defensive, hiding equipment and personnel.'

Russia and the UAE's partnership in Libya was remarkable, as
was their common enemy in Turkey. The UAE was in Libya as part
of its effort to counter the rise of Islamist parties. In doing so, it
backed Haftar's Libyan National Army (LNA) against the government in Tripoli. Despite being an ally of the United States and a
beneficiary of defence cooperation, the UAE was willing to align with
Russia, support the use of Syrian mercenaries and work alongside
the Wagner Group – by then subject to U.S. sanctions – to support
their ally in Libya. The use of mercenaries and front companies
allowed the UAE sufficient official deniability to avoid directly con-
tradicting their U.S. partnership. This alone was clearly not enough,
as the Pentagon took public note of the relationship between the
UAE and Wagner, and the UN criticized the UAE's chronic violations
of the arms embargo. Both Russia and the UAE were nonetheless
able to work as allies of convenience thanks to their use of ostensibly private structures, whether they were the Wagner Group or the
UAE's air bridge for Haftar.

This at-arms-length approach to an internationalized conflict
also allowed Russia and Turkey to avoid direct confrontation, even
as Wagner fighters were killed in large numbers by Turkish drones.
When Wagner fighters were killed by Turkish Bayraktar TB-2
drones, there would be no calls at home for taking action against
Ankara. In fact, Russia could continue to cooperate with Turkey
in many spheres. Such were the benefits of the deniability afforded
by leveraging 'non-state' networks, even when that deniability was
transparent to anyone who bothered to look.

Magnum Opus

In early July 2019 a Manta rigid-hull inflatable boat motored into the port of Valletta, Malta. It carried men from the UK, South Africa and Australia, who claimed to be oil and gas contractors fleeing violence in Libya.[15] In reality, they had been sent to Libya as part of an operation called Project Opus, which the UN claimed 'was designed to provide [Haftar]' with attack helicopters, intelligence and cyber capabilities, and to conduct kidnapping and targeted killings on his behalf.[16] According to investigations by the UN and the *New York Times*, they were sent by America's most famous private military contractor, Erik Prince, the founder of Blackwater.[17] It was a full-suite private military operation with smaller numbers than Wagner but promising vastly greater sophistication.

According to the UN, Project Opus was funded and organized through a complex network of companies registered around the world, but primarily based in the UAE. These companies, with names like Lancaster and Opus Capital Asset Limited, were managed by Australian national Christiaan Durrant and UK national Amanda Kate Perry, while the ground team was run by a South African named Stephen Lodge. The UN alleged that Erik Prince had presented their plan, packaged as 'Operation Regain Libja', to Haftar in Egypt in April of 2019, and that its managers began to execute the plan in the summer of that year.

The UN found that Durrant and his colleagues had originally planned to acquire surplus Cobra attack helicopters and MD 530F light attack helicopters from Jordan. The Jordanian armed forces were immediately sceptical of the purchasers and the legitimacy of their operation, and Durrant met Jordanian officers to assuage their concerns. He introduced himself as 'Gene Rynack', the name of Mel Gibson's character in the 1990 action comedy *Air America* about a CIA airlift operation.[18] The Jordanians cancelled the sale.

Project Opus's planners improvised and rapidly purchased utility helicopters from South African and UAE companies, along with an Antonov transport plane, a LASA T-Bird light attack aircraft and a Pilatus PC-surveillance aircraft from an Austrian company. The latter two planes were identified by the UN as being transferred from companies controlled by Erik Prince.[19] Opus moved its twenty contractors to Benghazi in late June, where they met the cyber and targeting teams already deployed. The planes and helicopters were dispatched to Libya at the same time.

When Haftar learned that rather than the fearsome attack helicopters he had been promised, the contractors were bringing utility aircraft, he was furious. The substitute choppers – agile Gazelles and hulking Super Puma transports – would have likely still made an impact on the battlefield, but he felt short-changed. He threatened the team's management. Lodge decided it was time to go – they were staying in a camp patrolled by armed men loyal to Haftar and it was no longer safe. They loaded onto their boats and crossed the 350 nautical miles to Malta. Around the same time, Jordanian authorities invited Durrant to leave their country.

The UN's report on Project Opus states that its directors made another attempt in the spring of 2020 to deploy helicopters from the UAE for assault operations on Haftar's behalf, but this too was cancelled in light of the Tripoli government's new air defence capabilities. Turkey had parked a fleet of vessels carrying a mid-range air defence system along the Libyan coast near Tripoli and had armed their allies in the capital city with improved weapons that could take down helicopters and drones. Throughout this time, the Pilatus surveillance aircraft that Opus had delivered to Haftar remained in eastern Libya, though the UN did not establish publicly whether Haftar made active use of the intelligence capabilities it afforded him.

In all, the UN Panel of Experts on Libya identified that approximately 'U.S.$20M was committed to the operation just for the funding of the equipment and private military operatives' salaries.[20] The ultimate source of most of these funds is not known. While Project Opus never materialized in the way its protagonists had envisioned, it represented the trend in using deniable private forces to turn the tide in conflicts like Libya. There are unsupported claims that Prince had engaged with Prigozhin and proposed collaboration, but it is more likely that they were both in Libya because it presented opportunities for their businesses. The Opus operation looked nothing like Wagner except in its fundamental logic, that privately organized forces could produce both financial and geopolitical dividends. The factor that ultimately led Opus to fail was also one of the most visible elements of Wagner's success in Libya: Wagner had a state backer willing to accept the risk of arming and funding a mercenary force, while Opus did not.

Flood of Dignity

While Opus fell out with Haftar, Wagner's men fought alongside the LNA. They fortified their strongholds at Al Jufra and Sirte and set their eyes on Libya's southern oil fields. The LNA was going to hold Libya's oil wealth hostage and deny the Tripoli government funding. Haftar's LNA took control of the Sharara oil field, which had previously produced 300,000 barrels a day under the management of Spanish, French, Norwegian and Austrian companies.[21] They were soon reinforced by Wagner and Sudanese mercenaries.

In April 2019, the LNA buttressed their Southern Campaign with a dramatic push to the west, making it all the way to Tripoli's outskirts. The internationally recognized government succeeded in rallying armed groups and its Turkish allies, halting their advance. Wagner Group forces dug in, aggressively mining and booby-trapping the suburbs. They stationed snipers at lookout points, making the outskirts of Tripoli a no-man's land.[22] The fight ground on, and scores of Wagner fighters were killed or injured by air strikes.[23] Among those injured was the long-time commander of the 1st Assault Detachment, Aleksandr 'Ratibor' Kuznetsov. He was flown back to St Petersburg and treated at the SOGAZ private clinic, owned by business associates of Putin's family. There, he was found by Reuters correspondents, bandaged, smoking a cigarette in the October cold. He told them that he had been 'fighting international terrorism to protect Moscow's interests' and admitted to his command role in a Russian PMC.[24]

Despite robust air defences via their Pantsirs and drone-jamming technology that even managed to take down an unarmed American UAV, Wagner was hurting. Throughout the end of 2019 and through mid-2020, Wagner lost men and Pantsirs in large numbers. Due to either poor battlefield performance or poor operators, more than $100 million worth of Pantsirs were destroyed, often by the very Turkish drones they were meant to repel. Photographs circulated, first of Pantsirs cruising the roads of Libya, emblazoned by Wagner's favourite Norse runes, and then later of a captured Pantsir being paraded through the streets of Tripoli.[25]

Wagner withdrew to its airbase strongholds aboard trucks and cargo planes, including those same ones owned by Emirati companies.[26] By October, the warring sides in Libya were negotiating a ceasefire. By then, Wagner had more than 7,000 personnel in Libya, including seven hundred Syrian mercenaries. While the LNA and GNA reached a ceasefire agreement that would require foreign fighters to leave Libya in three months, Wagner sapper groups planted mines around Sirte to prevent an advance by Tripoli and dug more than 70 kilometres (43 mi.) of trenches, scoring a vast stretch of desert from Sirte on the coast to their stronghold at Al Jufra.[27] The war was officially over, but in reality it had just reached a violent stalemate.

Wagner might not have succeeded in taking Tripoli with Haftar, but it won itself a regional hub that would play a key role in its operations for years to come. Libya's airbases would remain a launchpad for Wagner logistics further into Africa. The civil war in the CAR burned on, Sudan faced a new round of turmoil, and new frontiers were opening in West Africa. Just as importantly for Wagner's future, its commercial enterprises were growing fast. Libya would provide the air hub to supply them with men and equipment, and one of the avenues to carry out their plundered resources.

8

THE SAHEL: CRISIS AND OPPORTUNITY

Young colonels, tired of Western exploitation and corruption of civilian authorities, are taking power into their own hands. What we are now seeing is the New Liberation of Africa. Assimi Goita is the new African Che Guevara, and Mali is the country from which the patchwork quilt of Africa will begin to be pulled. I remind you that Russian President Vladimir Putin is also a colonel.

Maksim Shugalei, representative of the Foundation for Protection of National Values

France was on the way out of Mali. For nine years, French troops had waged a counterinsurgency campaign alongside local forces in five West African countries, fighting an array of Islamist groups that threatened to destabilize the region. The bulk of French forces were concentrated in the former colony of Mali, where 48 of their soldiers died during the nearly decade-long campaign. Now, in April 2022, they were preparing to leave. The new Malian military regime of Assimi Goita, which had taken power in a coup in 2021, made it abundantly clear that the French were no longer welcome. In February, he had expelled the French ambassador, and citizens poured into the street of the capital, Bamako, to celebrate.

As part of this departure, French forces withdrew from one of their bases in the middle of the country near a town called Gossi on 19 April. The next day, French drone footage captured Malian soldiers entering the base. They made camp, sleeping under the stars. Next to them, another unseen group of men slept in tents.

That night, an anonymous Twitter account claimed that it would reveal evidence of French human rights abuses in Gossi. It had a relatively small following, but French intelligence took note. The next day, a French drone captured Malian soldiers and foreign men in fatigues travelling to a site 3 kilometres (nearly 2 mi.) away from the Gossi base. In the footage, men in fatigues gathered around a mass of corpses and two of them began shovelling sand over the bodies. The others looked on. The drone rotated its angle and stabilized, remaining fixed on the bodies. The men on the ground began recording footage of their own: they stood aside while one of them circled the bodies with a camcorder. Shortly thereafter, the video shot by the soldiers on the ground was released on Twitter. The French military released their own drone footage, citing it as evidence of a staged massacre, undertaken by the Wagner Group.

Less than one month earlier, a massacre had taken place in the town of Moura, southwest of Gossi. It was a busy market day in Moura on 27 April and locals were crowded in the centre of town. Malian and Wagner intelligence sources indicated that 'armed Islamists' were organizing a meeting in the city and prepared a response.[1] Five helicopters approached Moura, huge Mi transports and Mi helicopter gunships. Four of them landed outside Moura, where Malian and Russian soldiers disembarked. The fifth helicopter came in low over the town and hovered. It opened fire in the direction of the market, causing the crowd to panic, while Russian and Malian soldiers marched into the town firing indiscriminately. They were met by small-arms fire from local militants. Like in Bambari in the CAR, militants hid among the local population. And like in Bambari, Wagner and its local partners responded by treating everyone as a potential threat. At least twenty unarmed civilians and around a dozen militants were killed.

After this initial violent episode, the massacre continued over four days as Russian and Malian soldiers went from house to house. The UN found that around five hundred people were executed on suspicion of supporting the insurgents. They were singled out for having beards, wearing clothing that indicated they were devout

Muslims, or simply acting afraid. Their bodies were thrown into ditches. Others were detained and tortured by beating and electrocution, but eventually released. At least 58 women and girls were raped by soldiers. Multiple eyewitnesses reported that the operation was overseen by a group of European soldiers whom the UN would identify as members of the Wagner Group.

The massacre in Moura was the best-documented mass atrocity perpetrated by Wagner in Africa. Their arrival in late 2021 sparked a significant change in Western attitudes towards the group and the mass killing in Moura raised alarms among humanitarians and regional experts.

Mali marked a new period of expansion and brutality by Wagner, as it proclaimed its intention to support a range of military governments seizing power through coups across the region. These new authoritarian governments characterized themselves by disdain for the European countries that had until then served as their primary security partners. They were fertile ground for Wagner information operations, and in some cases military assistance.

Wagner also promised a gloves-off response to insurgents, one that focused not on conditional offers of training and limited operations, but on the use of overwhelming force to find and kill insurgents and terrify the civilian populations that might support them. To the local security elites who felt patronized by European powers and as though a decade of security assistance had failed to achieve results, Wagner promised a way out – they could secure their regimes and fight back at the enemy, using any means available.

Wagner's expansion into the Sahel would create popular impressions in the West that every coup in West Africa was tied to Wagner. A region that had suffered years of insurgency that local governments and their European backers had failed to resolve was now seen primarily through the prism of Russia's nefarious involvement. This way of looking at the wave of coups obscured more than it revealed. The epidemic of military takeovers, often carried out by

Western-trained military officers, would continue for years, most often with Wagner's main involvement being coordinated disinformation online and the waving of Russian flags at protests. Mali was the exception.

Entry to the Sahel

Bisected by the Sahel, an arid band that divides the Sahara and sub-Saharan Africa, Mali is a country of 22 million people. It has been at war with a range of armed groups in a conflict that has escalated since 2012, fuelled by a scarcity of resources, a product of climate change and corruption. Libya's collapse in 2011 created ripple effects throughout the region, as armed groups marauded across the Sahel, extracting tribute to sustain themselves. Meanwhile, violent extremist groups in the Lake Chad basin conducted campaigns in Niger and Nigeria. These included Boko Haram and later the Islamic State – West African Province (iswap), which would conduct attacks from trucks and motorcycles in central and northern Mali.

France, the European Union and the United Nations all maintained missions in Mali to counter the threats of jihadist groups and banditry. These missions were widely recognized as some of their most dangerous deployments. Despite the size of their forces (France maintained around 5,000 soldiers in Mali), the threat from armed groups had grown in the ten years since Europe and the un began scaling up their involvement. The French presence was unpopular at home and in Mali – it was viewed as a legacy of colonial influence that had failed to make the Malian people safer.[2] With the 2021 coup that led Assimi Goita to power, Malian authorities became more openly hostile to France. The French began to prepare for their withdrawal and the Wagner Group prepared to replace them.

Wagner's entry to Mali started with a series of clumsy fakes. Wagner already had a network of accounts pumping out social media posts in French targeted at francophone Africans in the Central African Republic, but in 2021 they turned their messaging towards Mali. Their posts celebrated friendship between the new military government of Assimi Goita and Russia, attacked the French and European military presence in Mali and cheered the Wagner Group. Rumours were already circulating in international media about Mali's overtures to Wagner and their disinformation apparatus was happy to give these rumours oxygen.[3] Facebook accounts posing as Malian citizens and pages run by the Wagner network began sharing clearly photoshopped pictures of 'pro-Wagner' graffiti in Mali.[4] Fake Malian Facebook pages posted cartoons that showed Wagner fighters and Malians standing side by side, punching out insurgents. The day before Russian foreign minister Sergey Lavrov publicly denied Wagner's involvement in Mali in November, these same Facebook accounts posted photographs of 'Russian instructors training Malian soldiers'. In these photographs, apparent Wagner Group soldiers provided guidance to a pair of camouflaged and beret-clad African soldiers wearing patches for the Malian Armed Forces, FAMa. Closer inspection would reveal that these photographs were taken in the Berengo palace in the CAR.[5]

It was easy to be swept up in the proclamations of the Wagner Group's disinformation, believing that the group was behind all political upheaval in the region. But the messages were often simply reflections of existing sentiment in the countries that they targeted. The tide of coups across West Africa, the anti-European and authoritarian turn among these countries, the grinding insurgencies – all these things were real. They all spelled opportunities for Wagner, if not for direct engagement with these countries, then to tie them together with a story about the failure of Western involvement. There was a reason these narratives took hold: Western engagements in these countries had failed to quell insurgencies or deliver security and prosperity for their people. This was also largely the fault of the corrupt leadership in these countries, but the West chose which governments to support and how to support them. The real threat of Wagner in West Africa and across the developing world is not necessarily that it will lead to coups, but rather that it will attach itself to authoritarian governments, strengthen their kleptocratic and anti-democratic systems and magnify the violence that they are able to perpetrate against their local populations.

Such was the case in Mali. As Goita consolidated power, figures from Wagner were already in Bamako laying the groundwork. Their main interlocutors on the Malian side were Defence Minister Colonel Sadio Camara and Air Force Chief of Staff General Alou Boï Diarra.[6] Diarra was a smart leader who had rapidly climbed the ranks in Mali. Like a number of promising West African officers, he had studied at the U.S. National Defense University (NDU), where he was a distinguished graduate in 2019.[7] Camara also studied military arts abroad, at Russia's Higher Military College.[8] Diarra and Camara worked with the man identified by the U.S. Department of the Treasury and by French officials as Wagner's number one in Mali, a former *spetsnaz* soldier named Ivan 'Miron' Maslov.[9] Maslov had served in Wagner since the group's first incursions into Ukraine in 2014, according to Ukrainian intelligence. Wagner internal documents list him among the main points of contact in Sudan in 2018. He seems to have risen in the ranks as he worked for Wagner's internal security service, documenting theft, violations of rules and regulations and determining who would have their pay docked or face corporal punishment. The description of Wagner's base at Al Jufra in the previous chapter is drawn from a report that Maslov authored in November 2020.

Maslov was backed up by geologists and businessmen. This included Prigozhin's long-time associate Andrey Mandel, who had acted as a director on his companies receiving Russian state contracts and who had helped lead Wagner's entry to Sudan through his role in M Invest. A deal took shape, with some U.S. sources even claiming that Mali promised Wagner $10 million per month.[10] If this figure was offered by the Malian side, one must imagine that Wagner officials knew they were being taken for a ride. *Le Monde* later discovered 'accidentally published' budgets for Mali's intelligence service that documented that its budget had been increased in size by 30 per cent over the course of 2022, coming to around $130 million, a figure that neatly approached Wagner's alleged fee.[11] Whatever the value, UN and U.S. officials claimed that, by December, Wagner and Malian authorities had arrived at an agreement and inked a contract.[12]

Meeting the Enemy

By mid-December, Wagner's airlift began, using familiar Tupolev planes of Russia's 223rd Flight Unit, the same state airline that had carried their fighters into Syria, Libya, Sudan and the CAR.[13] They travelled to Bamako via other Wagner locations, from Moscow to Syria to Libya, before landing in Mali. Wagner got to work almost immediately, finishing construction of a base just south of the main airport in Bamako. Wagner rapidly deployed into the centre of the country and encountered militants of Jama'at Nusrat ul-Islam wa al-Muslimin (JNIM), an al-Qaida-aligned jihadist organization.[14] By early January, Wagner had already clashed with the group in the Mopti region, near towns like Moura.[15] Wagner Group soldiers, travelling with Malian FAMa, met familiar insurgent tactics. On patrol or moving between locations, they would hit an improvised explosive device and be ambushed by small teams of militants. On 30 January 2022 JNIM sources published video of their fighters unearthing the severed hand and foot of a man alleged to be a Wagner fighter injured in one such attack.

What we know of Wagner's campaign in Mali in 2022 is mostly the result of international investigations into incidents of mass violence and the claims of Islamist militants. This was not Syria or the CAR. They fought a different enemy in terrain they were not accustomed to. Unlike in Syria, in Mali Wagner did not enjoy the benefit of robust logistics in-country and was reliant on FAMa to move its men.[16] Unlike in Libya, Wagner was not acting in tandem with another major international backer like the UAE. France's original force in the country was a thousand strong, supported by more than a thousand additional French soldiers in Chad, with more in Niger, the Ivory Coast and Burkina Faso.[17] France had its own logistics and a superior capability to 'find, fix and finish' – counterinsurgency lingo for the cycle of identifying targets, locating and monitoring them and executing operations to destroy them. Wagner had small surveillance drones like the Orlan 10s previously used in the CAR, but France had both surveillance and combat drones like the U.S.-manufactured Reaper that allowed its forces to strike militants from great distances.[18] Wagner was forced to meet its enemy face-to-face, on unfamiliar ground.

Militant groups in Mali, like JNIM, but also the Islamic State Sahel Province (ISSP), claimed multiple attacks on Wagner Group fighters throughout 2022. Some of these were supported with evidence; others were not. Journalist and analyst Wassim Nasr identified eight claims by JNIM of attacks on Wagner from September to November 2022.[19] In response, Wagner employed the tactics on display in Moura.

On 5 and 6 March 2022, FAMa and 'white-skinned soldiers' entered towns in the Segou region of Mali near the border with Mauritania. In the town of Robinet El Ataye soldiers gathered the town's Malian and Mauritanian men and boys at gunpoint, bound and blindfolded them, and looted their houses. More FAMa units arrived and began beating the prisoners. Some of the prisoners were released; others were led away. Relatives of the villagers found their bodies the next day. Twenty-nine Mauritanians and four Malian men had been shot and their bodies burned.[20]

A litany of such events was recorded by international monitors from the United Nations, Human Rights Watch, the Armed Conflict

Location and Event Data Project (ACLED), the International Federation for Human Rights and international journalists.[21] Witnesses accused Wagner of summary execution, torture, abduction, looting and rape. The group operated in tandem with Malian forces, predominately targeting communities believed to be sources of supplies or recruitment for militants.[22] Like in the CAR, ethnic communities like the Fulani, who had been targeted for recruitment by militant groups, were frequently victims of such raids.[23]

The outcome of these tactics appears to have been an increase in militant violence. As ACLED documented, 2022 became the deadliest year for Mali since the crisis began in the Sahel a decade earlier. This was at least partly the result of Mali's new political stance and its more brutal conduct, which created recruitment opportunities for jihadist fighters. When the French and other European forces departed Mali, the Malian government also tightened measures restricting freedom of action for MINUSMA, the UN mission in Mali, particularly their ability to move peacekeepers by ground and air.[24] Malian authorities repeatedly denied MINUSMA's flight requests, and hindered their logistics and ability to combat insurgents.[25] Steadily, UN members began pulling their participation from MINUSMA. It wasn't just European powers either. Egypt and Côte d'Ivoire both withdrew their involvement in 2022.[26] In their eagerness to wage a total war against insurgents, the government of Assimi Goita had alienated most of Mali's international partners. Mali and Wagner would be going it alone.

Expand and Embed

By June 2023 Wagner's bases occupied a crescent across the central part of Mali and were staffed by 1,200 to 1,600 men.[27] Many of these were former French bases, now home to both FAMa and Wagner. Wagner used military camps in places like Sofara in the centre of the country as both bases of operation and detention facilities.[28] Like in the CAR, Wagner expanded its impact by working not only with the armed forces of their host country, but with pro-government armed groups. These included the Dogon village self-defence groups under the Dan Na Ambassagou organization, and Tuareg militias like the Imghad Tuareg Self-Defence Group and Allies (GATIA) and the Movement for the Salvation of Azawad (MSA).[29] Tuareg fighters with their signature *litham* mouth veils and Dogon militias bearing distinctive peaked caps have been a fixture in Mali's decade-long insurgency crisis and have a long history of armed defence of their communities. These armed groups coalesced into organizations in the last ten years that are largely ethnically delineated and opposed to Islamist militants and separatist armed groups in their territory. Consequently, their aims have overlapped with those of the Malian government. Even the French have worked alongside these groups in their fight against JNIM and ISSP.[30]

This doesn't mean that they are official forces or even always aligned with the government – pro-government militias like Dan Na Ambassagou, GATIA and MSA walk a fine line of working together with the Bamako government and effectively replacing that same absent government in their home regions. They have time and again knocked heads with a government that wants greater control over them.[31] Wagner has encouraged collaboration with these groups, who themselves have documented histories of attacking civilians.[32] Their effectiveness has been mixed, as they fight a range of insurgent groups that are larger and better armed.[33] They do, however, allow Wagner to further extend its reach and establish greater local influence, building relationships with not only the Malian government but de facto authorities in the provinces. Like in the CAR and Sudan, Wagner's relationships in Mali are diverse.

As Wagner consolidated its presence in Mali, violence escalated and the group's clashes with insurgents intensified. Into the autumn of 2022, Wagner, together with its local proxies, more actively engaged in attacks on civilians and fell victim to attacks by

JNIM and ISSP.[34] In towns like Nia Ouro in central Mali and Gouni in the southwest, Wagner arrived with FAMa forces and local militias in September.[35] Locals fled, and Wagner and its proxy forces would pillage the towns. In some cases, civilians were allegedly threatened, executed or subjected to sexual violence.[36] In central Mali, FAMa and local forces would routinely enter the town of Sofara and carry out mass arrests. In October, Wagner was documented taking part in these arrests of up to a hundred people. Many of those arrested disappeared.[37]

The tempo of pillage continued, with locals claiming that FAMa and pro-government militants, together with Wagner, stole cattle.[38] In herding communities, this was a grave crime. Cattle raiding serves not only to provide raiders with income from reselling or butchering the cattle, but to deprive local communities of resources. Islamist insurgents have seized on these rumours to recruit and propagandize, claiming to have recovered cattle stolen by FAMa and Wagner.[39]

While much of this violence and pillage was based on profiling of ethnic communities targeted for recruitment or where insurgents were believed to live, Wagner and FAMa's raids were also driven by a local intelligence network of collaborators and informants.[40] This bred paranoia and suspicion of outsiders in the towns and villages that Wagner and FAMa patrolled, perpetuating the cycle of violence. With little prospect of a decisive victory against well-armed and well-resourced insurgents in such a vast territory, Wagner is locked into a quagmire in Mali, using its force to extend government control and capture territory, but without providing long-term solutions to Mali's security crisis. Their presence ensures the continuation of violence, but if they were to leave, the Goita government would be left with little external support.

The Bridgehead from Bamako

In the last four years, history has moved fast in West Africa, and Wagner has been well placed to seize on the region's political turmoil. Alongside coups in Mali in 2020 and 2021, there were also military takeovers in Guinea and Burkina Faso. In 2023 the militaries of Niger and Gabon overthrew their governments as well. All these countries were victims of the region's insurgency crisis, were governed by increasingly repressive leaders dogged by accusations of corruption, and were propped up by flagging security assistance from the USA and European countries. Coup leaders courted popular support by antagonizing their former colonial masters, the French, and the regional political and economic block, ECOWAS. These conditions created opportunities for Russia to enter the region and Wagner gave them the mechanism to do so.

Wagner failed to deploy forces to any West African country other than Mali, but this did not stop rampant speculation in the Western press and policy circles about Wagner's role in coups across the region.[41] Wagner's often-inflated influence in the region has produced an information and policy feedback loop that both assists the Wagner Group and hinders African and Western efforts in the Sahel. In response, U.S. and European policymakers have applied the same framework of 'great-power competition' that they had when Wagner entered Sudan and the CAR, and like in those countries, it has failed to push Wagner out.[42]

A large part of Western concern over Wagner's foothold in the region is a result of the public embrace of Wagner by coup leaders and their supporters. As they seized power in Mali, Burkina Faso and Niger, crowds have poured into the streets, waving banners and chanting slogans.[43] Some of them carried Russian flags. Stranger still, others raised the flag of the Wagner Group and posters with pictures of Evgeniy Prigozhin.[44] The Wagner posters that featured specific memes and in-jokes of the group may have been provided by local actors paid or supplied by Wagner.[45] Mostly, it was a direct reflection of the widespread anti-French and anti-Western sentiment in these countries and a testament to the rise of Wagner as a brand identity, a symbol of all things anti-Western and pro-military.

Even as Russia officially condemned some of these coups, the broader Wagner network worked to tie them to a pro-Russian and, just as importantly, pro-Wagner narrative.[46] Prigozhin, together with other network actors ranging from Maksim Shugalei to Wagner representatives in the CAR, described these coups as part of an anti-colonial revolution across sub-Saharan Africa.[47] In this revolution, these countries would be supported by Russia, in the same way as African anti-imperialist movements in the Cold War, such as FRELIMO in Mozambique or the MPLA in Angola, had been supported by the Soviet Union. Wagner propaganda and the statements of Prigozhin all implied Wagner support for these coups and sometimes hinted at direct involvement. Unfounded rumours spread that coup leaders had plotted their takeovers with Wagner.[48]

In January of 2022, Paul-Henry Sandaogo Damiba, a French-educated and American-trained lieutenant colonel in Burkina Faso's military, overthrew the Burkinabe government. Within days, claims circulated in Western media not only that the new military government was seeking to employ Wagner, but that they may have overthrown the former president for his refusal to do so.[49] Wagner's mouthpieces had already been seeding hints at their involvement or future business with the military government. A day after the coup, Aleksandr Ivanov, head of the Wagner front organization Officers Union for International Security in the CAR, published a statement that read,

> I believe that if instructors from Russia were invited to train the army of Burkina Faso, they will be able to do it effectively ... the Officers Union for International Security is ready to share the experience gained in CAR on how to

organize the work quickly and efficiently in order to build a combat-ready army and bring the security situation under control in a short time.[50]

The statement was widely reported in international media. Anyone following Wagner and Ivanov knew that he was among Wagner's least reliable spokespeople, who mostly issued tepid statements that followed the lead of Prigozhin and other mouthpieces like Shugalei. However, the environment was ripe for this fear to take hold, and u.s. defence spokespeople refused to confirm or deny the allegations of Wagner's involvement in the coup.[51]

By September, Damiba was himself overthrown by one of his military colleagues, a young captain named Ibrahim Traore. Traore, who had been a soldier in MINUSMA, was also alleged to have been working with Wagner.[52] Within a day, Prigozhin had released a statement congratulating Traore and describing Burkina Faso as having cast off the 'yoke of the colonialists'.[53] The new military government, much like the previous one, also sought a rapprochement with Russia as they expelled French forces.[54] American and European analysts and journalists penned dozens of pieces anticipating Wagner's arrival in Ouagadougou. Wagner would never succeed in dispatching forces to Burkina Faso. As we will see later, Russia would not gain a military foothold in the country until Wagner suffered a dramatic and painful transformation a year later.

Less than a year after Burkina Faso's second coup, Niger's military staged its own, overthrowing President Mohamed Bazoum. Like the coups in the region that preceded it, the new military government of Abdourahamane Tchiani cited among their grievances frustration with civilian corruption, the inability of the civilian government to confront the insurgency and the heavy-handed involvement of France. Like the other coups, Tchiani identified France and ECOWAS as his foes and Russia as a potential ally. Prigozhin soon published a recorded statement:

What happened in Niger is the struggle of the people of
Niger with the colonialists who tried to keep them in the
same state that Africa was in hundreds of years ago . . .
International missions with tens of thousands of soldiers
were not able to protect the population . . . This is the high
effectiveness of Wagner, because one thousand Wagner
soldiers can restore order and destroy terrorists.[55]

In Niamey, there were public demonstrations in support of the
coup government. Demonstrators carried a poster with a picture of
Prigozhin that read, 'Wagner, protect us.'[56]

u.s. officials were clear this time that they did not believe that
Wagner had supported the coup but suggested that Wagner might
attempt to establish itself in Niger.[57] Malian and French diplomatic sources told the media that Niger's military government had
contacted Wagner during a visit by one of their officials to Mali.[58]
Niger, up until then one of the United States's most crucial coun-
terterrorism partners in West Africa and host to a u.s. drone base,
appeared to be in danger of becoming another Russian mercenary
stronghold. The United States was playing it cautiously, refrain-
ing from calling the military takeover a coup while engaging
with the coup leadership to dissuade them from partnering with
Wagner.[59] ecowas deployed a standby force and weighed intervention. Islamist militant forces took advantage of the chaos to launch
attacks on Nigerien military forces. Wagner's future role in Niger
remains unclear.

Sudan's Civil War

In Sudan, a similar form of political turmoil was taking place on an
even larger scale. In late October 2021 the military seized power from
the civilian-led government in a violent coup. Unlike in West Africa,
the crowds that poured into the streets in Sudan overwhelmingly

opposed the military takeover. The same grass-roots movements that had toppled the military dictatorship of Omar al-Bashir were unwilling to quietly let the military turn back the clock. The military suppressed them, killing dozens of protestors and arresting anyone who opposed them.

The Wagner Group kept quiet. It had a smaller force in Sudan than elsewhere but maintained active operations in gold mining and political interference. Men from units including the 1st and 10th Assault Detachments remained in the country, mainly to provide security. Tensions were growing between the rival military factions in Sudan: the Sudanese Armed Forces (SAF), under its leader, Abdel Fattah al-Burhan, and the Rapid Support Forces (RSF), under Hemedti. The SAF wanted to see the RSF formally integrated with the Sudanese military, while Hemedti and his officers wanted to retain their power.

The RSF tested the resolve of the SAF until matters came to a head in April 2023. It is unclear who fired the first shots, but the RSF was swift in seizing SAF bases and taking control of large areas of Khartoum. The SAF retaliated with its superior air power, launching air strikes on RSF locations in the capital. Within days, a war was raging across the country the likes of which had not been seen in Sudan for decades. As was so often the case in Sudan's history of political violence, it was the civilians caught in the crossfire who suffered the most. From the cities of Khartoum and Port Sudan to the towns of Darfur, regular Sudanese were trapped between the warring sides.

Wagner had done business with the military and the ascendant RSF and was well placed to choose its champion. Wagner's numbers in the country, however, were small and they could hardly play a decisive role in the ground war. On top of that, the group had little to gain from choosing one side in what was likely to be a grinding war of sizable forces, each backed by various international powers. The SAF benefited from powerful regional partners like Egypt and

Gulf powers like Saudi Arabia, while the UAE backed the RSF with arms and equipment.[60]

In April, Sudanese sources told international media that Wagner and the UAE's mutual ally in Libya, Khalifa Haftar, was airdropping Wagner-supplied man-portable air defence systems (MANPADS) to the RSF to help them counter SAF airpower.[61] The U.S. Treasury confirmed these claims a month later.[62] Satellite images revealed movement of Il-76 transport planes along Wagner's familiar route from Syria to Al-Khadim airbase in Libya prior to the reported delivery of MANPADS in a pattern that online aviation researchers identified as unusual.[63] There is as yet little hard evidence of the nature and scale of Wagner's alleged support for the RSF.[64]

The course of events in Sudan presents some of the best and worst of Western efforts to counter Wagner. The U.S. decision to publicize information about Wagner's role in the delivery of weapons systems to the RSF is helpful to demonstrate to international stakeholders the role that Wagner plays in the civil war in Sudan and could be used to apply pressure to the UAE. The disclosure mirrors earlier intelligence sharing by the United States with Chadian authorities. In February 2023 the *Wall Street Journal* reported that the United States shared information with Chad on the coordination between the Wagner Group and Chadian rebels, including possible plots to overthrow Chad's president.[65] U.S. officials commented publicly that they had exposed a plot by Wagner's leadership, including Prigozhin, to work with Chadian rebels to destabilize the government. This wasn't entirely far-fetched, given that Wagner had been stationed alongside hundreds of Chadian rebels of the Front pour l'alternance et la concorde au Tchad (FACT) at Al Jufra in Libya and had crossed paths with Chadian rebel groups in the CAR. The dilemma of studying intelligence is that we seldom know about the cases in which it is successful – it is entirely possible that U.S. intelligence disclosures to Chad helped to prevent Wagner's activity in that country.

For all the benefits of the U.S. engagement with Chad, the prudent decision to share intelligence on Wagner with partners and the public was marred by the nature of the Chadian government itself. Ruled by President Mahamat Idriss Deby, Chad is a military dictatorship that has been controlled by the Deby family dynasty for thirty years. Mahamat Idriss Deby's father, Idriss Deby, was president of Chad until he was killed by FACT rebels in April 2021. The United States and France have been criticized by civil society in Chad who oppose the Deby family's undemocratic rule.[66]

As we have seen throughout Africa, illegitimate, unstable and repressive governments make for fertile ground for networks like the Wagner Group, even when those governments are friendly with the West. Western engagement in Sudan failed to empower civilians and to isolate the coup government, laying the groundwork for the country's current civil war. European diplomats lent legitimacy to leaders like Hemedti by publicly meeting with him to discuss the RSF's 'reform efforts', and Western sanctions did not comprehensively target the true financial power base of the RSF and SAF.[67] It was this financial power base that formed the crux of their relationship with external actors like Wagner and allowed them to retain power after the overthrow of Bashir. Civil society organizations in Sudan had long sounded the alarms about the military and the RSF's capture of the economy and the threat it posed to Sudan's democratic future, but Western countries nonetheless chose a more moderate stance that ultimately empowered Sudan's most repressive actors.[68]

If we want to prevent Wagner from spreading, entrenching corruption, defending dictators, immiserating vulnerable populations and prolonging civil wars, we need to focus on a more holistic approach that denies Wagner the ability to take root. This includes sanctions, but not only against Wagner. Financial restrictions should be used to limit the financial resources that authoritarian leaders use to wage war, pay patronage and maintain an iron grip on their countries' economies. In cases like Sudan, but also beyond Africa in countries like Myanmar, civil society often provides the best cues for this policy.[69] Western policymakers should take civilian grievances seriously and evaluate the calls for sanctions by local organizations on their own merits.

More importantly, Western governments need to look more critically at their partnerships and objectives in Africa. Paradoxically, the more Africa policies focus on great-power competition, the worse they seem to perform. Rather than focusing on boxing out China and Russia, especially actors like the Wagner Group, Western governments and institutions should focus on the types of partnership they want to see flourish. This means a more principled approach to choosing partners. Authoritarian governments may make for helpful security partners in the short term, but they lead to the type of instability that malign networks like Wagner can prey on in the long run. It also means considering development and aid as security priorities in and of themselves and binding these closely to a commitment to transparency. Local corruption, corporate secrecy and suffering economies are fertile ground for networks like Wagner, whether they trade in resources, arms or violence. Working in Sudan, I found that transparency and the rule of law were among the most powerful weapons that local civilian leaders wielded against malicious foreign interference. Concrete steps such as publicly available corporate registries can allow local journalists and civil society to understand who owns their economies, while independent and empowered judiciaries can prevent local officials from engaging in corruption together with foreign interlopers, whether they are international oil companies or mercenaries.

These must be true partnerships, not just relationships in which Western governments present the terms on which their aid and investment are contingent. As such, Western governments and institutions need to demonstrate commitment through action. This includes greater legal cooperation with African states, whose efforts at international legal coordination, ranging from recovering assets looted by deposed autocrats to prosecuting war criminals abroad, are often stymied by a slow-moving international legal system hostile to judiciaries of developing states.[70] The same international legal system that has created quagmires and roadblocks for the international justice and asset recovery efforts of countries like Nigeria, Egypt, Libya and Sudan has also enabled Prigozhin to launch legal attacks on his critics abroad, as we will see in Chapter Nine. It is imperative that these mechanisms, such as mutual legal assistance that allows countries to request law enforcement coordination to prosecute crimes committed within their borders, are made more available to African states.

Countering criminal networks in Africa also means holding our allies to the same standards that we hold African countries. Western partners like the UAE, Saudi Arabia and Israel also play significant roles in African security, development and politics. Western responses to criminal activity by state or private networks from these countries has diverged greatly from our condemnation of Chinese- or Russian-sponsored organizations. Consider the cases of Israel Ziv and Dan Gertler, two Israeli nationals conducting business in Africa. Ziv, a retired general in the Israeli Defence Forces, was sanctioned by the USA in 2018 for allegedly providing $150 million in weapons to the South Sudanese government while it was under an international arms embargo.[71] While his sanctions announcement accused him of corruption and organizing mercenaries to attack oil fields, his designation was mysteriously lifted after efforts by an international law firm to earn him relief.[72] In 2017 Gertler was also placed under U.S. sanctions for his role in 'hundreds of millions of dollars' worth of opaque and corrupt mining and oil deals' in the Democratic Republic of Congo.[73] Sanctions on Gertler were temporarily lifted in the late days of the Donald Trump administration before they were reintroduced under President Biden.[74] There is no evidence that these actors were backed by the Israeli government, but Israel has also failed to adequately investigate their crimes.

As we have seen with the cases of Project Opus and the UAE's coordination with Wagner in Libya, it is not always Russia behind harmful mercenary activity in Africa. Corporate secrecy in the United Arab Emirates enables vast corruption and illicit resource extraction throughout Africa, whether corrupt government officials are buying secret real estate in Dubai or selling gold through Emirati intermediaries. Shadowy aviation companies based in the UAE have been used by arms dealers in Africa since the days of legendary trafficker Viktor Bout. The UAE has dispatched mercenaries, including Americans and Brits, to fight in Libya and Yemen.[75] The United States, the EU and the UK variously maintain relationships of legal cooperation, arms sales and diplomatic coordination with the UAE despite this.

Western governments will have to expend political capital and show they are willing to walk the walk, even if it leads to friction with valuable regional security partners. Demonstrating commitment to partners or principles always comes with costs, and this is a cost that Western states will have to be willing to bear if they want to resist networks like the Wagner Group. Wagner can show commitment through its willingness to deploy men to fight and die on behalf of foreign governments, an area in which Western governments are – with good reason – hard-pressed to compete. But there are other ways to show commitment. In a conversation with a former U.S. special forces officer, I explained my thoughts on this area of Wagner's advantage, its willingness to accept risk versus the U.S. force protection bias, our avoidance of risking the lives of soldiers in foreign wars. 'If our main objective is to stay safe,' he replied, 'then that is best achieved by staying home.' This is true not only of security support, but of our resolve to hold our international partners to account. Resisting Wagner and networks like it will require Western governments to bear costs, not necessarily in sending their troops to fight, but in compelling their regional security partners to make good on their promises to restrict, prosecute and deny safe haven to corrupt and criminal organizations.

9

PILLAGE

The [Western elite] did not become wealthy by chance.
They achieved a lot … they largely took their position
by robbing other peoples in Asia and Africa.
Vladimir Putin speaking at the Strong Ideas
for a New Time forum, July 2022

The drive north from Khartoum traces the Nile. On your left is green: date palms crowd the river between small towns. On your right is red: sand and dramatic black rock outcroppings, punctuated by gas stations, the tall, flaming rigging of oil refineries, and occasional verdant circles of crops. Farmers sell fruits and tea at roadside stalls shaded by tarps and umbrellas. The road is travelled by white Hyundais and Toyotas and trundling cargo trucks. Past the grand, jagged pyramids of Meroe is the rail crossroads at Atbara. Just north of Atbara, 320 kilometres (200 mi.) from Khartoum, is the mining town of al Ibediyya. Artisanal miners cart gold ore into the town from remote sites in the desert, where they auction it off to local buyers who process out the gold using dangerous mercury – a risky but profitable venture. By the time I visited Sudan in 2021, this market was dominated by the Russians, who would buy both gold and processed ore in al Ibediyya before loading it into trucks to carry it 25 kilometres (15 mi.) into the desert to their enormous facility. It had hardly existed just two years earlier but now it was a well-guarded compound of towers and scaffolding surrounded by high fences under a red Soviet flag.

The company running its operations near al Ibediyya was popularly known as 'the Russian company'. In its corporate registration documents, stored among the towering, dusty stacks of folders in Sudan's corporate registry in Khartoum, it is identified as Meroe Gold – the company owned by Prigozhin's M Invest.

Nearly 2,000 kilometres (1,240 mi.) away in the CAR, another huge processing facility sits in a red clay scar in the forest. Around 60 kilometres (37 mi.) from Bambari, where Wagner fired into a mosque in 2021, this is the Ndasimma gold mine, the CAR's first industrial mining facility. Excavators belch smoke as they pass its looming tank batteries and murky storage ponds, travelling the short distance south to the cavernous open mining pits, where more than three hundred local artisanal miners work.

Al Ibediyya and Ndasimma were two of the most impressive jewels in Wagner's crown, but they were by no means the only ones. They were owned by Meroe Gold, later renamed al Solag, and Midas Resources. Both were local companies and bore the mark of local connections. The domain registration for the Midas Resources now defunct website provides the contact information for William Wabem Ndede, a Central African diamond merchant related to CAR president Touadera.[1] Meroe's transformation to al Solag was conducted by Sudan's Ministry of Mining and it achieved its first contracts through coordination with officials in Bashir's government.[2]

These and other Wagner companies registered in Madagascar, Sudan and the CAR were diversified beyond just mineral resources. Back when al Solag was called Meroe, it also registered an agricultural arm that ran a farm further south along the Nile. In Bangui, Wagner companies run a brewery that produces their own Africa Ti L'Or brand beer and Wa Na Wa brand vodka.[3] Wood International Group SARLU, formerly Bois Rouge SARLU, harvests timber from the CAR and exports it to Denmark, France, China and Pakistan.[4] Diamville, a company directed by the former driver for Dmitriy Sytiy, one of Wagner's managers in the CAR, exports diamonds to the UAE and Europe.[5] These companies buy their equipment from

Russia, China and South Africa, and import it over Wagner's air bridges and through third countries like Cameroon.

Wagner's businesses abroad are diverse and locally connected, and seem resistant to international sanctions. They trade with the same cluster of Prigozhin-associated Russian companies like M Invest and Broker Expert. When the USA or the European Union places sanctions on a Wagner company, that company can continue business as usual by working through unscrupulous middlemen in countries like the UAE or change its name to hide its identity. These companies have one other major characteristic in common: no one can give a convincing estimate of what they're worth.

Balancing the Books

Wagner operates in historically opaque markets. The Central Bank of Sudan estimates that around 70 per cent of Sudan's gold production is smuggled out of the country, bypassing tax and reporting requirements. Wagner has been documented misreporting its gold exports and carrying it out on flights from Khartoum airport. The situation is even worse in the CAR, where Wagner operates mining sites in areas forbidden under international agreements designed to curtail the trade in conflict diamonds. Despite these restrictions, Wagner's Diamville was noted as one of the top four diamond exporters in the CAR by the American aid agency USAID in spring 2022.[6]

Investigators have attempted to ascertain Wagner's actual income from its African operations. In some cases, customs documentation illuminates the value of its exports: Wagner's timber enterprises exported around $270,000 worth of wood via Cameroon from April 2022 to June 2023, according to customs documents reviewed by Bloomberg.[7] That same investigation found that Wagner's timber operations could yield up to $5.4 million annually – not accounting for the challenges of transporting wood, hiding its origin and finding buyers. Those same challenges are true of diamonds and gold. Politico has quoted U.S. officials claiming that Wagner could generate up to $1 billion annually from Ndasimma alone.[8] CNN concedes that it is nearly impossible to estimate the profits of Wagner's Sudan ventures, particularly when the value of gold smuggled out of Sudan sits anywhere between $1.9 billion and a staggering $13.4 billion annually.[9]

After working with journalists on the ground and international investigators, and reviewing thousands of leaked documents that include balance sheets and receipts, I still couldn't give you a reliable figure as to Wagner's international profit. I could tell you, for example, that Wagner struggled to make money in its early days in Sudan – a presumption based on balance sheets from that time – or that it has routinely been short-changed by local partners from Syria to Mali, as documented in managers' correspondence. I could point out that in Libya, a massive Wagner deployment, there is no solid evidence of a real extractives operation. But these attempts to divine a dollar value for Wagner's resource ventures fail to consider the non-financial benefits it provides the group.

While many models of Wagner activity draw a direct line between resource extraction, mercenary operations and political interference, the truth is that the profitability of a natural-resource market isn't a good predictor of Wagner's involvement in a country. We have already addressed the Libya example, but let's also look at Mozambique and Madagascar. Wagner's involvement in Mozambique was more blood than treasure. It fought a fraught counterinsurgency campaign, putting less energy into trying to secure resource deals. In Madagascar it was all treasure, no blood. Wagner focused on creating a joint venture with Madagascar's state-owned mining company and tried to pay off local presidential candidates with suitcases full of cash. Wagner changed its model to suit what its curators thought would be most likely to achieve long-term influence. Mozambique's security market was much more open than its resource market – Wagner would have a hard time competing with Total, for example, but it could undercut South African PMSCs – while the opposite was true in Madagascar: there was more money to be made in mining than in violence. In both cases, Wagner's efforts failed, not because it didn't turn a profit, but because it failed to make sustainable local connections.

Industry and Influence

Eeben Barlow, the director of influential South African PMSC Executive Outcomes, faced a myriad of accusations of trading in 'blood for oil' or 'blood for diamonds' in EO's operations in Angola and Sierra Leone. But as Barlow pointed out when he was accused by Russian media of advising the Russian government on the use of PMCs in 2019, it is very difficult to pay contractors in carats of diamonds or barrels of oil.[10] This, of course, obscures the very real ways in which resources can be exchanged for guarantees of security – 'I bankroll your security now to guarantee greater profit through access to resources later' – but it is still an important factor in how we understand Wagner's model. Wagner may be partly financed through the resources it collects abroad, but its primary funding source is the Russian state, both through direct contracts and through Prigozhin's preferential access to lucrative government contracting. This is evidenced by Prigozhin's and Putin's later statements and a comparison of 'the Company's' income from contracting in Russia versus verifiable profits abroad.

Why, then, the focus on diamonds, gold, oil and timber, let alone beer and vodka? The answer is not just financial, but political. In each of the countries Wagner is active in commercially or as a fighting force, it has launched political-interference operations. Like its commercial activities, these are shrouded in a series of front organizations. AFRIC, the 'Association for Free Research and International Cooperation', was a Prigozhin project active in sending election observers, releasing illegal polling data and coordinating with other Prigozhin-linked disinformation campaigns in South Africa, the Democratic Republic of Congo, Zimbabwe, Madagascar and Mozambique.[11] AFRIC dispatched non-Russian observers to a number of the elections that it monitored, though these were invariably figures from the far-right or conspiracist fringe in their respective countries. There was also the Foundation for the Defence of National Values, which ran disinformation campaigns in the United States and sent Maksim Shugalei on his ill-fated trip to Libya – and later sent him on trips to countries including Afghanistan after the Taliban takeover.[12] The group's most robust disinformation campaigns were enacted in the countries that Wagner had the greatest presence in: Sudan, the CAR, Libya and Mali. These were aimed at supporting their local partners, burnishing the image of Russia, and spinning a positive narrative around Wagner itself.

Commercial enterprises went hand in hand in these activities. Through business, Wagner could capture local elites in more meaningful and sustainable ways than just through guns and Facebook posts: through money. Wagner's enterprises gave the group consistent contact with leading economic players in these countries and let it build financial relationships, thereby encouraging local elites to support Wagner's long-term presence. This could range from paying off militias in the CAR to striking a mutually beneficial deal with the Bashir government in Sudan. Because Wagner was engaged in countries that were so afflicted by corruption, it could leverage kickbacks to make itself favoured for the security not only of the leader, but of the ruling financial elite. After all, national leaders could be overthrown, as Bashir was in Sudan – it pays to be diversified.

This is, of course, not the only factor incentivizing the commercial side of Wagner. Maintaining international businesses provided Prigozhin with a financial lifeline if he was cut out of his lucrative contracting arrangement with the Russian government. There is also the matter of the larger strategic significance of some of the resources that Wagner is invested in. With Russia's invasion of Ukraine, a few observers pointed to Wagner as a valuable source of gold, diamonds and other precious metals for the Russian state. It is difficult to ascertain exactly where the resources that Wagner plunders end up, aside from a few exceptions where investigators have identified the UAE as a key transit point, and at least some diamonds bound for Belgium.[13] It is possible that more of the gold and diamonds mined by Wagner find their way back to strategic reserves in Russia, but this is not supported by documentary evidence.

To better understand what motives besides naked profit drive Wagner's commercial activity, we should look to the CAR and Sudan. In the CAR, the mine at Ndasimma was formerly run by Canadian company AXMIN, which had owned the rights to it since 2010. AXMIN was unusual among the mostly small-scale mining operations in the CAR, many run by small teams of Chinese miners. There was a reason why few were willing to take the risk of running a larger operation. In late 2012, AXMIN's site at Ndasimma was occupied by Seleka rebels. By 2013, AXMIN reported that all its facilities and equipment had been stolen or destroyed, resulting in losses of approximately $38 million. They declared force majeure.[14] The CAR government ignored AXMIN's continuing legal claim to the site when it handed it to Wagner.

Similarly, there are reasons why Meroe Gold was able to claim such a significant place in Sudan. First, the company benefited from the existing work of the Russian–Emirati gold firm Alliance for Mining, a subsidiary of the Dubai-based Emiral, a company directed by former KGB officer Boris Ivanov.[15] Alliance was successful in Sudan, leading Meroe Gold to recruit some of its former staff to make sense of the local gold market. Second, it established commercial links with all the major security players that could make or break its operation, doing business with the Sudanese Armed

Forces' Military Industrial Corporation, the Rapid Support Forces' Esnaad Engineering and the Sudanese intelligence services' Aswar.

Wagner's commercial activities required substantial upfront spending, an enormous appetite for risk and a willingness to engage in flagrant corruption, on top of the ability to leverage security guarantees for local hosts. Few other truly private enterprises would be willing to accept these terms – not just because of the reputational risk, but because they are in many ways unwise investments. Most international businesses holding mining concessions in African states with fragile security are more than happy to sit on their holdings, either to flip them down the line or to wait out the instability. Not so for Wagner, which can establish its security independently and pay off militias, and is willing to accept its own security forces dying in the line of duty.

Just like the myriad flights of ostensibly privately owned aircraft from the UAE to Libya, or the fleet of similarly 'private' vessels running from the Black Sea to Syria in the Syrian Express, these activities only make sense when we look at them through a geopolitical lens. They are uneconomical, providing benefit for the companies that partake only so long as the countries they are acting on behalf of offer them substantial benefits in return.

If Wagner's primary motive was profit, it could very easily run a more conventional set of businesses with less risk, more opportunity and likely greater margins. Take, for example, Russian diamond giant Alrosa. Alrosa is largely active in Russia itself, but also in Africa, in countries like Angola, Botswana and Zimbabwe. Up to 2022, Alrosa rivalled even the titanic De Beers in terms of value produced, with a revenue of $3 billion in 2020. Alrosa relies on having an at least palatable reputation to maintain access to its international markets, even after being sanctioned by the United States and others because of Russia's invasion of Ukraine. Diamville and other Wagner mining companies do not enjoy such a competitive market of buyers.

The Wagner Group's commercial network was not principally interested in profit. It was interested in seizing opportunities created by instability and by its own unique offering to get into places that larger firms cannot. Once there, it can establish influence for the Russian state and for its curators, namely Prigozhin. Wagner and Prigozhin could then use their success abroad to shore up their security, influence and access to rents at home. Major international mineral companies profit in the long term due to patience; Wagner's companies do not subscribe to this virtue. Because they are willing to guarantee their own security in-country and offer their local partners benefits that no reputable firm could, they can fast-track themselves from exploration to extraction and export. This comes with enormous overheads that eat into profits and means that their international markets are significantly smaller. But this hit to profitability is a secondary concern if you can demonstrate success to the Kremlin and make yourself indispensable to the Russian state.

The Nature of the Network

Wagner's commercial enterprises are an adhocracy that sometimes engage closely with the security and political elements of Wagner, and sometimes operate almost entirely independently. Their finances are overseen by a smaller cadre of administrators, mostly in St Petersburg, who are housed within the structures of the Concord group of companies and firms like Evro Polis. This group of administrators, many of whom are indistinguishable on paper or in person from the countless similar accountants and middle managers across Russia, oversee a huge number of corporate entities. Leaked Wagner administrative documents indicate that the network maintained, in all, 368 companies in Russia in 2021. Most of these were disposable, spun up to take the place of companies that were heavily sanctioned or otherwise compromised. A small core of them were more regularly leveraged for Wagner's finance and logistics.

The companies that Wagner has most actively leveraged to pay people and companies and to move employees and equipment are (non-exhaustively) Broker Expert, M Finance, M Invest, Breeze LLC, Agro Capital, DM LLC, Mercury and Evro Polis. All of these firms are Swiss army knives, deployed for whatever purpose necessary. One of these companies, Paritet Film, is a Russian firm created primarily to produce Prigozhin's series of Wagner films. According to customs data, in 2021 Paritet also sent products that include helicopter components and batteries to a CAR company called Mining Industries SURL. These products were no doubt useful for filming Prigozhin's Wagner epics *Tourist* and *Granit* in the CAR, but also may have had applications for Wagner itself, particularly where helicopter parts were concerned.

This network also includes companies that Prigozhin used to maintain an iron grip on the catering and construction market for the Russian military, like Obshchepit and Main Line LLC. They served his vanity as well: he used a series of companies in his sprawling network to effectively 'launder' his private jets by transferring their ownership across his Seychelles companies to Russian firms with names like S-Logistic LLC. One of the Seychelles companies that Prigozhin previously used to hold his aircraft also may have been used as a vehicle to employ private military contractors, based on the résumé of a former Moran Security employee.[16]

In this way, Prigozhin could use his seemingly bottomless well of companies both in Russia and abroad to secure contracts with the Russian state, run his mercenary empire and hold onto his toys. This was enabled not just by corruption in Russia, but by global corporate secrecy. Prigozhin was known to have used companies not only in the countries in Africa in which the Wagner Group was active, but in Czechia, the Seychelles, the UAE and Hong Kong, and to have registered his vessels and aircraft to the Cayman Islands and the Isle of Man. This is the real value that Prigozhin brought to Wagner in its iterations from 2014 to 2022, and the element in which he could truly stake his claim: the corporate infrastructure that undergirds Wagner's success.

Sanctioning the Chef

The Wagner Group is just one of countless similar Russian illicit networks that have penetrated the global financial system, all of them using secrecy and anonymity to allow them to continue to turn a profit on the one hand and serve the interests of the Russian state on the other. These networks are difficult to restrict by sanctioning, because they can so quickly create new companies or open new lines of business in friendlier third countries. Prigozhin demonstrated that while he would defy sanctions, he recognized their usefulness at home, where he could cite his sanctioning by the West as evidence of his resolve in support of the Russian state. That doesn't mean he passively accepted being subject to international financial restrictions. Prigozhin used law firms in Washington, DC, and London to hinder attempts to hold him accountable.

Beginning in 2018, a series of Prigozhin's firms, several of which had been involved in shipping goods to Syria, Sudan and beyond, contracted with a Russian law firm. They began Project Shakespeare, an international effort to strike back at the sanctions and indictments targeting Prigozhin for his role in the Wagner Group. The Russian firm he contracted, Capital Legal Services, worked with international firms like Reed Smith to fight the U.S. Department of Justice's indictment of Prigozhin for election interference. The DOJ indictment ultimately failed.

To fight EU sanctions, Capital Legal Services engaged its sister firm, the conspicuously named Discreet Law, to launch a libel case against Eliot Higgins, the founder of Bellingcat. Bellingcat had exposed Prigozhin's connections to Wagner time and again, using leaked data and public information. If Prigozhin's team could win a case against Higgins, it would both bolster Prigozhin's argument to have sanctions lifted and create a chilling effect on any journalist who wanted to investigate him – even if they were on the other side of the world. In this case, Capital Legal Services worked with London firm Phillips Lewis Smith and well-known media barristers such as Justin Rushbrooke and solicitors such as Roger Gherson.[17] Gherson was even granted approval by the UK Treasury to represent the sanctioned Prigozhin. Discrete Law asked for documents from Prigozhin to submit to UK authorities to check for money laundering. Prigozhin submitted a gas bill in his mother's name and his lawyers claimed that she paid the bills at his residence.

All of this was put to a halt by Russia's invasion of Ukraine in February 2022 and Prigozhin's later public statements about Wagner, but it was exceptional how far the case was able to go. The international financial system allowed Prigozhin to move the money necessary to run a mercenary company, spread disinformation and enjoy the perks of his wealth. The international legal system allowed him even to strike at the journalists who investigated him, even those ostensibly safe in London. Only following the Russian invasion of Ukraine did he find his freedom of action truly limited.

But just how limited was it? Sanctions certainly had an impact on Prigozhin, as they have had an impact on the Russian economy. As Prigozhin's role in Wagner and global information operations became more overt, we can see how his network and assets withdrew to Russia. He re-registered his planes and yacht in Russia. His daughter no longer competes in showjumping competitions in Spain. In other ways, he succeeded in evading sanctions. The EU lifted sanctions on his mother, Violetta Prigozhina, on 8 March 2023, on the grounds that family relations were not strong enough to accuse her of involvement in his criminal activities, even though she had previously acted as an officer in his companies. Wagner continued to move men and equipment into places like Syria, Libya, the CAR and Sudan, and kept exporting gold and diamonds, timber and liquor. Prigozhin continued to pay his fighters and his army of trolls, and to earn money from lucrative government contracts. Wagner expanded into new domains, even as pressure ratcheted up.

How does a network that is sanctioned by the UK, the EU and the USA continue to operate on this scale? It would be one thing if, like many Russian companies, most of its business was in Russia and friendly neighbouring countries. But Prigozhin's and Wagner's work was international. Part of the problem lies in their agility and part of it lies in the gaps in the international sanctions enforcement framework.

Prigozhin's network in Russia and abroad could quickly create new legal entities, much faster than the U.S. or the UK Treasury could designate them. This means that at least part of the burden for stopping networks like Prigozhin's falls to international financial institutions to identify sanctions and money-laundering risk. As we can see from the example of Project Shakespeare, many firms failed to do the necessary due diligence or simply turned a blind eye.

Leaked internal files from Prigozhin's network show how they were able to pay for services, including in Europe, long after Prigozhin himself was sanctioned by the EU, the United States and the UK. Expense records document that, in August 2021, Prigozhin's network was still contracting with a German social media analytics firm, paying them in euros. Account statements from a crypto-currency site record how they paid translators around the world in bitcoin and traded in cryptocurrency through intermediaries in places like Czechia. At least one of their accounts was shuttered by an online crypto marketplace in 2020, costing them around $10,000 in bitcoin – but they continued to make payments through a myriad of other accounts on the same platform.

Prior to Russia's invasion of Ukraine, the broader Wagner network sent political technologists and other network employees to their sites aboard flights that transited through Europe, even chartering aircraft via companies with European branches. While increased scrutiny on Wagner reduced the network's overt footprint in Europe, they could withdraw to other safe havens.

The Finer Things

It isn't just Prigozhin's mother who has walked between the raindrops of international sanctions. Prigozhin had two daughters, Polina and Veronika, and a son, Pavel. When Polina and Pavel were children, Prigozhin authored a children's book for them. Later, as young adults, he continued to spoil them.

Polina and Veronika are both amateur showjumpers and have owned a number of horses that they have ridden in competitions across Europe. Navalny's Anti-Corruption Foundation (ACF) even found that they continued to compete after Russia invaded Ukraine.[18] Polina, the eldest daughter, at one point registered a company in Germany to manage her horses. According to her Facebook page, she still lives in Hanover, Germany.

All three children have been involved in their father's business empire. Prigozhin gave them director and shareholder roles on his many companies and placed them at the helm of businesses like hotels and real-estate development companies in St Petersburg. Pavel has even been involved in Wagner. Prigozhin claimed that he fought with Wagner in Syria and continued to serve as a member. There is little evidence of Pavel's combat experience, but ample video and photographs of him riding on his father's private jets, sunbathing nude on his father's yacht, and drinking with his sisters, friends and wife around a campfire on holiday.

Pavel's wife, Ekaterina Inkina, is herself the daughter of another St Petersburg catering magnate, Sergey Inkin. Inkin's company has won catering contracts with Russian companies like Gazprom subsidiaries and companies owned by officials of United Russia, Putin's political party. These in-laws have been subject to none of the scrutiny that Prigozhin himself contended with. As identified by Navalny's ACF, the Inkin family own a home in the beachside town of Forte dei Marmi, Italy, worth more than €3 million. There is no evidence that Prigozhin's family has been able to travel to this property since the start of the war, but there are other beaches in the world.

In early June, videos began appearing on Telegram of Veronika Prigozhina. They were video messages that were clearly not intended to be shared beyond a few of her friends. 'How's life in Russia?' she pouts into the camera, smoking a slim cigarette. 'It must be cold there.' In others, she monologues about her life. In some, she is clearly drunk, sobbing out barely intelligible apologies to her friends. In still others, she lounges on a beach, skyscrapers in the distance. Her mother, Lyubov Prigozhina, wanders into the shot.

Many of these videos were recorded in Dubai. They were very clearly extracted from Veronika's phone illicitly, likely leaked online as part of an effort by Russia's Defence Ministry to discredit Prigozhin. They showed that his family was able to enjoy life outside Russia, particularly in the UAE. They were in good company: many wealthy Russians moved their assets to Dubai as Russia became more bellicose and Europe became less welcoming. Working at the C4ADS non-profit investigative organization in 2022, my team found dozens of such properties in Dubai, from a former prime minister of a Russia-backed breakaway republic in eastern Ukraine to Duma deputies and business associates of both Chechen strongman Ramzan Kadyrov and Belarusian dictator Aleksandr Lukashenko.[19] Prigozhin's family appear to be among them.

Wagner allowed Prigozhin and his family to enjoy a lifestyle accessible to only a small number of people in Russia. While his more conventional government contracts were a source of great wealth, Wagner set him apart. By 2022, with Wagner's operations stretching from Syria to West Africa, Prigozhin's fortune rested on the Wagner Group . He would do anything to keep it.

PART THREE
BLOWBACK

10

CRY HAVOC

The place to prove you're right is on the battlefield.

Evgeniy Prigozhin, interviewed by Russian media on 24 May 2023[1]

I t is not clear when Putin made the final decision to invade Ukraine, one that blindsided most of Russia's military leadership. In the months leading up to the invasion, Russia had amassed men and equipment near the border, justified as part of exercises or to deter Ukrainian aggression. When the first troops crossed the border, it was evident that this was not going to be a repeat of 2014. Russia's aims were much greater, as it sought to seize Kyiv and remove Ukraine's leadership, installing its own leaders and turning Ukraine into a vassal state. And Ukraine was better prepared – the country had fought this enemy for eight years with Western training and security assistance. Most fundamentally, Ukraine's survival as a nation was at stake.

Russia's invasion of Ukraine on 24 February 2022 was the culmination of eight years of undeclared war. Up to then, the war was fought with limited numbers of regular Russian troops, fighting alongside separatists and irregular units, including organizations like Wagner. After the wild early days of the war in 2014, it had morphed into a lingering low-intensity conflict. The scale of violence had decreased, but there were still combat and civilian deaths in the news to remind Ukrainians that part of their country was occupied. Internally displaced Ukrainians still couldn't return home and life in the occupied territories was a bizarre theatre of statehood by the self-proclaimed Donetsk and Luhansk People's Republics. Repression was widespread, particularly for media or citizen journalists investigating corruption. Wagner's assassination campaign of wayward militant leaders running counter to Kremlin aims of a negotiated settlement in 2014 and 2015 had effectively suppressed the more troublesome pro-Russia forces in eastern Ukraine, but that didn't mean that Russian-backed separatist authorities would integrate with Ukraine. Now, they merely insisted on terms that, while less outrageous to the international community, would undermine Ukrainian sovereignty and dash any hope of EU or NATO membership.

During this time, Russia leveraged public–private partnerships not only in deploying paramilitary forces to Ukraine, but to pillage the occupied territories. While Wagner was exporting gold, diamonds and timber in Africa, other Russia-based networks were extracting wealth from eastern Ukraine. These organizations didn't traffic in force like Wagner, but their model bore other similarities. Moscow-friendly Ukrainian businessman Sergey Kurchenko ran a wide range of companies that were authorized to export coal and metals from the people's republics. Like Prigozhin, he was selected, likely by Russian security services, to have a near monopoly on this industry. Kurchenko's companies, like Gaz Alliance and Vneshtorgservis, could turn a handsome profit by extracting coal and scrap metal in the occupied territories, transporting those products into Russia and then selling them on the international market as Russian-origin goods. Kurchenko used a range of Russian and international front companies in places like Hong Kong to hide the origin of his products. Just like Wagner, this model let Kurchenko's enterprises sell on international markets, to customers in places like Germany and the United Kingdom. He sold to pariah states and Russian-sponsored breakaway territories too, providing coal to a Russian–North Korean joint venture and to companies in the unrecognized Republic of Abkhazia.

This state of affairs was grievous for Ukraine's sovereignty and development and cost Moscow relatively little. It was all the more unusual, then, that Russia decided to attempt a full military invasion. Aside from Putin's vision of Russia's historical destiny, this decision was clearly linked to Russian security services' view of the Ukrainian military as dismally unprepared to defend its borders.[2] Consequently, neither Putin nor the security services expected that they would need to rely heavily on mercenaries.

Still, the scale and ambition of the invasion demanded that Russia commit greater resources to this fight. Putin knew this, even if he believed that Ukraine would fall in three days, as his cadre of spymasters was telling him. Fortunately for him, the security services had themselves been developing their own solution to the challenge of manpower.

Feud

Since the GRU's early days in Syria, General Vladimir Alekseev, its deputy head, had been a friend to Wagner. In a document that Wagner's leadership prepared for the GRU in 2018, presenting an abridged history of the group, they explained that, in Syria, 'We carried out our activities independently and in close coordination with the GRU under the leadership of General Alekseev.' But after several years of increasingly wayward behaviour by Prigozhin, the security services didn't want to rely on Wagner alone for deniable mercenary forces.

Shoigu never liked Prigozhin. According to Ministry of Defence sources interviewed by the Dossier Centre, Shoigu had originally ruled out including Prigozhin in the 2014 efforts to amass PMCs, volunteer units and irregular forces.[3] But Prigozhin had been able to push his connections around Shoigu to secure access to valuable contracts and then built relationships with other corners of the defence establishment, including Alekseev. Syria gave Prigozhin more opportunities to build bridges in the MOD. He became familiar with respected and high-ranking officials that had risen in the

Ministry before the arrival of Shoigu, men like Sergey Surovikin and Mikhail Mizintsev.

The tenure of Shoigu's predecessor, Anatoliy Serdyukov, was characterized by dramatic reforms to the Russian military which made the careers and personal fortunes of Prigozhin, Mizintsev and Surovikin. Serdyukov instituted the privatization drive that landed Prigozhin his near monopoly on military catering contracts starting in 2011. He appointed Colonel General Mizintsev to head the organization that would become Russia's National Defence Management Centre, second to the defence minister in its responsibility for the oversight of Russia's armed forces. He also created Russia's Military Police and made Afghanistan and Chechnya veteran General Surovikin its chief.

Serdyukov saw his aggressive reorganization of the military as vital to rescue a fighting force that was then on the brink of financial collapse. He planned to institute professionalism and to clean out a bloated officer corps. These moves were unpopular in many areas of the military, particularly among the comfortable leadership who were now expected to prove their utility; if they failed to do so, they were simply made redundant and forced out.[4] By 2011, Russian law enforcement had launched investigations into corruption under Serdyukov. These were both likely well founded and almost certainly politically motivated. During these investigations, law enforcement happened to expose Serdyukov's extramarital affair. This humiliation sealed his fate. He was sacked, but considerately dispatched to a comfortable retirement at Russian arms manufacturer Rostec. His replacement was Shoigu, a skilled political operative and close friend to Putin who took a much more cautious line in his reforms. Prigozhin, Mizintsev and Surovikin saw Serdyukov's revolutionary changes in the ministry as part of their success, and Shoigu's relative conservativism and politicking as an obstacle to their careers, their personal fortunes and Russia's ability to win wars.

The seeds of mutual distrust between Shoigu and Wagner were also planted in Syria. In Palmyra, former Wagner fighters indicate that Prigozhin conflicted with Shoigu over the Ministry claiming credit for 'Wagner's victories'.[5] Their relationship was already cooling, in no small part due to the increasing number of public disclosures about Wagner that embarrassed the Ministry.[6] Some Russian media claimed that Wagner had undertaken its ill-fated assault near Khasham that had resulted in the deaths of eighty Wagner fighters on its own initiative, outside the guidelines of the Russian military leadership.[7] The subsequent decision by the Russian General Staff to tell the Americans that they had no personnel at that location, paving the way for the aerial bombardment of Wagner forces, served to create a deep rift between Prigozhin and Russia's top brass.

Prigozhin later published his own version of the events at Khasham. It is hardly a reliable account – he conflates the Kurdish SDF with ISIS, for example – but reflects the attitude of many Wagner fighters towards the event. Prigozhin claimed that not only was Wagner's advance on Khasham coordinated with the Russian military, but that they promised to cover the mercenaries with air defence and provide support from Sukhoi multirole aircraft.[8] The day after the battle, he claims,

I flew to Moscow and urgently tried to get an appointment with Shoigu to find out what had actually happened. The Minister did not receive me. I tried him 10, 11 times, but he didn't have time to talk. I finally caught him at a reception at the Kremlin. I approached him and asked: 'Can I talk to you about the situation that occurred on February 8 near Deir ez-Zor?' He calmly and arrogantly replied: 'You wanted to be a hero? You became a hero. All the heroes are now here in this hall,' – here, he waved his hand around those in expensive suits – 'But you simply lost the plot.'[9]

Prigozhin was just as troublesome in other quarters. A 2020 Russian court case documented how associates of Prigozhin and the Wagner Group had bribed an employee of a cellular network with $20 to give them access to the phone of a man named Aleksandr Vinokurov. Vinokurov was a successful businessman on the board of the largest Kentucky Fried Chicken franchisee in Russia. He was also the son-in-law of Russia's minister of foreign affairs, Sergey Lavrov. The court case names Aleksandr Maloletko as the man who allocated the money for the operation. Maloletko also appears in Wagner's personnel lists, identified as a 'tracker'. He was awarded the CAR's Cross of Military Valour by President Touadera.[10] For anyone watching, it seemed clear that Prigozhin had his men hack into the phone of Russia's chief diplomat's family member. This maybe wasn't a surprise, given that Wagner was often at odds with Russian diplomats in the CAR and that Prigozhin had an abiding suspicion of plots by state officials to sabotage him.[11]

He was also picking fights with his former allies. Aleksandr Beglov, the former deputy head of the Presidential Administration whom Prigozhin claimed years earlier had raised his plans for a catering company to then president Medvedev, was now governor of St Petersburg. In 2019 Prigozhin's media empire and spin doctors had helped Beglov to win the gubernatorial election.[12] It seems that Beglov didn't feel he owed Prigozhin and began to box his companies out of lucrative deals in the city. Prigozhin struck back, mobilizing bots and his media companies to smear Beglov for incompetence. It started as a typical feud between elites, but it was emblematic of Prigozhin's abrasive style and relentless antagonism of anyone who obstructed him.

As reported by Russian journalists at Meduza, Prigozhin took pot shots at higher-placed elites, like deputy head of the Presidential Administration Sergey Kiriyenko.[13] Prigozhin had some well-placed friends, but was making still more powerful enemies. The trouble was that he was useful and unique. Moscow had plenty of pliant businessmen and commercial networks that they could leverage for their purposes abroad, including even privately funded paramilitaries. They didn't have other private war fighters. Other PMCs could protect Russia's interests as guards or private security, but Prigozhin had a monopoly on the market for mercenaries that could take the battle to the enemy.

Breaking the Monopoly

We don't know exactly when or why a cadre of GRU officers decided that they needed to create an alternative to Wagner. Maybe they were instructed directly by Shoigu, maybe even by Putin himself. Maybe it was an internal decision, decided by men like Alekseev who realized that reliance on Prigozhin meant exposure.

Russia's military intelligence had plenty of options to work with. Much as Wagner was kick-started with pieces from other PMCs, they could choose between a myriad of security companies to use as the basis for a new private army. Of these, the most mature was Redut.

You might remember Redut from Wagner's time in Syria. There, they had defended the phosphate assets of Putin's friend Gennady Timchenko and his StroyTransGaz. In the process, they had recruited former Wagner fighters and military veterans alike. Mostly, they had performed site security rather than the grand offensives that Wagner led in places like Palmyra. They were not as large or aggressive and they had stayed out of the limelight. They were also closely tied to the GRU, located at a site abutting the base of the 45th Airborne Spetsnaz. Redut shared roots with Wagner – it traced its name back through the earlier Redut Antiterror, through the Redut Security that Evgeniy Sidorov of both Moran and Slavonic Corps had founded.

Alekseev took a more active role sometime in 2021, putting his trusted representative Anatoliy Karaziy in charge. Little is known about Karaziy but Russian investigators with the Insider found that he was a former member of the GRU *spetsnaz* and a a possible family member of Alekseev.[14] Leaked Wagner documents from 2020 indicate that he was a member of the group, further corroborated by the reporting that found he managed intelligence for the group. The revitalized Redut began recruiting aggressively and shopping for new bases in places like occupied Crimea and the military production capital, Tambov. They succeeded in bringing over numerous former Wagner fighters as well as soldiers from the 16th GRU Special Forces Brigade near Tambov.

New recruits of Redut would sign a contract with an entity called RLSPI. Radio Free Europe dug into this mysterious acronym and found the résumé of one it's former employees, which includes its other name: Military Unit 35555, a 'regional laboratory for socio-psychological research under the Ministry of Defence'.[15] This corner of the GRU had a history in Ukraine. Unit 35555 is within the GRU's 78th Intelligence Centre in Rostov in southwestern Russia, at the same location as the 175th Communications and Control Brigade, which had previously dispatched GRU officers to eastern Ukraine to coordinate militias in the Luhansk People's Republic.[16]

This unit is a key node in the GRU's coordination with Wagner as well. As far back as 2014, Wagner was receiving weapons through Unit 35555, from AKM rifles to AGS-17 automatic grenade launchers and Nona-S self-propelled mortars.[17] They would continue to supply Wagner through at least February 2022.[18] Mapping this tangle of units and their ties to Wagner and Redut, we can see part of the structure by which the GRU equipped its 'PMCs' with both men and arms. Alekseev used the same structure to establish Wagner's rival that his directorate had used to arm Wagner.

Redut swelled to include thousands of men across several detachments, with names such as 'Veterans', 'Bears', 'Hooligans', 'Wolves', 'Marines', 'Axes', 'Ilimovtsy' and 'Storm'. Redut was ahead of the curve in what would become a panoply of organizations variously called PMCs, reserve units and volunteer battalions, all aimed at recruiting and deploying men. The Insider cites a GRU source who claims that Prigozhin was outraged by the recruitment of Wagner men. He contacted Alekseev and threatened to 'deal with' Karaziy if he didn't cease recruitment of Wagner's men. Alekseev defused the tensions.[19]

By February 2022, the Ministry of Defence considered Redut ready, and just in time: Russia was preparing to invade Ukraine. Already, small groups of men were reportedly undercover in Kyiv to stage sabotage operations and even to attempt to assassinate Ukrainian president Volodymyr Zelenskyy. The men of Redut were reportedly among this number.[20] Some of their men were deployed to the Donbas to stand by for the invasion.

On the night of 23 February, the war began for the mercenaries. Days before, a team of Redut's soldiers had crossed the demarcation line on the Seversky Donets river near Stanytsia Luhanska. They crept through freezing rain past the village of Bolotnoye, observing Ukrainian positions through their night vision equipment. They received a command to withdraw on the afternoon of the 23rd. They pulled out and transmitted information on Ukrainian locations.

On the morning of the 24th, Russian rockets struck targets in cities across Ukraine. Men and equipment rolled across the border. The invasion had begun.

Crossing the Line

Prigozhin finally managed to get Alekseev to answer his phone. He had been calling him since 23 February to no avail. The next day, Alekseev answered, and the men spoke for two minutes. We don't know what they discussed, but in the weeks to come one thing would be clear – Wagner wasn't to have a role in this war, at least not yet.

Redut's soldiers entered Ukraine from multiple directions in the first days of the war, pushing towards Kyiv. They immediately met with catastrophe. One unit, crossing from Belarus, was hit by friendly fire, mortally wounding one of their men. Elsewhere, they met fierce resistance. Russian service members and Redut contractors had expected to be welcomed by Ukrainian civilians as saviours and had assumed that the Ukrainian military would be so cowed by the shock and awe of the first wave of attacks that they would surrender or flee. But Ukraine was prepared, not only with Western training and equipment, but with greater morale and more effective leadership than the Russian forces. Redut fighters described to Russian journalist Lilia Yapparova the massive losses they experienced in eastern Ukraine. This included witnessing the destruction of a Russian motor rifle brigade attempting to cross the Seversky Donets river, the same river that Redut reconnaissance teams had crossed the day prior to the invasion.[21]

Redut's losses were so great that the Ministry of Defence reportedly recalled them to their base at Kubinka. Deputy Defence Minister Yunus-bek Yevkurov commanded the Redut fighters present to sign contracts with the armed forces directly. Wagner-friendly networks circulated rumours that their performance was so poor that the FSB had detained a Redut official. As with Slavonic Corps, there were consequences for failure in the world of Russian PMCs.

Nevertheless, Redut's campaign continued. Alongside Russian armed forces, they took part in the occupation of towns throughout the country. In September 2022 soldiers of Russia's 16th Separate Spetsnaz Brigade entered the town of Borova, east of the Seversky Donets river. Redut soldiers were among them. At least two of these men had been recruited from Wagner. Ruslan Kolesnikov, aged 55, and Mikhail Ivanov, aged 46, had joined Wagner in 2018 and 2017, respectively. In Wagner, they had been known as 'Bulat' and 'Pokrov'. Kolesnikov had been a sniper in the 7th Assault Detachment and had served in Syria. He had fought in Ukraine before with other irregular units. Ivanov had joined at the height of Wagner's campaign in Syria.

On 1 September members of the 16th Spetsnaz under the command of Kolesnikov and his superior, a man named 'Amur', captured a local resident. They put a bag over his head and drove him to a nearby village. There, they had prepared a 3-metre-deep (10 ft) pit, where they left their captive without food or water. They had identified the local man as having served in the Ukrainian military and proceeded to torture him for two days to pressure him into identifying other veterans in Borova. He was eventually released, but two other locals were abducted. Kolesnikov, Ivanov and their men threatened one with amputation. The other they beat with a hammer.

The Ukrainian military retook the area less than a month later and captured Kolesnikov, Ivanov and two other soldiers. They identified Kolesnikov as the detachment commander and Ivanov as a private. All four men were tried for violating the Geneva Conventions by imprisoning and torturing civilians and with violating Ukraine's territorial integrity. At the trial, Kolesnikov, wearing glasses and a parka, explained that while he and Ivanov were Redut fighters, they were established under the 16th Spetsnaz Brigade. Ivanov apologized for his crimes against 'Slavic brothers'. They pleaded guilty and were sentenced to eleven years in prison.

The roles of the regular military and PMCs were blurred, as entities under the Redut umbrella were employed to recruit additional manpower for the front. I asked Marat Gabidullin, a former Wagner fighter who also worked for Redut in Syria, to explain how Redut and others compared with Wagner in this war. They 'can't compete on any level with Wagner,' he said matter-of-factly.

All the other [PMCs] are a way to replenish the armed force. This is a substitute for total mobilization – they attract those people who don't want to serve in the army but are ready to fight. They are needed first to cover the flanks, for actions in the rear echelons and to close gaps. Nothing more.

In the months to come, this would emerge as a key function of these other structures. After the failure to take Kyiv in the early days of the war, Putin and his inner circle were forced to come to terms with the fact that they were in for a long and grinding fight. They would have to balance their requirements for men, necessary to win the war that Putin had staked his legitimacy on, with the public backlash that would result from mass conscription. At this time, still in the first month of the war, they turned to Wagner.

Call to Arms

On 19 March Alekseev called Prigozhin. They had several conversations that day.[22] Within 24 hours, Wagner was in the war. The group's role was limited at first, while Prigozhin focused on recruitment and mobilization, but it would grow to new heights.

Russia had made progress in its initial advance, but its forces were largely stalled by the time Wagner entered the fray. Russian soldiers held suburbs near Kyiv, as well as territory through eastern Ukraine, and in Kherson in the south. Many Western analysts and journalists observed the catastrophic state of Russian operations, including images of a kilometres-long traffic jam of Russian vehicles and abandoned Russian tanks being towed away by Ukrainian tractors, and surmised that the invasion was a failure. While it was true that Russia had failed spectacularly to achieve their original aims of swiftly taking Kyiv, both sides were in for a war of attrition. Russia would leverage PMCs to help sustain its assault.

By late March, U.S. intelligence began referencing Wagner's deployment to Ukraine.[23] There was rampant speculation among international media that Wagner was withdrawing its forces from Africa to support the war.[24] Most of these claims were unfounded, or encouraged by Wagner-friendly sources that were keen to emphasize Wagner's importance for the Russian war effort. Wagner undoubtedly withdrew some men from African deployments, but to completely abandon its progress in these theatres would have been immensely costly for both Wagner and the Russian state. Part of Wagner's advantage for Russia was that it enabled Russian security structures to balance multiple priorities at once – with African projects shopped out to Wagner, resources were freed to support the invasion.

Wagner's leadership was cognizant of this, as they were cognizant of Russia's tenuous position in Ukraine. They weren't about to put all their eggs in one basket. Some Wagner commanders were directed back to Russia to prepare for deployment to Ukraine, but the bulk of forces in places like the CAR and Mali remained, while Wagner's presence in Syria, Sudan and Libya had already been substantially reduced prior to the war.[25]

Through March, there were additional rumours of Wagner's role. German intelligence indicated that Russian PMCs, possibly Wagner, played a role in the occupation of Bucha, a town north of Kyiv.[26] Over the course of this occupation, civilians were arbitrarily arrested, tortured and executed. When Bucha was retaken by Ukraine in late March, journalists entered the town and documented the aftermath with images of dead civilians in the streets and accounts of mass killings. Evidence of the Wagner Group's involvement was not conclusive, but its role in later abuses would be. What was clear was that the Russian forces were engaging in brutal tactics to suppress populations in occupied territory and exact vengeance against former Ukrainian service members and regular civilians alike.

There was other evidence of Wagner's presence. In early March, Ukrainian sources posted photographs of dog tags they found among dead Russian soldiers that included contact information and text in English, French and Arabic that read 'Please help and contact us.' A Web address listed on those dog tags linked to a defunct website. I ran it through an archive service and found the old version of the site, one page of text that reads, 'Keep this man alive and you will be awarded. If the man is dead – bring his remains back and you will be awarded [*sic*].' The languages on these tags aligned with the regions that Wagner had deployed to, from Syria to francophone Africa. If not evidence of Wagner's deployment to Ukraine, this at least suggested that men who had fought with Wagner brought mementos with them on their current deployment with the military.

Once they were deployed in earnest, Wagner were immediately used as shock troops. The most authoritative account of Wagner's early days in the field, compiled by Russian journalist Lilia Yapparova, details their early efforts in Mariupol in southern Ukraine, where sixty Wagner fighters were killed or wounded. Other sources from Redut claimed that up to half of a Wagner detachment was destroyed conducting a frontal assault without air or artillery cover. These same sources alleged that the commander of this assault was executed for poor performance and indicated that his name was 'Lotos'.[27] If they meant Anton 'Lotos' Elizarov, commander of the 7th Assault Detachment whom we met in the CAR and in Libya, they were mistaken. He was about to emerge as one of Wagner's most public leaders in their new, more overt iteration.

Popasna

By April, Wagner had a critical mass of fighters who were prepared to deploy. Since the start of the war, Wagner had been recruiting aggressively through online advertisements, social media posts and job postings to the Russian hiring site Avito. These were principally conducted under the brand name 'Zvezda' or 'Star', but the contact information matched Wagner recruitment material and Zvezda's representatives confirmed to Russian journalists that they were hiring for the 'orchestra', one of Wagner's euphemistic titles.[28] Wagner sources told Russian journalists that part of Wagner's recruitment infrastructure had been effectively seized by the state to let them piggyback on Wagner's brand for recruitment. Even with the Ministry of Defence skimming recruits, Wagner still managed to swell its ranks.

Wagner also had a clear set of tasks. The territories held by Russian forces formed a horseshoe in eastern Ukraine. Near the middle of this vice were the towns of Popasna and Lysychansk and the city of Bakhmut. These would be the key targets of Wagner's campaign.

When Prigozhin appeared in an image taken on 16 April at Pervomaisk, Ukraine, alongside nationalist Russian lawmaker Vitaliy Milonov, Wagner was already in battle nearby. It had made the first push into the town of Popasna, a road and rail junction that had been a fixture in the war even before 2022. Here, Wagner had the benefit of additional artillery support, the backing of Russian airborne forces and support from Ramzan Kadyrov's Chechen fighters.[29] Its fighters also employed tactics that they would continue to use throughout their time in Ukraine: they used drones to direct artillery fire and infantry attacks and automatic grenade launchers for indirect fire in urban combat.[30] Nonetheless, Wagner sources reported serious losses over the course of the assault.[31] The Ukrainian military posted images of dead soldiers that it stated were Wagner fighters, along with CAR francs and Libyan dinar recovered from their bodies. They claimed that these men were themselves Libyan mercenaries employed by Wagner – a claim that proved impossible to verify. But despite taking heavy losses, Wagner, with support from other Russian forces, ultimately prevailed.

Russian artillery fire softened Ukrainian positions, destroying homes and infrastructure in the process. From there, Wagner infantry units fought from house to house. In May, pro-Wagner Telegram channels published drone footage showing Wagner fighters clearing buildings. Between ruined buildings, the combatants were often mere metres away from their enemy. A small unit of Wagner soldiers

'M' designation Wagner fighter, an officer who has completed several tours with the Wagner Group. This fighter is equipped with protective gear similar to that worn by Western militaries, including a high-cut helmet that can carry night vision optics, ear protection, modern plate carrier and encrypted radio. Slung on his back is an AS Val, a compact rifle with an integrated suppressor. He carries an AK-12, a fifth-generation Kalashnikov rifle, that is fitted with a U.S.-produced aftermarket stock and optic, as well as a Russian suppressor. His armaments and equipment are distinctive among Russian forces in Ukraine, most similar in appearance to those of Russian Special Operations Forces (SSO).

ultimately forced eight Ukrainians to surrender and led them off camera at gunpoint.[32]

Their units fought under the command of experienced Wagner officers. Part of the 5th Assault Detachment had been withdrawn from Libya and was dispatched in the direction of Popasna under the command of Aleksey 'Terek' Nagin.[33] Nagin had previously fought in Syria and served as the chief of staff for Wagner in Libya. Before Wagner, he had served in Chechnya and in Georgia. He was also unique among Wagner fighters for his extracurricular activities – he was a writer on Prigozhin's propaganda movie *Sunlight* about the war in Ukraine in 2014, and later co-wrote *The Best in Hell*, which would be shot on location in Popasna. Nagin was joined by commanders who included Nikolai 'Bes' Budko, whom we met in Mozambique and the CAR in Chapter Six, when he served as commander of the 4th Assault Detachment.[34]

Alekandr 'Ratibor' Kuznetsov, commander of the 1st Assault Detachment and perhaps Wagner's most legendary commander after Utkin, was already in Ukraine. He led his troops southeast of Popasna, where they took the town of Novoaleksandrivka. Prigozhin claimed that Ratibor's men killed one hundred Ukrainian soldiers in that battle, hauled their bodies into trucks and delivered them to occupied Pervomaisk to demonstrate their success.[35]

In Ratibor's telling, he had received a call from Utkin, who told him, 'Ratibor – are you ready to defend the motherland?'[36] He was sent to Pervomaisk, where a Russian commander ordered him to assault Novoaleksandrivka. His men advanced towards the southeastern flank of Popasna. At first, they moved under cover of night. They took Ukrainian positions silently, entering their underground fortifications and killing with knives. As they continued, they met well-organized resistance. They fought across open fields, facing artillery and machine gun fire. Ratibor would dispatch small groups of his fighters to flank fortified Ukrainian positions and eliminate them to clear the way.

They advanced along dirt roads into the suburbs of Popasna, scanning the high ground. Directly beside the road, obscured by brush, a Ukrainian soldier lay hidden. As Ratibor and his men approached, the man began firing at them, killing three of Ratibor's men, including a unit commander he had known since his time in Chechnya.

The battleground became more urban. Ratibor took twelve Ukrainian soldiers prisoner. Eventually, they entered Popasna itself. Ratibor's units fought from building to building. Together with units like Terek's, they pushed the Ukrainians out of the city. By early April, Wagner fighters were posing for photographs in front of the Popasna city administration building. A few days later, Vitaliy Milonov, Prigozhin's chum and hanger-on, was photographed in the same spot alongside Wagner propagandist Maksim Shugalei.

While Wagner was taking Popasna, the Russian military was struggling elsewhere.[37] The superior experience of Wagner's men, their greater flexibility in the field and the success of tactics that they used in urban combat had set them apart. For their efforts, participants were awarded medals by the Russian state.[38] More importantly still, Prigozhin was secretly recognized with the Hero of Russia medal.[39] Russian state media even began obliquely referring to the 'military orchestra' on the front line, referencing Wagner's exploits.

Popasna was a breakthrough for Wagner. Its forces had proved their effectiveness relative to a flagging set of operations by the Russian military, reflecting positively on Prigozhin and negatively on the defence leadership with whom Putin was becoming increasingly frustrated. Prigozhin's own media companies dispatched correspondents to Popasna to interview Wagner combatants, show them in action and display their tactics. They bore the signature symbols of Wagner. They even drove in Evro Polis's own Wagner Wagon armoured vehicles seen in places like the CAR and Libya.[40] Wagner was slowly coming out of the shadows.

Prigozhin leaned on Popasna for his myth making. Months later, his Aurum media production company would release the movie co-written by Wagner commander Nagin, shot in Popasna. The movie, which on release didn't specifically name Wagner, was nonetheless another clear effort to tell a positive story of the group and tie them to a larger patriotic movement in Russia. The movie opens with a dedication: 'We have a contract. With a company. With the motherland. With our conscience. We will fulfil it to the end. Dead or alive.'

Lysychansk

From the centre of the horseshoe of Russia's offensive line, Wagner had punched through. Beyond lay a series of towns of strategic value for Russia to consolidate control of the Donbas. There was Sloviansk, close to the M03 highway between Kyiv and the major city of Kharkiv, and Kramatorsk, a major Ukrainian industrial centre. To get to these towns, Wagner would have to push through Bakhmut.

Before that, there were the last two Ukrainian footholds in the Luhansk region: Severodonetsk and Lysychansk, facing each other on opposite banks of the Seversky Donets river.[41] The two cities held around a tenth of their pre-war populations. Without running water, gas or electricity, civilians huddled in shelters. In the distance, an oil refinery burned for months after being hit by Russian shells. The Ukrainian units protecting the towns were exhausted and nearly surrounded by Russian troops and artillery.

By June, both cities were decimated by indiscriminate Russian shelling. Ground assaults were incessant. Another 10,000 civilians had fled as Russian troops, Chechen units of Ramzan Kadyrov's 'Akhmat' unit and Wagner fighters assaulted the town. Wagner continued their role as shock troops, reinforced by rotating Russian forces, including conscripts drawn from Russia's Far East, and mobilized men from Donetsk and Luhansk.[42]

By July it was over. A combination of overwhelming artillery fire and waves of soldiers, many used as cannon fodder, forced the Ukrainians out of the city. On 3 July Shoigu told Putin that they had taken the city and that all significant points in Luhansk had been captured.[43] The Ukrainians reported that they had identified at least 150 civilian casualties.[44]

Wagner fought on, taking the Vuhlehirska Power Station to the south by early August. Its forces repositioned to push further west, towards the strategic cities of Sloviansk, Kramatorsk and Bakhmut. It would be their biggest battle yet and the one that would not only decide Wagner's fortune but lead to the greatest threat to Putin's authority that he had yet faced.

Wagner's next fight would demand more men, equipment and determination than they had ever mobilized before. To claim victory, they would have to use a new and terrible weapon, one familiar throughout the history of war, but alien and repugnant, even to many Russians supportive of Wagner. They called it Project K.

11

THE MEAT GRINDER

I have never been a chef; I used to be a restaurateur and quite successful. I can't cook myself. They should have just come up with 'Putin's butcher' instead.

Evgeniy Prigozhin, interviewed by Russian media on 24 May 2023[1]

The day before Russia claimed victory in Lysychansk, Russia opposition bloggers began reporting on a new development in Wagner's story.[2] Over the summer, Russian journalists confirmed it: Wagner was recruiting from prisons.[3] It seemed entirely plausible given Russia's difficulties in mobilizing enough men to go to the front. It was, however, unusual that Prigozhin would be given licence to go to Russian penitentiaries and either force men into service or make them the offer of fighting in exchange for their freedom. Under Russian law, only the president can pardon a convict, so it wasn't clear how Wagner was given the right to bestow amnesty.

On 14 September 2022 Prigozhin reinvented himself and Wagner. I opened Telegram for what had become a daily ritual of observing new developments in the war and reading the perspectives of Russian combatants on what had happened the day before. I had grown accustomed to seeing unusually overt mercenaries, faces still covered, standing amid rubble and describing the war in Ukraine. I was surprised this time to see a man who looked unmistakably like Prigozhin himself.

He stood in a grey prison yard, surrounded by hundreds of convicts, all clad in black and wearing caps. Prigozhin, usually photographed in a suit, was wearing a martial beige jacket. There were medals pinned to his chest. He spoke loudly and clearly. 'I am a representative of a private military company.' He paced, cap in his hand. 'You've probably heard of it. It's called PMC Wagner.' Prigozhin had made winking references over the years, but he had denied in court and in public statements that he had anything to do with Wagner. Now he was going back on his denials, even as he sued international journalists for tying him to the PMC. And he didn't stop there:

> This war is hard. It can't be compared to Chechnya or anything like that, even remotely. Sixty percent of my guys are shock troops and you will be one of them. All of those who die, the bodies are taken to the place specified in your will. In six months, you go home having received a pardon.

Prigozhin was transparent regarding his expectations of the men. 'Those who get there and on the first day say, "I ended up somewhere I shouldn't have," we designate them as a deserter and then comes the execution by firing squad.'

'You have five minutes to make your decision.'

As Prigozhin walked out of the yard, the stars of the Hero of Russia and Hero of the Luhansk People's Republic were visible on his jacket.

Over the summer and into the autumn, Wagner would create an enormous penal battalion the likes of which had not been seen in Russia since Stalin deployed *strafbat* of commanders accused of indiscipline in the Second World War.[4] By some estimates, Wagner's numbers would balloon to 5,000 men, most of them convicts. From their beginnings as a handful of fighters eight years earlier, Wagner would become a true army. Up to a third of them would die in Ukraine.

Wagner called its prison recruitment drive Project K. Wagner drew primarily from violent offenders but had some reservations about those convicted for sexual crimes and would not recruit those convicted of terrorism.[5] Convict recruits were designated with an identification number beginning with the letter 'K', while recent recruits for the war were denoted by 'A' for 'Army', and legacy fighters who had been with Wagner before 2022 were marked as 'M'. 'K' soldiers received various levels of training. Some reported that they were loaded onto transport aircraft with hardly any preparation, while others received several weeks of instruction.

By most accounts, a significant number of convicts volunteered. These included those serving long sentences for which Wagner represented perhaps their only chance at freedom, but also impulsive young men drawn by amnesty and cash rewards. Tens of thousands agreed to fight.

Wagner's drive from Russian prisons was successful not only because of the limited prospects that convicts otherwise had, but because Prigozhin could speak to them in a familiar language. He had, after all, served nearly a decade in prison himself. He had clout, emphasized by his theatrical arrival by helicopter and the grudging subservience to him demonstrated by the prison guards.[6] Even organized-crime figures who were serving long prison sentences joined Wagner: Bellingcat identified that Andrey Berezhnykh, Sergey Maksimenko and Igor Kusk, three organized-crime bosses, all over the age of fifty, had joined Wagner and died in Ukraine.[7]

Prigozhin and even Utkin toured prisons throughout Russia in the summer and autumn, promising amnesty, 200,000 roubles a month and sizable payouts to convicts' families in the event of their deaths.[8] Wagner grew by orders of magnitude just as Russia was struggling to continue to staff its war effort. Putin knew that average Russian citizens would be supportive or at least acquiesce to the war as long as they didn't personally suffer. Mass mobilization would mean that Russian families would lose fathers and sons. Wagner already helped to resolve this conundrum – it was easier to hide their casualties, and besides, they were mercenaries, not conscripts. With convicts, the public would care even less.

'K' designation Wagner combatant, a convict recruited in 2022 to fight in Ukraine. Wagner convict recruits carried a variety of equipment and arms, with their quality determined based on what was available and the soldier's performance on the battlefield. This recent recruit is equipped with limited gear similar to that carried by many regular Russian units in Ukraine, including a standard-issue 6B27 helmet and chest rig. He carries a common AKS-74 automatic rifle fitted with a Russian muzzle brake. Unlike most Russian units, he is not equipped with a plate carrier and may go into combat unarmoured.

These were murderers, robbers, rapists, the worst of society. If they died in attempting to redeem themselves in service to Russia, so be it. This callousness let Wagner employ grim tactics to overwhelm Ukrainian forces in the Donetsk region.

Going Public

Prigozhin's appearance on video at a prison, later identified as a penal colony in Russia's Mari El Republic, marked an escalation in Wagner's growing publicity. For years, while Prigozhin maintained outright denial of any involvement with Wagner, his media structures would celebrate the 'instructors' that his companies sent abroad. Propagandists within these media holdings, men like Kirill Romanovsky and Oleg Blokhin, would embed with Wagner fighters and report on their exploits in Syria and Africa. Prigozhin wanted to keep his men in the public eye. It grew the Wagner brand and emphasized to common Russians and the Kremlin leadership alike the significance of his work.

Up to now, Prigozhin-friendly media had avoided referring explicitly to 'Wagner' or tying him to the organization. Beginning with Popasna, this started to change. A group of war correspondents, known in Russia as *voenkory*, were dispatched alongside Wagner fighters to film and interview them in action. Prigozhin outlets like RIA FAN shared this material, which found its largest audience on Telegram. A cottage industry of Wagner-themed channels developed. At its core were Reverse Side of the Medal, abbreviated as RSOTM, run by a Wagner veteran known only as 'Admin', and Prigozhin's Press Service. Around them were circles of accounts that would repost their material or collect submissions from fighters at the front, with names like Grey Zone or Soldier of Fortune.

This material at first gave insight into the fighters of the Wagner Group and elevated their visibility in Russia. The masked men of

Wagner looked different from most of the Russian military. They had better equipment and generally looked closer to special forces units of Russia's sso than to the other Russian units on the ground. They wore high-cut ballistic helmets and frequently wielded more modern rifles, such as the jagged, black AK-12. They were covered in patches that advertised their membership in the group. Wagner put its most experienced and best-equipped men front and centre, an advertisement to would-be recruits and Russia's elite.

Wagner was just as intentional in how it represented convicts. The hordes of Russian criminals recruited by Wagner were seldom as well outfitted and cut a much more dismal image. Wagner found ways to use them in its publicity campaigns nonetheless. Where prisoners had performed command responsibilities, they were rewarded. If they fell in combat, as they often did, Prigozhin frequently made good on his promise of a hero's burial, at least frequently enough that it could be publicized. In a series of videos released by his press service, Prigozhin and Wagner commanders presided over awards ceremonies for former convicts, recognizing them with medals like Wagner's Platinum Star. Prigozhin himself loudly proclaimed that many of them made excellent fighters.

Eventually even Russia's state-run propaganda network Russia Today would air a documentary on 'Project K', valorizing the convict recruits who fought in Ukraine to 'redeem their guilt with blood', a line directly borrowed from Stalin's July 1942 order instituting penal battalions.[9] It was a sign of just how far Prigozhin's efforts had come in bringing his activities into the light. Russian state media not only named Wagner, but showed Prigozhin speaking to his soldiers.

Russia Today's documentary would air in March 2023. By that time, things were more complicated. Wagner and Prigozhin still got a call-out, but some direct mentions of Wagner ended up on the cutting room floor. Since Prigozhin had gone public, he had taken a new tack, from celebrating Wagner to denigrating Russia's military leadership. By that point, he had achieved a much greater platform. Wagner had taken the national stage as it engaged in the fight that would ultimately determine the fate of Prigozhin's 'private army' in the city of Bakhmut.

Westwards

Over the summer, Russia's advance had slowed.[10] They captured and occupied territories in places like Kherson in the south and held an advantage over Ukraine in artillery and ammunition but were quickly encountering manpower limitations.[11] After Russian forces retreated from the strategic city of Lyman in eastern Ukraine, elite dissatisfaction with the conduct of the war came to a head.

In September, Russia instituted partial mobilization, a seemingly haphazard and unpopular process of conscripting mainly reservists to fight in Ukraine.[12] Ramzan Kadyrov and Prigozhin were both critical of the military's approach to its manpower issue, particularly the tendency to shelter officers and senior leadership. 'First of all, those who have received benefits from the Ministry of Defence throughout their lives should be mobilized,' Prigozhin said in a post on 1 October. 'As well as representatives of government and law enforcement agencies. Last but not least, mobilize those who have never held a machine gun in their hands, including those who completed a year of military service and fired three rounds.'[13]

Ramzan Kadyrov, who was also playing a key role in supplying forces to cover the shortage of soldiers, chimed in. 'The defence of this area was led by the commander of the Central Military District, Colonel General Aleksandr Lapin,' he wrote.

> The insult is not that Lapin is incompetent, [but] the fact that he is protected by the leaders at the top of the General Staff. If it were up to me, I would demote Lapin to private, deprive him of his awards and, with a machine gun in his

hands, send him to the front line to wash away his shame with blood.[14]

Despite the populist jabs Prigozhin took at the Ministry of Defence, these failures were an excellent opportunity for Wagner to highlight their relative success. Wagner pressed slowly west towards Bakhmut. They had set up shop along the way, installing forward headquarters in places such as Popasna. Military correspondents who had been reporting from the front milled about, snapping photographs and chatting with soldiers. One of them, Sergei Sreda, met Wagner fighters for a photo op on 8 August. He shook hands with Prigozhin and stood next to masked men in front of a run-down building. The images were shot about 3 kilometres (2 mi.) from where *The Best in Hell* was filmed. In one photograph, the building's street address was visible: 'Mironivska 12'. Sreda posted the images to Telegram: 'Arrived in Popasna, dropped into the headquarters of PMC Wagner. They treated me like one of their own. They told some funny stories.' Major Wagner channels like RSOTM, always eager to repost images of Wagner fighters, shared Sreda's post.

On 14 August, a rocket roared into the building at Mironivska 12. It had been fired from a U.S.-supplied HIMARS multiple rocket launcher system, a precision weapon that was dialled into the exact location of Wagner's Popasna base. Wagner fighters carted out casualties on stretchers. Ukraine likely had other sources of intelligence but the Russian media was quick to point out that Sreda had published photographs showing the location just days before. He deleted his post.

There was immediate conjecture about Prigozhin's where-abouts. Had he been killed in the blast? Had the Ukrainians waited until they had other sources that told them where he was? Within a day, Prigozhin appeared, decked out in camo, sporting a boonie hat, posing triumphantly in the rubble. He was accompanied by

Andrey Bogatov, the Wagner fighter and Hero of Russia who had lost his hand in Syria. Despite the embarrassment and apparently avoidable death of his men, Prigozhin delighted in the opportunity to reveal that he was still alive.

About 20 kilometres (12½ mi.) away, Russian forces were getting closer to Bakhmut, their most successful front that month. They were reinforced by Wagner as they advanced along Patrice Lumumba Street, which ran into the heart of the city. Aleksey 'Terek' Nagin led the men of his 5th Assault Detachment under the cover of Russian artillery. The fields surrounding Bakhmut were already pockmarked by shells. Most of the city still stood, with its Soviet-era mid-rise apartment buildings, churches and locally famous winery. Russian forces approached from the east and south.

The scale and intensity of fighting around Bakhmut steadily escalated into the autumn. Ukrainian and Russian forces exchanged artillery and mortar fire. Russia used TOS-1A 'Sunlight' multiple rocket launchers, the namesake of the first film, co-written, by Aleksey Nagin. The TOS-1A fires munitions that vaporize a fuel mixture on impact, filling the air with flammable gas. A second explosion ignites the mixture, producing a devastating pressure wave that creates a fireball. Russian artillery and thermobaric weapons pounded Bakhmut and the nearby town of Soledar, reaching Ukrainian forces even when they were sheltered in basements.

The battle took a heavy toll on Russian forces as well. A Russian motor rifle division that had previously held around 12,000 men was almost completely destroyed by the end of September.[15] Aleksey Nagin himself was killed on 20 September. In Russia, he was given a burial with honours and Prigozhin met his family to express his condolences.

Hell on Earth

Wagner was betting it all on Bakhmut. Prigozhin claimed that he himself had chosen the battle, but it was more likely that the Ministry of Defence had assigned Wagner to that axis of the conflict. It wasn't necessarily a glamorous one, but in the autumn and winter of 2022, other options for Russian forces weren't much better. Wagner's long-time associate Sergey Surovikin was by now commander of Russian forces in Ukraine. For months, he had nothing but bad news to break to Putin. In early November, he announced that Russian forces would withdraw from Kherson in the south, one of Russia's most visible early victories in the war.[16] In September, Russia had been pushed back from Kharkiv in the north. Surovikin would eventually be sacked for demanding strategic withdrawals and failing to satisfy Putin's grandiose aims.

Bakhmut lacked the strategic value of other objectives in the south and north, but it served a purpose. Ukraine had to choose to fight at Bakhmut or in deeper territory, such as the cities of Kramatorsk and Sloviansk. Russia endeavoured to use this axis to exhaust Ukrainian forces, compelling them to expend men and ammunition that might be used elsewhere. Every Ukrainian soldier fighting in Bakhmut was one more who wasn't fighting somewhere like Zaporizhzhia or Vuhledar. This logic cut both ways: it is more costly to attack a position than to defend it. Conventional wisdom holds that the attacker needs a three-to-one manpower advantage. But with Wagner and their dispensable army of convicts, Russia could employ a grim calculus. Wagner prison recruits were less valuable to Russia than Ukraine's soldiers were to Ukraine. It didn't matter if Russia suffered greater casualties in absolute terms; the relative impact on Ukraine's armed forces would be worse.

The battle in Bakhmut became one of attrition. It led many foreign observers to note an apparent return to First World War-style trench warfare. This was a fight based first on artillery and then on savage, close-quarters urban combat. Throughout the winter, Russian artillery levelled Bakhmut, making the town unrecognizable. The surrounding areas were riven with trenches and cratered by shells. The forests around the city were dead, the trees splintered. Winter settled and froze the mud. Bakhmut seemed to burn incessantly.

The Wagner Group wasn't the only Russian force fighting in Bakhmut, but it was the most numerous. Wagner employed a set of strategies that leveraged both its expendable prison troops and its more experienced and valuable fighters. We know about these tactics from the first-hand accounts of Ukrainian soldiers and commanders, expert observers and information shared by Russian Telegram channels, including documents that purport to be recovered Ukrainian assessments of Wagner tactics. They paint a picture of a methodical and costly, but effective, approach, one that relied on terrifically dangerous infantry assaults and the overwhelming use of artillery.[17]

Before an assault, Wagner field commanders collected intelligence on Ukrainian positions using commercial drones, such as the compact, Chinese-made DJI.[18] Based on their observations, commanders would assess the resources necessary to take a Ukrainian position, in terms of both men and artillery ammunition.

Wagner's artillery, placed further back in the field and dispersed, would begin to fire on the Ukrainian positions. Artillery units would use long-range towed weapons, such as colossal 152 mm howitzers, to strike the Ukrainians. As the bombardment commenced, drones remained overhead, observing the battlefield. In the rear, drone operators worked with commanders to relay corrections to artillery and fire groups. While the Russian military typically conserved ammunition, Wagner shelled with abandon, preventing Ukrainian forces from fighting back or holding forward positions to observe Russian lines.[19]

Assault groups of anywhere from half a dozen to fifty men would get ready to take their positions. These smaller units, comprising the full assault detachment, allowed Wagner to over-whelm Ukrainian positions through persistent attacks. During the day, they would approach Ukrainian positions on foot, unac-companied by vehicles, trying to maintain the element of surprise. They stayed low, but, without tanks or armoured transport, they were vulnerable. These first forays towards a position were usually carried out by convict recruits, who would try to get within the dis-tance of well-lobbed grenade of the Ukrainian position. Then their assault would begin.

With the Ukrainian units suppressed, disorientated and seeking shelter from the volleys of shells and grenades, the infantry assault group would try to take the Ukrainian position. This was a dan-gerous proposition – if the Ukrainians were prepared, the Wagner fighters attempting to enter a building or a trench made for easy targets. Thousands of Wagner convict recruits died in this fashion, killed by Ukrainian small-arms fire and even their own artillery. Mobile 'fire groups' supported the assaulting infantry from nearby, using mortars and AGS automatic grenade launchers, a favourite of Wagner that they had employed since their time in Syria.

If the assault group was rendered ineffective, a new one could quickly take their place. If they succeeded, another assault group would follow in their footsteps and consolidate control of the pos-ition. This second approach was much safer and more likely to be executed by more experienced or valuable Wagner fighters, who would then be able to fortify the new position and relay informa-tion to command staff. They would shelter and wait for subsequent orders, while evacuation units would carry out wounded men.

Often, the subsequent order was to press forward to the next position. Wagner's artillery would adjust their aim and the horrible cycle would begin again: bombardment, assault, con-solidation. Many assaults on Ukrainian positions would fail time and again, as Wagner's convict recruits would throw themselves at entrenched Ukrainian units. New groups were rapidly rotated in to replace them, the bodies of fallen men piling in the fields and streets.

As night fell, Wagner's more senior fighters would don night vision and thermal optics. These tools would allow them to continue their attack and provided an advantage over the Ukrainian forces, the majority of which were forced to fight in the dark or expose their positions with lights. The assault would continue, seeking to exhaust the Ukrainians, who had no choice but to fight off wave after wave of fighters. Pounded by artillery, mortars and grenades, emptying magazine after magazine towards the enemy, the Ukrainians were often left to retreat or face annihilation.

For those Wagner fighters unwilling to press the advance or who tried to desert, retribution was swift. Aside from widespread reports of the execution of retreating convict units, there was more appalling evidence of the killing of deserters by sledgehammer.[20] Rather than disown the recorded executions, Prigozhin endorsed them. He made the sledgehammer Wagner's calling card, gifting embossed hammers to friendly politicians, and sent a hammer smeared with fake blood to the European parliament. In another reference to 'the orchestra', he packaged the hammer in a violin case.[21]

Soledar

In this fashion, Wagner crept further forward. By November, it was focusing its attacks on the southern outskirts of the city, but it would rapidly switch the axis of its advance to keep Ukrainian units on the back foot. Wagner refocused on the town of Soledar to the north in December. Anton 'Lotos' Elizarov oversaw the assault, which he planned in coordination with platoon commanders such as 'Chief', 'Dopusk' and 'Lebed'.[22] These men gave an interview to Russian propaganda mainstay Vladimir Solovyev in February 2023, in which they described the battle. While all the Wagner fighters hid their faces, they are partially identifiable.

'Chief' was likely Viktor Shevchuk based on his call sign, appearance and experience. Shevchuk had joined the Company in 2015, and risen in the ranks to command a platoon, serving in places like the CAR and Libya. Solovyev noted that another commander, 'Lebed', held seven medals for courage more than any other Russian service member. Based on his distinguished service, he may be Andrey Lebedev, a Slavonic Corps veteran who was part of the anti-aircraft crew that downed Ukraine's Il-76 at the Luhansk airport back in 2014 and who narrowly escaped death at the hands of U.S. air strikes at the Battle of Khasham in 2018. We know he was gravely injured at Khasham and was awarded a medal for courage as a result. Some sources reported that he had died from his wounds, but leaked Wagner documentation indicates that he survived. According to Wagner's records, by 2019 Lebedev held four medals for courage and an Order of Bravery and served as a commander of a unit in the 5th Assault Detachment. In contrast to Chief and Lebed, 'Dopusk' was recruited from a prison colony but had evidently been promoted to command a unit. This mixture of Wagner's old hands and new recruits who had proved themselves was representative of the front lines of their Bakhmut assault.

According to Elizarov, his men applied flexible strategies to draw Ukrainians out of their fortified positions and expose them to ambushes. Using heavy shelling and experience in urban combat, Wagner took Soledar in January, establishing quarters for his men and their equipment in the town's deep gypsum mines.

Prigozhin announced victory at Soledar on 10 January 2023: 'A "cauldron" was formed in the middle of the city, in which urban battles are taking place. I want to emphasize again, that no units besides Wagner took part in the assault on Soledar.'[23] On 13 January he published a message saying that Russian officials 'are constantly trying to steal victory from the Wagner PMC and talk about the presence of unknown people to belittle [Wagner's] merits.'[24]

When the Russian Ministry of Defence published its announce-ment of victory at Soledar on 13 January, there was at first no mention of Wagner.[25] A few hours later, they published another statement 'clarifying' the composition of Russian forces attacking Soledar and saying that the 'direct assault on the city of Soledar ... was suc-cessfully accomplished by the courageous and selfless actions of the volunteers of the assault detachments of the Wagner PMC'.[26]

Something was brewing behind the scenes. The grievances that Wagner had so long nurtured towards the Ministry of Defence for claiming credit for their sacrifice, and the mutual distrust that ministry leadership held for Wagner, were spilling into public view.

Shell Hunger

By February, the Battle of Bakhmut had been raging for half a year. The toll on both sides was enormous. Wagner continued to make progress, but at a glacial pace – where they succeeded in taking territory, they were seizing metres a day, fighting from building to building. They were receiving some support from the 106th Airborne, but even more vitally, Wagner continued to receive ammunition. The scheme for this transfer continued to use the GRU's unit 35555, the same one that had supplied Wagner when it was first in Ukraine and that been used to create a structure for recruits to contract with the rival PMC Redut.[27] But Prigozhin felt that it wasn't enough. On top of that, Wagner was being cut out of its other key advantage – prison recruitment.

On 9 February Prigozhin announced through his press service, a Telegram channel that was quickly becoming his key mouthpiece, that Wagner had stopped all recruitment from prisons.[28] His mes-sage was uncharacteristically terse and restrained. He followed this statement with a flurry of complaints directed at 'bureau-cracy' in Moscow that he blamed for slowing Wagner's advance. 'Bakhmut would have been taken before the New Year, if not for our monstrous military bureaucracy,' he said in a 16 February interview with Russian media.[29]

He spoke in front of the charred tail of an Su-24M tactical bomber. It had belonged to an aircraft flown by Aleksandr Antonov and Vladimir Nikishin, a commander and navigator, respectively, flying for the Wagner Group. They had been shot down near Bakhmut while providing air support for ground troops. Wagner mythology claimed that, after being hit by a missile, they had piloted their doomed aircraft into a column of Ukrainian vehicles. The remains of the bomber were a symbol of Wagner's sacrifice, which Prigozhin used to emphasize the story he told about betrayal by Russia's top brass through artificial 'shell hunger' – the denial of critical ammunition. This dramatic device – parading Wagner's losses to emphasize their valour in contrast with the Russian military's sclerotic and corrupt leadership – would become a trope in Prigozhin's emerging information campaign.

Prigozhin was shuttling back and forth from the front lines at Bakhmut to the familiar environs of St Petersburg. He wasn't commanding at the front lines; he was fighting a narrative war. On 21 February he published an audio statement that the Ministry of Defence was guilty of 'direct obstruction' to prevent Wagner from receiving ammunition. He equated this with 'high treason' and pinned the blame for the death of Wagner fighters on the military leadership.[30] His statements were accompanied by videos that appeared across Russian social media in which masked Wagner fighters would demand relief from the Ministry of Defence: 'Help us and provide the ammunition.'[31] When asked about these videos, Prigozhin used the opportunity to highlight the assistance Wagner was receiving from outside the Ministry of Defence. He indicated that one of Kadyrov's commanders, Apti Alaudinov, had helped to arrange for the transfer of mines and tank shells. He rewarded Alaudinov with Wagner's new symbol of friendship, an engraved sledgehammer.[32]

Some of Prigozhin's complaints were likely well founded. Wagner was cut out of the prison recruitment game as the Ministry of Defence sought to shoulder in, though by that time it was much slimmer pickings in the prison colonies.[33] Most able men who were willing to volunteer had already joined Wagner, leaving only either those who wouldn't go unless coerced, or those whom Wagner had rejected for reasons of mental or physical fitness. The shell hunger claims may have reflected an element of reality, but the real story was more nuanced than the version Prigozhin pushed.

Other major figures in the patriotic infospace chimed in. Prigozhin was not alone in both championing the invasion and criticizing the Ministry of Defence. Major paramilitary figures who had played a key role in Russia's war in Ukraine since 2014 – people like Igor 'Strelkov' Girkin and Aleksandr Khodakovsky of the 'Vostok' Battalion – were supportive of Russia's war but felt the conduct of the invasion was disastrous. Girkin was the most visible of these figures. A former FSB officer who had organized paramilitary forces in the early days of the war and had coordinated separatist actions with Russia's security services, Girkin had become a critic of even Putin himself. He felt that the Russian president simply had not gone far enough.

Such men were not fond of Prigozhin, however. Khodakovsky described Wagner's 'shell hunger' as a consequence of the group simply receiving the same amount of ammunition as everyone else after months of enjoying preferential treatment: 'We envied Wagner in a good way when they had their own front-line aviation assets, two iskanders and one kalibr [missiles] per day, and when they applied for 2.5 thousand rounds [of ammunition] for training . . . the results do not just have to do with numbers.'[34]

This change in treatment was quite likely the result of a shake-up at the top of Russia's military leadership. In January, after failing to conduct the war on terms aggressive enough to satisfy Putin, Surovikin was sacked from his role as head of Russian forces in Ukraine and replaced with chief of the General Staff Valeriy Gerasimov. Among Gerasimov's key dilemmas was the diversity of Russian forces in Ukraine and their lack of coordination.[35] Moscow had relied on paramilitaries, Wagner and forces like Kadyrov's Akhmat to pad out their numbers, but these different groups didn't fall under a unified command. As a result, Russia's invasion effort was suffering. Fixing this problem meant bringing Wagner to heel. It didn't help Prigozhin's case that Gerasimov and Shoigu were united in their distrust of him.[36]

While both Shoigu and Gerasimov began their efforts to curb Wagner's wayward behaviour and subordinate them to Ministry control, Prigozhin read the writing on the wall. Even a modest reduction in ammunition taken together with the end of prison recruitment likely heralded more severe measures in the future. He would first try to get Putin's direct support. Failing that, he was going to use his platform to make as much noise as possible until he simply couldn't be ignored.

On 22 February Prigozhin made his first major escalation. He called on the Russian public to lobby the government to supply Wagner. Then he reposted two photographs originally uploaded by 'Vladlen Tatarskiy', a military correspondent supportive of Wagner. The first image showed an order sheet for ammunition, the second showed rows of corpses arrayed on a snowy field. These were the bodies of fallen Wagner fighters.[37] The message was clear: these men are dead because we are being denied ammunition. Their blood is on the hands of the military's top commanders.

Talking about Russian losses in these terms, let alone exposing the bloody reality publicly, was taboo. Prigozhin had crossed a line. International media reported that he was shortly thereafter summoned to a meeting with Putin and Shoigu.[38] We don't know what the three men discussed at this meeting, but it appears that Putin pressured them to resolve the issue between themselves. Putin had generally stayed out of the matter though Prigozhin's public statements appeared to be, at least in part, an appeal for him to intercede on Wagner's behalf.

Either at this meeting or soon afterwards, an agreement was made. Within hours of posting the images of dead fighters, Prigozhin claimed that the shortage of ammunition had been resolved.

Today at 6 AM, they reported that the shipment of ammunition had begun. On paper for now, but as we were told, the main papers have already been signed. I would like to thank all those who helped us make this happen. You saved hundreds, maybe thousands of lives of guys who defend their homeland, gave them the opportunity to live on.[39]

The truce was short-lived and Prigozhin was back on the offensive by 5 March. He claimed that a group of mobilized men who had expressed their preference to join Wagner had been blocked by military police and dispersed among different units. He also complained that the ammunition had still not materialized. 'We're still figuring out what the reasons are – ordinary bureaucracy or betrayal.'[40]

Prigozhin knew that time was ticking. He was being cut out. On 9 March he published an audio statement claiming that he had no longer had access through official government phone lines and that he was denied access to 'agencies responsible for making decisions'. 'Now I can only ask through the media . . . I will most likely be doing just that.'[41]

War Tourists

Increasingly, Prigozhin began appearing in video shot in the territories of Bakhmut held by Wagner. By now, he had traded his suit and tie for camo and a plate carrier. He carried a compact AKS-74U rifle and wore body armour like his commanders. He spoke at length on the progress of the fight, standing alongside Elizarov and Vladimir 'Mekhan' Titov, another assault detachment commander who had served with Slavonic Corps before joining Wagner. Titov attempted to hide his identity but had retained his call sign documented in Wagner leaks. He painted the Egyptian ankh symbol on his rifle and equipment, a habit he had maintained since 2014.[42] Titov had taken over the detachment originally commanded by Nagin before the latter was killed in September.

Prigozhin was doing two things at the front: he was portraying himself more overtly as a military figure, one with the guts to go to the front unlike top Russian commanders. He was also elevating the assault detachment commanders as public figures in their own right. Elizarov had already appeared alongside Prigozhin and provided comments to media on a number of occasions, but now he was joined by others, such as Boris 'Zombie' Nizhevenok, Aleksandr 'Brodyaga' Bogatov and Mekhan. In months to come, they would be used to broadcast Prigozhin's narrative about Wagner's effectiveness and the betrayal by the Ministry of Defence. Even the reclusive Ratibor would have his day in the sun.

The recorded forays Prigozhin made into Bakhmut became increasingly brazen. He was still always kept well beyond Wagner's lines, but these stunts elevated his stature within the community of 'super-patriots' online, in the military and security services and in the controlled field of Russian politics.

This circle of patriotic agitators was grabbing headlines in Russia in ways that they didn't intend. The military correspondents or *voenkory* that had followed Wagner into Popasna and now into Bakhmut were fulfilling a unique role in the information space during the war. They posted unsanitized dispatches from the front to Telegram and social media sites such as VKontakte, which contained perspectives that Russians weren't seeing in state media. Most of this was worded cautiously and targeted 'bureaucracy', striking broadly appealing anti-elite chords. These figures weren't reaching audiences on the scale of Russian state media, but particularly for young or politically engaged Russians, they were a window into the war that wasn't available elsewhere.

One of them was 'Vladlen Tatarskiy'. Tatarskiy's real name was Maksim Fomin, a convicted bank robber who had served first as a combatant within paramilitary units in Ukraine before then transitioning to become a propagandist who crowdfunded volunteer units, supplied them with drones and, most of all, celebrated the exploits of Wagner. A portly man with a round face and short beard, Fomin was a friend to many vocal Wagner veterans and one of the key figures in Prigozhin's home front effort.

This domestic information campaign consisted not only of online propaganda, but of regular 'patriotic meetings' such as a series called 'Cyber Front Z'. These groups would gather in cafés and in the newly branded 'PMC Wagner Centre', an unoccupied, modern-looking high-rise office building in St Petersburg. Prigozhin had bought the property, to the consternation of his now-enemy Governor Beglov, and smacked a giant sign that read PMC WAGNER on the side. The building was still mostly empty, primarily being used to host groups such as Cyber Front Z or patriotic youth groups. It didn't seem as though there was much of a plan for the 'Wagner Group Centre', but it nonetheless grabbed Western headlines and gave Wagner a symbol of its seriousness at home. Prigozhin's spin doctors and their friends used the space for various events, including those with speakers such as Maria Butina, the Russian activist that the USA convicted of acting as an unregistered foreign agent, or Wagner-themed video game tournaments. These were well attended by the usual set of militant wannabes and nationalists.

This cast of characters also held events at Prigozhin's restaurant, Street Food Bar No. 1, located not far from the main offices of his corporate operations on Vasilyevsky Island in St Petersburg.

On 2 April Fomin was appearing at an event in the café when one of the attendees, an auburn-haired young woman, expressed her gratitude for his work and gave him a gift. It was a cheap bust in his likeness. He thanked her, laughed that the statue looked skinnier than he was, and continued his conversation with the audience. Several minutes later, an explosion ripped through the café. Fomin was killed instantly, while 24 others were hospitalized.

The woman who had given Fomin the bust, which was found to have contained a bomb, was arrested. The story immediately became murky. Ukrainian authorities blamed the attack on Russian elite infighting. Russian statements accused Ukrainian agents of planning the bombing. Pro-Wagner circles celebrated Fomin as a martyr.

Prigozhin topped all demonstrations of support for Fomin the next day. In ghostly green night vision, Prigozhin could be seen journeying into the centre of Bakhmut alongside Wagner fighters. Wagner had pressed into the interior of the city, as documented in near-daily updates from Prigozhin. He clambered over a pile of rubble that had once been the city administration building and planted two flags: a Russian flag scribbled with a dedication to Fomin and a black Wagner banner. He proclaimed that Bakhmut, which he called by the city's old Soviet name, Artemovsk, was now 'Russian in a legal sense'.

It was clear to even the most ardent nationalists watching that this didn't constitute a meaningful victory at Bakhmut, but it made for a powerful visual for the benefit of Russian audiences. It also allowed him to piggyback on the national news of Fomin's assassination. It was notable, after all, that whoever had planned Fomin's death had staged it within a stone's throw of Concord companies' corporate offices. Whoever killed Fomin had set off a bomb on Prigozhin's doorstep.

Competition

In the spring of 2023, other players began entering the PMC game in Ukraine. They included some familiar names such as the revamped version of Redut that had arrived before Wagner. There were also new players, a series of structures connected to both Redut and Russian energy giant Gazprom with unassuming, oil-themed names, like Potok ('Stream'), Fakel ('Torch') and Plamya ('Flame'). Disentangling these entities became challenging as Redut alone maintained a variety of units with names such as 'Patriot' and 'Wolves'. More confusing still, these 'PMCs' were hardly PMCs at all, by virtue of not only the heavy-handed involvement of the GRU, but their overlap with other reserve and 'volunteer' structures that the state encouraged politicians and businessmen to form to get more men to the front.

This marked what could be deemed the fourth revolution of PMCs in Russia: the first being the advent of private security in the aftermath of the Soviet Union's collapse, the second being the explosion of the market during the global War on Terror and the third being the more combat-oriented operations of Slavonic Corps and the Wagner Group. Until now, no other Russian PMC was engaged in direct combat operations as Slavonic Corps and Wagner were. Now, Russian security elites, starting with GRU Deputy Chief Alekseev's efforts to develop Redut, were looking to diversify the field.

On 4 February 2023 Russian prime minister Mikhail Mishustin signed an order allowing Russian energy conglomerate Gazprom Neft to create a 'private security organization'.[43] Experts disagreed about whether this constituted an effort by one of Russia's largest companies to create a PMC to rival Wagner. I fell into the camp of sceptics. Gazprom had maintained a relatively toothy private security force historically, and Russian critical infrastructure was now under threat of Ukrainian drone strikes and sabotage deep within their territory. Russian lawmakers were floating the idea of domestic companies buying their own air defence systems to defend against UAV strikes.[44] Couldn't this just be an effort by Russia to allow its strategic industries to defend themselves?

On 29 April the Education Department of the Russian city of Prokhladny, located in southwest Russia's Kabardino-Balkarian Republic, posted a memorial for a local citizen killed in Ukraine. Fifty-three-year-old Erast Yakovenko had died as 'a true defender of the motherland'. He had 'fulfilled his duty in the Northern Military District as part of the Potok (Gazprom) Detachment'. An investigation by the BBC found that Yakovenko had military experience with the Soviet military in Poland, had served in Chechnya and had joined the Terek Cossack Army. More recently, he had been a senior security guard in Gazprom's Southern Interregional Security Directorate.[45]

A few days earlier, Russian *voenkory* posted a video of masked fighters from Potok in Ukraine. They carried black rifles and wore mismatched military uniforms. One of them read a prepared statement, addressed to Putin. They claimed that they were Gazprom security officers, recruited by their management, but that they had not been adequately equipped. The fighter addressing the camera said that they had been promised contracts with the Ministry of Defence but were dispatched to Ukraine under the control of PMC Redut. They said that they were near Bakhmut, taking over positions on the flanks from Wagner and that Wagner fighters had threatened to kill them if they retreated.[46]

The rumours around the 'Gazprom PMC' were taking shape. According to an investigation by the *Financial Times*, recruitment had begun in August 2022, with Gazprom units of 'Fakel' being trained near Tambov at the Tregulyai training grounds, where Redut soldiers were also trained. It was near the base of the 16th Spetsnaz that Redut recruited from.[47] Gazprom units of 'Fakel' were deployed to Soledar as early as October.[48] They were promised competitive pay and to return to their jobs after their brief contracts were concluded. Their relatives noted in private correspondence that many had died.

Redut appeared to have a role in the 'Gazprom' PMCs and to be creating new units of its own. Their 'Veterans' detachment, which used a symbol featuring Putin's portrait, trained at the same grounds in Tambov as Gazprom units.[49] Their units signed contracts with the Ministry of Defence and drew funding from wealthy Russians and nationalist organizations such as the imperialist Pravaya Rossiya.[50] Russian conscripts claimed that some of them had been transferred to Rostov and abruptly handed over the 'Wolves' detachment, where they were pressed into signing contracts.[51] These claims implied that the 'PMCs' were not only assisting with recruitment, but helping an overburdened Ministry of Defence to train, arm and field conscripts that they otherwise didn't have the bandwidth to handle.

Prigozhin named Redut and Gazprom's units such as Potok in a 21 April monologue in which he drove near the front lines in an SUV, past bombed-out factories and barren fields. He was clearly irked by the rise of what he called 'micro-PMCs':

> Everyone thinks that like Wagner they can save the motherland. In order to somehow dilute PMC Wagner, to make it so that it's not one great force that can play such a role in internal politics – and everyone talks about how 'when there is a fight for power, everyone needs a private army', – those people who have money, they think it's cool to create a PMC.[52]

He visited units of Potok fighters, most of whom appeared to be filthy and dishevelled, and expounded on their lack of equipment and training.

> You can't just construct a building, buy a professor's hat and create Harvard University. For this you need years and

specialists. In just the same way, Wagner is a private army of the new generation, a private army with an ideology. You can't just make a PMC, recruit common people and make such an effective structure.

He had a point. Gazprom's structures and Redut were clearly not aiming even truly to compete with Wagner in any field besides recruitment. Marat Gabidullin had served with both Wagner and Redut in Syria. I asked him about the difference between Wagner and the other PMCs. He had little faith in their effectiveness:

The organizational staff structure of [other PMCs] is similar to a battalion tactical group [of the Russian military], but without the amount of equipment and firepower. There are not particularly many of them because they are most often a temporary formation, which eventually dissolves.

This was consistent with the roles that Redut and Gazprom's units were taking on, including around Bakhmut. In this, they blended with other semi-formal structures dedicated primarily to getting men to the front, even if they were poorly equipped. This included reserve units called 'BARS', and 'volunteer' units with names such as the Sudoplatov Battalion. Rather than being true PMCs, Redut and Gazprom's structures fit into this amalgam of entities supported by both state and private funding that sought to reinforce Russia's regular forces.

His Majesty's Convoy

Not all PMCs fit into this mould, however. Notably absent from most of Prigozhin's tirade against the 'micro-PMCs' was the one most clearly connected with Wagner: the Crimea-based PMC Convoy. Their commanders include Konstantin 'Mazay' Pikalov, who had worked with Wagner in Madagascar and the CAR, and Vasiliy 'Yaschik' Yashchikov, who claims to be descended from a member of His Majesty's Convoy, a Tsarist-era praetorian guard that is the PMC's namesake. The Russia-appointed head of occupied Crimea, Sergey Aksyenov, appears to be its primary patron, but most of its money flows from the Russian government and structures owned by Putin's friend, the billionaire Arkady Rotenberg.[53]

Unlike Redut and Gazprom's units, Convoy seems less concerned with the numbers of men it can field. As Wagner did in the early days, it refers to its units as reconnaissance and assault brigades, or RShRs. These units mainly conduct small, targeted operations in southern Ukraine, documented in drone footage that they publish online. In this material, we see commercial drones dropping bombs on Ukrainian roadblocks, or destroying buildings where they claim Ukrainian sabotage units have taken refuge. Most of their photographs and videos focus on the training of their men. In these videos, they present a more professionalized image than do the other newer PMCs. Their fighters could easily be mistaken for Wagner combatants based on their body armour and weaponry – the same helmets, plate carriers and customized rifles. Their sniper units wield Russian Lobaev Arms rifles with U.S.-manufactured Nightforce Optics scopes, and they use the same types of Chinese commercial drones that a variety of Russian forces employ for reconnaissance and to drop munitions on enemy positions. They are distinguishable by their patches, the yellow cartoon head of a fanged dog, but their fighters sometimes sport Wagner patches as well, more a sign of the ubiquity of the Wagner brand and the conflation of 'Wagner' and broader Russian PMCs than a representation of any formal affiliation.[54]

Convoy had existed in one form or another since 2009 under Pikalov, who appears as a director on security companies registered as early as 2004. Its earliest iteration was a blend of security company and imperial nostalgia. Pikalov co-founded the original

Cossack organization with Cossack activists and historians and Yashchikov, then a patriotic blogger. They enlisted the support of Prince Dmitriy Romanov, the second cousin of Tsar Nicholas II, then living in Denmark.[55] Romanov wrote to the authorities in St Petersburg endorsing the formation of the organization, which was officially recognized in 2009. The Cossack organization Convoy was the sole founder of Military Security Company Convoy LLC, which Pikalov created to undertake activities to defend 'the interests of Russia in difficult conditions'.[56]

Aside from Pikalov's activities with Wagner, Convoy itself could scarcely be called a PMC before 2022. The Cossack organization and its associated security company mainly provided security for church events and patriotic classes for children, and squabbled with other Cossack organizations over legitimacy and official recognition in St Petersburg.[57] Pikalov was a security guard and Cossack aficionado, not a soldier or spy, but that didn't stop him from having broader ambitions in the military and security market. He flew near the Ukrainian border with members of Wagner and Moran Security leaders such as Vadim Gusev in 2014 and 2017.[58] Then he set his sights on Africa. His efforts there didn't amount to much. Convoy proposed to create a 'smart-city' project in Burkina Faso, essentially an Orwellian network of surveillance and law enforcement coordination, but this appears to have resulted in little more than a PowerPoint presentation. Pikalov also attempted to broker the sale of Russian rifles to Madagascar, but this also fell through. His most significant private military activities before 2022 were in piggybacking on Wagner's success in Africa.

When Russia began its invasion of Ukraine, he had another opportunity. Through his contacts, possibly a friend who had served in the GRU before becoming an official in the northern Russian region of Karelia, Convoy established itself anew. It would now be based in Crimea, next to the base of Russia's 126th Separate Guards Coastal Defence Brigade, which took part in battles near

Kherson. It would operate through the 165th Training Centre, a defunct Soviet-era training base that hosted soldiers from Soviet allies such as Mozambique's FRELIMO and Angola's MPLA.

By autumn 2022, money started to pour in. Convoy received 440 million roubles, or around $4.5 million, in just a month and a half.[59] That money came from the Russian state bank VTB, structures owned by Putin's childhood friend Arkady Rotenberg and mysterious Russian coal companies. Convoy used this money to buy arms and equipment, expand its base and swell its ranks to somewhere around three hundred to four hundred men – a much smaller number than that of Redut's or Gazprom's units, but easier to rigorously train and outfit. They undertook combat operations around Kherson, and began a propaganda drive, giving interviews to state television and posting advertisements on Russian social networks.

Convoy benefited handsomely from state and private funds, but it is difficult to assess whether it is truly more effective than other PMCs such as Redut or those under Gazprom. As other PMCs and volunteer and reserve units do, Convoy sits in a grey territory between the military and informal structures. Russian journalists discovered that Convoy is legally a BARS reserve unit and that its fighters sign a contract with both Convoy and the Ministry of Defence when they enter.[60] But rather than try to maintain access to resources by simply getting bodies to the front as Redut does, Convoy seems to have chosen a more specific niche, conducting constrained operations with the use of smaller numbers of men.

Convoy was still in no position to rival Wagner. Prigozhin's 'private army' stood alone as an unofficial structure undertaking major offensive operations. Convoy and the other semi-formal structures that bore the 'PMC' label watched with interest as Wagner struggled to take Bakhmut, to wring resources out of the Ministry of Defence and to justify to Russia's leadership that they were vital to the war effort. Pikalov and his compatriots knew that if

Wagner succeeded, it could convince Putin of the necessity of units of this type. On the other hand, if Wagner failed, it might mean new business opportunities for other organizations. These other PMCs waited in the wings, not wanting to stake their legitimacy on a single, grand campaign like Wagner, satisfied that there would be place for them in Russia's composite of formal and informal forces, no matter the outcome.

Ultimatum

While other players entered the war and Prigozhin railed against the Ministry of Defence, the Battle of Bakhmut dragged on. It was May, and the siege was now in its ninth month. All eyes were on the city, which had risen to outsize symbolic significance in the eyes of Ukrainian, Russian and international observers. Wagner was gradually taking the city itself and Ukrainian forces now only held a small area on Bakhmut's western edge.

Prigozhin was considering what would happen after Bakhmut. It was widely accepted that Ukraine was planning a spring counteroffensive to take advantage of Russia's difficulties in advancing over the winter. Wagner was an assault force, and the prospect of defending Bakhmut against a coming Ukrainian counteroffensive was singularly unappealing. At the same time, their numbers were too exhausted to push beyond Bakhmut towards the next series of Ukrainian cities. Prigozhin and Wagner's Council of Commanders, comprising Utkin and the most accomplished assault detachment commanders, both realized that there would be little glory in reversing roles to hang on to the city with their diminished forces. They prepared their narrative both to cast Bakhmut as a victory belonging to Wagner and to pave the way for their speedy exit.

During this period, Prigozhin posted almost daily updates on the advance of Wagner forces and their losses. Dozens of metres were taken at the cost of dozens of men each day. The United States estimated that Russia had suffered 100,000 casualties with 20,000 killed in the previous five months alone, mainly in Bakhmut. Prigozhin himself attested to the fact that more than 20,000 Wagner fighters were killed at Bakhmut.[61] He claimed that half of these were convict recruits, though their proportion in losses is almost certainly higher. Ukrainian losses had also been significant, though difficult to reliably estimate. Prigozhin emphasized the scale of Russian deaths, which he continued to blame on poor supply of ammunition. He referred to Bakhmut as 'Operation Meatgrinder', casting Wagner's efforts as a success in tying down and exhausting Ukrainian forces.

Wagner needed a victory, and needed it fast. It selected 9 May, Russia's holiday celebrating victory in the Second World War, as the target.[62] The date was significant symbolically, and if Wagner could pull it off, it would have enough forces left to pull out and reconstitute back in Russia. But success by 9 May wasn't a foregone conclusion. Ukraine was staging pinprick attacks in and around Bakhmut to challenge Wagner's advance, leading Prigozhin to claim that the counteroffensive was already beginning.[63] He was anxiously lobbying either for the support Wagner needed to secure their definition of victory, or, in the worst case, to be able to blame their failure on betrayal by the Ministry of Defence. The shock value of showing dead Russian soldiers had won him attention before, so he tried it again. This time, he was going to push the envelope as far as he could.

'Shoigu, Gerasimov, where is the fucking ammunition?' He snarled into the camera. Behind him were rows of the mangled bodies of Wagner soldiers. He gestured to the dead men. 'If you had given us the required amount of ammunition, their number would be five times less. They came here as volunteers and are dying for you to live in your redwood offices. Keep that in mind.'[64]

Less than twelve hours later, on 5 May, his press service posted a video in which he stood before a horde of masked Wagner fighters.

He listed Wagner's successes in the war. He stated that Wagner would withdraw on 10 May since they had been completely cut off from ammunition since 1 May.[65] In his telling, Prigozhin was refusing to let his men continue to die at the hands of Russia's military leadership, who out of corruption and jealousy had snatched defeat from the jaws of victory. The next day, he posted an official request to Chechen leader Ramzan Kadyrov asking to transfer Wagner's positions to Chechnya's Akhmat units. This was more than a shot across the bow. It was not only an attack on the Ministry of Defence, but a threat to further undermine the military's control of the war by empowering Kadyrov.

Once again, this risky tactic appeared to work. Despite all conjecture by Western observers that Prigozhin had gone too far, he reported on 7 May that he had received guarantees of ammunition. He appeared to believe the promises this time because Wagner's old ally in the ministry, Surovikin, was being placed in charge of coordination with the Defence Ministry.[66] On top of that, Colonel General Mizintsev, who had been head of the National Defence Management Centre and Russia's deputy minister of defence for logistics until he was fired in late April, came over to Wagner as its 'deputy commander', ostensibly under Utkin.[67] The pieces were in place for a more believable detente between the ministry and Wagner.

Few were surprised when this arrangement fell apart as well. Russia's military leadership knew that they could not allow threats of desertion to go unpunished, not when they were pushing for unity of command. In a 27-minute video released on 9 May, Prigozhin visited Wagner units manning artillery, Grad rocket launcher systems and Pantsir air defence systems. He said that the ministry had informed him that his men would be charged with treason if they tried to withdraw. 'They simply and brazenly deceived us,' he said. He also accused the Russian military of deserting its positions around Bakhmut. The whole video soured what was supposed to be a day in celebration of Russian victory. In a short aside, Prigozhin wondered, 'The happy grandfather thinks he is fine, but what if it turns out he is a complete arsehole?' 'Grandfather' is a well-known nickname for Putin, leading Russian and international press to speculate whether Prigozhin finally intended to go after the boss. He demurred, saying he meant Ministry leadership.

Wagner's ultimatum had failed. The Ministry had called Prigozhin's bluff and so Wagner fighters had little choice but to battle on at Bakhmut. Prigozhin continued his public counts of remaining territory, mingled with snipes at the Ministry. He no longer listed Wagner's losses.

On 14 May, 1.69 square kilometres (⅔ sq. mi.) remained.

On 15 May, 1.59 square kilometres (⅗ sq.mi.) remained.

On 16 May, Prigozhin claimed that they cleared one of the last blocks of apartment buildings still held by the Ukrainians; 1.46 square kilometres (½ sq. mi.) remained.

On 17 May, 1.28 square kilometres (⅖ sq.mi.) remained.

On 18 May, Prigozhin reported that Ministry of Defence troops had retreated, exposing Wagner's flanks. Nevertheless, they advanced. 'Let's finish this business.'

On 19 May, Prigozhin reported that only 0.5 square kilometres (⅕ sq.mi.) remained. Heavy fighting continued. 'We are close to fulfilling our mission.'

'Victory'

Ratibor roared. In one hand he held a Russian flag scrawled with the words '1st Assault Detachment', in the other a Wagner flag. From atop a ruined building on the western edge of Bakhmut he bellowed, 'For the PMC! Victory!' Two Wagner fighters planted the flags on top of the building, shouting, 'Bakhmut is ours!'

Prigozhin recorded a statement announcing the successful conclusion of 'Operation Meatgrinder' in Bakhmut. 'For 224 days, these guys assaulted this city.' He thanked the fallen Wagner soldiers, the Russian people, Surovikin, Mizintsev and, of course, Putin. He slammed Gerasimov and Shoigu. 'Sometime in history, they will answer for their actions, for their crimes. We have prepared a list of those that helped us and those that actively opposed us, practically assisting the enemy.' Prigozhin said that on 25 May Wagner would withdraw from Bakhmut to their camps in Russia, to reconstitute and rest and be prepared to answer the country's call again if they needed them. They would hand over their positions to the army.

Prigozhin addressed Zelenskyy. 'Your guys fought bravely; they fought well. If you continue this path, you can become the second-greatest army in the world, after the strongest army in the world, PMC Wagner.'

On 21 May Prigozhin and Troshev sent a letter to Shoigu sarcastically wishing him a happy birthday. They sent him a book on Wagner as a gift.[68] The same day, Putin delivered a statement that congratulated Wagner and the Ministry of Defence for taking Bakhmut.[69]

Wagner began its withdrawal to its rear bases in Ukraine. Against all odds, its forces had prevailed. It had suffered tens of thousands of losses, but the core forces survived. Wagner had been recognized by Putin himself for all its sacrifice. It had won a battle of more symbolic than strategic significance, but it was a loss for Ukraine – a tragedy both in lives lost and as one of the only areas where Ukrainian forces had been beaten back in recent months.

Prigozhin knew that Wagner's struggle didn't end with Bakhmut. He had identified that the more serious threat to himself and the Company was inside Russia. Prigozhin had succeeded in making very powerful enemies and was finding that, even after he delivered a victory, Putin wasn't willing to intercede on his behalf. Away from the battlefield, Wagner would still have to justify its existence. Bakhmut alone would not be enough to guarantee Wagner or Prigozhin's survival and influence.

The Long Road Home

As Wagner withdrew, Prigozhin continued to drive his narrative besmirching the Ministry of Defence. He drummed up Wagner's civil defence efforts, training civilians from the Kursk and Belgorod regions near the border to resist Ukrainian incursions into Russian territory. Given a series of recent embarrassing successes by Ukrainian-aligned armed groups in infiltrating Russian territory and Ukrainian drone strikes on targets that included the Kremlin itself, there was ample opportunity to make Russia's military leadership look bad. But these efforts to expand to Wagner's territorial defence role were rebuffed by the Russian leadership.[70]

The withdrawal of Wagner from Ukraine wouldn't be easy for either Wagner or the Defence Ministry. As early as 4 June, Prigozhin claimed that their routes of retreat had been mined by the military. He accused a drunk commander of a Russian motor rifle brigade of ordering his troops to fire on Wagner soldiers earlier in May. It was impossible to verify either claim – was Prigozhin spoiling for a fight, or was the military really looking to kill Wagner soldiers as they were on their way out of Ukraine?

Regardless of whether these events were fabricated or exaggerated, Wagner opted to escalate. Its forces captured Lieutenant Colonel Roman Venevitin, the commander of the unit that Prigozhin claimed fired on his troops. Wagner fighters debriefed him on camera. It was clear that they had beaten him. He confessed to firing on a Wagner vehicle while he was drunk 'due to personal animosity'. Venevitin was, in many ways, an easy target, having been previously accused by men under his command of threatening them with execution if they didn't follow his illegal orders.[71] He was eventually freed and published a series of statements in which he accused Wagner of torturing him and other soldiers to force a confession.[72]

In late May, anonymous Telegram accounts had published videos of Prigozhin's children on holiday in northern Russia. He had responded by saying that these videos were hacked from his family's phones by a cyber unit in the Ministry of Defence.[73] Immediately after Wagner took Venevitin prisoner, other channels began posting new material, focusing on Prigozhin's youngest daughter, Veronika. These videos were considerably more embarrassing as they showed that his children were living lavishly abroad despite Prigozhin's populist criticism of Russia's elite. The videos were risqué and depicted Veronika as entitled and indulgent. It was both a reprisal and a warning. Prigozhin chose not to respond directly.

Wagner and the Ministry were locked in a stand-off. Prigozhin had been so dogged in his criticism of the military that he had succeeded even in alienating his erstwhile ally, Kadyrov. Wagner's publicity campaign continued, with recorded segments of Lotos travelling around Bakhmut to 'help out' the Russian units that had taken over. Wagner continued their activities in Africa, including delivering L-39 trainer jets to the CAR aboard Ministry of Defence transport aircraft.[74] Prigozhin continued to embarass the Ministry look bad, while the Ministry did its best to carry on business as usual.

It was an arrangement that couldn't last, and Shoigu and Gerasimov decided to force the issue. On 11 June the Ministry of Defence announced that all 'volunteer' fighters, including PMCs, would have to sign contracts with the Ministry of Defence by 1 July. Prigozhin at first responded by declaring that Wagner fighters would not sign any such contract. He insisted that it was unnecessary given their coordination through Surovikin and their service to the Russian state. 'Whatever happens after this order – we will not be given weapons and ammunition – we will figure it out as it comes.'

The contract mandate was a step that would achieve unity of command, subordinate groups like Wagner to the Ministry of Defence and force Prigozhin to either give up or fight. He stood to lose the personal control he had wrested over the Wagner Group.

While it was a GRU creation, his corporate infrastructure and force of personality had given him more control than Wagner's original authors are likely to have ever envisioned. Now he stood to lose it all – his Africa holdings, his lucrative state contracts and, most of all, his key lever to attain power, influence and wealth. The Ministry of Defence contract mandate was a move of sufficient significance as to have required clearance from Putin. Wagner was cornered.

12

MUTINY

Having gone through such a difficult path of war for 10 years, sacrificing the lives of our comrades, we will not allow the memory and military service of PMC Wagner to our Great Motherland to be erased.
Aleksandr 'Ratibor' Kuznetsov, 12 June 2023[1]

If Shoigu and Gerasimov were going to compel Prigozhin to surrender Wagner or fight, he had resolved to fight. He appears to have sincerely believed that the majority of Russia's armed forces shared not only Wagner's frustrations with the Ministry's leadership, but that they would be willing to back him if push came to shove. On top of that, he seemed to hang on to the hope that if he could prove his effectiveness and the Ministry's weakness to Putin, the boss would come down on his side. It was a strange reflection of Putin's own delusions that Ukraine would crumple from the first days of the Russian invasion and that Russia could easily install a puppet government. It may have been that Prigozhin, like Putin, was surrounded by confidants who shared his blind spots and told him what he wanted to hear. He may have just been desperate, found that brinksmanship had worked so far, and preferred to burn out than to fade away.

After the Ministry's announcement of mandatory contracts for all 'volunteers', Prigozhin began to prepare for war. It had not been enough to attack Russia's military leadership in the information space to try to expose their failures, or even to take Bakhmut while the Russian military failed elsewhere. Prigozhin, together with Wagner's Council of Commanders, decided that through a stand-off, preferably bloodless, they could make Putin see the light.

We don't know who in Wagner or the Ministry of Defence may have known about this plot in advance, or even what the original plot may have been before it went off the rails, but we can make some deductions. Within Wagner, the top command echelons are likely to have been informed in order to facilitate preparation. Foot soldiers appear to have been kept in the dark, even unit commanders.[2] But the men closest to Prigozhin – Utkin, Troshev and favoured assault detachment commanders like Ratibor, Lotos and Mekhan – were likely in the loop.

Based on intercepted communications and satellite imagery, intelligence agencies in the West expected that Wagner might attempt an armed rebellion. Intelligence sources claimed that Wagner had originally planned to descend on Rostov, the headquarters of Russia's Southern Military District, not far from the border with Ukraine and Wagner's base at Molkino, during a visit by Shoigu and Gerasimov.[3] Wagner had friends there and it seemed the most likely place they could expect support, or at least limited resistance. From there, Prigozhin likely aimed to lobby for Shoigu's and Gerasimov's replacements, no doubt figures friendly to Wagner – people like Surovikin, for instance. While this may have seemed like a long shot, as it required Putin to negotiate with a putschist, Prigozhin may have surmised that Putin would have little choice if the military's top leadership was effectively out of the picture. If the armed forces sided with Prigozhin, as he expected, all the better.

Wagner was amassing its ammunition, fuel, armour and air defence. This might have been disguised as preparation to turn over equipment to the Ministry. Later leaks reported by Russian opposition Telegram channels alleged that Troshev had sent a letter to the authorities in Rostov, advising them that Wagner would be transiting to the city with arms and equipment in order to transfer them to the Ministry of Defence.[4]

Western officials told the *Wall Street Journal* that General Surovikin was in on the plot. This may have been the case, or it may have been a ruse to further divide Russia's command staff. Earlier, Western intelligence leaks indicated that Prigozhin had contacted Ukrainian intelligence, offering the locations of Russian troops if they should agree to withdraw from Bakhmut.[5] These claims were similarly problematic to verify and Prigozhin made light of them.

Russian intelligence, namely the FSB, had also discovered Prigozhin's plan.[6] They might have intercepted Wagner communications, been tipped off by an internal source or been leaked the information by one of Wagner's 'allies' in the security structures who were in on the plot. At some point on 22 or 23 June, Prigozhin learned that the cat was out of the bag. He accelerated his plan to avoid being headed off. It was now or never.

Rostov

In the evening of 23 June, Prigozhin's press service published a slew of explosive statements. Chief among these was a lengthy video in which Prigozhin boldly proclaimed that the war in Ukraine was baseless. He said that Ukraine didn't pose a threat to Russia and that the pretext for the war was a lie: 'The Russian Defence Ministry is deceiving the public and the president.'[7] Prigozhin gave himself an out by saying that the war itself was justified as a 'holy war', focusing his criticism on the Defence Ministry's false narrative of an impending Ukrainian invasion of Russia. But try as he might, it was impossible for him to criticize the decision for the war without also criticizing Putin. It was Putin's war, after all.

Like Putin with the invasion itself, Prigozhin also needed a false pretext for his operation. He released an audio message claiming an unprovoked attack by the Defence Ministry:

> We were ready to go to the Ministry of Defence and give up our weapons and find a solution for how we would defend our country in the future. But the scum did not calm down.

Today, seeing that we are not broken, they carried out strikes, rocket strikes, on our rear camps. A huge number of our fighters died, our military comrades. We will take the decision how to respond to this atrocity. The next step is up to us.[8]

Pro-Wagner Telegram channels posted a video that claimed to document the treachery. It played like a found-footage horror movie: the man filming ran along a path through the forest, swearing in horror and confusion to one of his comrades. They came to a clearing, where an explosion had reduced trees to matchsticks. 'Holy shit,' the cameraman exclaimed. The camera surveyed the destruction. The segments cut to another shot, looking into a trench. Fires burned, surrounded by fallen trees. The video cut again to a burned body lying in the underbrush. Another cut revealed a severed limb.[9]

The video was theatrical and almost certainly faked. The damage visible in the shots was not consistent with a rocket strike – the leaves and trees showed no signs of fire damage – and the remains shown in the video appear to have been exposed to the elements for some time.[10] But it was enough to justify Wagner's reprisal.

'The Council of Commanders of PMC Wagner has come to a decision. The evil carried out by the country's military leadership must be stopped,' Prigozhin announced at 9 p.m. on 23 June.

I ask you not to resist. Anyone who tries to offer resistance – we will consider this a threat and destroy it immediately, including any roadblocks that get in our way, any aircraft that we see above us. Justice will be restored in the military and after that, justice for all of Russia.

That night, a convoy of Wagner soldiers began moving from eastern Ukraine. They were thousands strong, travelling in buses, cars, tanks, armoured vehicles and mobile air defence systems. Both

Wagner fighters and Russian security services were caught off guard. Many Wagner fighters called up or told to stand ready in reserve were not sure who to support.[11] Russian authorities, for their part, seem to have read Prigozhin's statements as bluster until they started receiving reports of Wagner forces moving on Rostov.[12] The FSB's National Anti-terrorism Committee opened a case against Prigozhin for 'calling for an armed rebellion' at around 10 p.m.[13] Convoys of trucks were seen leaving the Ministry of Defence in Moscow. At 1:30 a.m., Russia's Channel One aired an emergency broadcast, stating that Putin was informed of what was happening and that the FSB had declared Prigozhin's order 'criminal and treasonous'.[14] Security forces raided the houses of some known Wagner fighters, detaining some men and simply warning others to stay put. Websites of Prigozhin's Patriot Media Group were blocked in Russia.[15]

Prigozhin continued posting audio statements into the early hours of 24 June. He claimed that military was attacking Wagner with helicopters and artillery, but that they had been welcomed by border guards with open arms. He claimed that the Ministry was hiding 2,000 bodies of Russian servicemen in the Rostov morgue. He claimed that Gerasimov had dispatched planes to strike Wagner but that the pilots refused. He seemed to be making it up as he went along.

The Ministry responded with their own videos. In a statement published to Telegram at around midnight, Wagner's long-time ally in the military, General Surovikin, sat in a white room, a suppressed PP-2000 sub-machine gun in his lap. He glared into the camera and urged Prigozhin personally to halt the rebellion. 'Before it's too late, you need to obey the will and orders of the democratically elected President of the Russian Federation.' Within the hour, another video appeared, this time with Lieutenant General Alekseev, Wagner's champion in the GRU since their time in Syria. He called Prigozhin's actions 'a stab in the back of the country and the president', and pleaded with him to stop.[16]

The military and intelligence services were telling Prigozhin that he could not count on his allies to back him. There would be no mass defections or support from the top. The convoy continued towards Rostov nonetheless.

Early on Saturday morning, Wagner's forces rolled into the city. As Prigozhin had anticipated, there was no real resistance, and Wagner tanks and armoured vehicles drove down Rostov's streets unhindered. Their dismounted infantry were at first cautious, guns at the ready, but within a few hours a strange calm took hold. Wagner soldiers went into local convenience stores and bought coffee. They sat on their tanks and smoked as locals walked among the armed men taking selfies. Rostov's governor announced that locals should stay indoors and warned that 'public transit may be affected.'

At 7.30 a.m., Prigozhin and his Wagner fighters were in the headquarters of the Southern Military District. They had taken the nearby airfield, where Prigozhin claimed that they were allowing strikes on Ukraine to occur as normal. On video, Defence Ministry staff could be seen milling around the complex despite the presence of armed Wagner men.

In a video uploaded to a Wagner channel at around the same time, Prigozhin confronted Defence Ministry staff at the Rostov headquarters. Alekseev had come out to talk to Prigozhin, accompanied by Deputy Minister of Defence Yunus-Bek Yevkurov, a sixty-year-old veteran who had fought in Kosovo and Chechnya. Prigozhin, surrounded by Wagner men, shepherded the two generals to a corner of a courtyard. They sat down to talk, Prigozhin with a rifle hanging from his shoulder.

Prigozhin brought up an attack by Russian helicopters on the Wagner column that had moved to Rostov.

'They fired at us and we shot them down.'

'You shot them down?' Yevkurov answered, incredulously.

'We shot them down. Three already. And we'll shoot them all down if you keep sending them. Because you're hitting innocent civilians. You're destroying civilians, you blew up a bus full of people and you have no conscience about it.'

Yevkurov tried to answer, and Alekseev tried to butt in, but Prigozhin took issue with being addressed in the informal register when Yevkurov referred to him by *tiy* ('you') instead of the more formal *viy*. Yevkurov asked what they should do.

'Once again: we came here. We want to get the Chief of the General Staff and Shoigu,' answered Prigozhin.

Alekseev scoffed and waved his hand dismissively, 'take them!'

Prigozhin continued, deadly serious.

'We'll remain here until we have them. We'll blockade the city of Rostov and go to Moscow.'

Yevkurov asked Prigozhin to withdraw his troops, but Prigozhin firmly declined. The men lapsed into another disagreement. Yevkurov sipped from a mug; Alekseev sat with his hands on his hips. He couldn't believe what he was hearing. Finally, Yevkurov asked Prigozhin, 'You believe everything you're doing right now is right. Is that correct?'

'Absolutely correct,' answered Prigozhin, arms resting on his body armour. 'We're saving Russia.'[17]

March for Justice

Prigozhin stayed in Rostov while the bulk of Wagner's forces moved up the M4 highway towards Moscow. The taking of Rostov had been bloodless, but the road north would be a different story. The convoy from Rostov was met by another contingent crossing the border from Ukraine. They crossed at the Bugayevka border crossing where the guards laid down their weapons. Wagner fighters photographed them standing by the side of the road.

The Moscow region introduced a 'counterterrorist operation' regime, began blocking roads and dispatched armed units from the Russian National Guard and other forces.[18] They used construction equipment to gouge trenches in the highway near Moscow and arrayed construction trucks on roads to block them. The Defence Ministry published a statement asking Wagner fighters to surrender.[19] Putin, Shoigu and Gerasimov were conspicuously absent.

The military dispatched aircraft to intercept the convoy. Shooting began at around five o'clock in the morning near Voronezh.[20] An Mi-35 attack helicopter was struck, falling to the ground and sending up a plume of smoke that was filmed by confused locals. Before 10 a.m., Wagner forces had downed another two helicopters, Mi-8MTPR intelligence and electronic warfare aircraft.[21] Most of the crew of these helicopters were reported to have survived.

Near the Ukrainian border, an Ilyushin Il-22 plane circled. It was packed with eight to ten crew and a full suite of intelligence and communications equipment. This was an air command post, one of the more unique aircraft in Russia's Aerospace Forces. Wagner's air defence targeted the plane and scored a direct hit. Its wing sheared off and it tumbled towards the ground engulfed in flames. On impact, it was completely flattened and scattered debris over kilometres of ground. All of its crew died.

As Wagner pressed north towards Moscow, Putin finally appeared. In a televised address at 10 a.m., he spoke with barely disguised fury:

> I address the citizens of Russia, the personnel of the armed forces, law enforcement agencies, and the special services, the soldiers and commanders who are now fighting in their positions, repelling enemy attacks. I am also addressing those who were drawn by deception or threats into a criminal gambit, pushed onto the path of the serious crime of armed rebellion.

He repeated Alekseev's words, calling Wagner's action 'a stab in the back to the country and its people'. He invoked the Russian Civil

War, in which 'Russians killed Russians, brothers killed brothers.' Putin promised, 'We will not let this happen again. We will defend our people and our country from any threats, including from internal betrayal, and what we are faced with is precisely betrayal.'

Putin asked Wagner fighters to defect. He recognized Wagner's 'heroic' sacrifice in Bakhmut and Soledar but said that its men had been betrayed by the organizers of the rebellion. 'Everyone who deliberately took the path of betrayal, who prepared an armed rebellion, took the path of blackmail and terrorist methods, will suffer inevitable punishment – before the law and before the people.'[22]

Recent history indicated that Putin had pronounced a death sentence. Treason was the cardinal sin which the law and security services would punish with or without trial. The journalists and politicians who had been killed within Russia, like Anna Politkovskaya and Boris Nemtsov, were accused of betraying their country. The former members of the security services who had been assassinated abroad were also killed for their perceived treachery. Aleksandr Litvinenko, a former FSB officer, had been poisoned with radioactive polonium in London in 2006 for his leaking of state secrets. Sergey Skripal, a former GRU officer, was also poisoned, with a nerve agent, in Salisbury in 2018 for acting as double agent for British intelligence. Opposition politician Aleksey Navalny was likewise poisoned in 2020, accused of being a 'fifth columnist' undermining the Russian state, before dying under suspicious circumstances in a Russian prison in 2024. Putin seemed to be determined to convince Wagner's fighters to surrender or be destroyed. For Prigozhin, there would be no amnesty.

This placed Prigozhin in a position in which surrender seemed tantamount not only to the end of Wagner, but to Prigozhin's own prosecution, if not his death. The main force of Wagner's fighters in Russia pushed on towards Moscow. Around noon, the convoy passed the major Russian city of Voronezh, where they were intercepted by Kamov Ka-52 'Alligator' attack helicopters. They thundered overhead, drawing curious onlookers from their offices and apartments.

It was a bizarre reflection of the Battle of Khasham, but this time Wagner was prepared with air defences. A Wagner Strela-10 surface-to-air missile system stopped in its tracks on the highway, its missile turret pivoting to track a helicopter that was banking over the city. It fired, setting off car alarms a block away. The helicopter pilot activated his missile countermeasures and a pair of incandescent flares arced away from the craft. Wagner's missile narrowly missed the Kamov and soared into a neighbourhood. Either the helicopter's flares or the missile itself landed on an oil depot, setting off an explosion that shook the entire city and sent up a fireball a hundred feet into the air. Civilian onlookers cried out in terror and scattered for cover.[23]

Russian air strikes took out at least two transport trucks, two pickups mounted with machine guns and an armoured vehicle. Thirteen Russian service members were killed, and more were injured, making 24 June one of the bloodiest days for the Russian Aerospace Forces in the entire war. Wagner's casualties remain a mystery.

Wagner proceeded through Lipetsk Oblast, coming within 300 kilometres (186 mi.) of Moscow. Russian forces had established defences along the Oka river near Moscow and blocked off roads – it was clear that if Wagner was going to enter the capital, more blood was going to be spilled.[24]

I was returning from holiday and in the process of boarding a transatlantic flight. Friends and colleagues were messaging me: 'Is this it?' Was Putin's government and military so weak that Wagner would be able to enter Moscow? Or would Putin come back from the brink, destroying Wagner and Prigozhin? Were we watching a civil war unfold?

What none of us knew at the time was that an odd collection of powerful men was working behind the scenes to somehow, some way, put a stop to the mutiny. Improbably, they made a deal.

Bargain

Aleksandr Lukashenko has been president of Belarus for nearly thirty years. Recognizable by his stature, comb-over of silver hair and dark triangle of a moustache, he has been frequently photographed alongside Putin and has long been seen as one of Russia's closest allies. In practice, Belarus has found itself very much the junior partner to its larger neighbour and Lukashenko hasn't always enjoyed abiding by the terms of his relationship with Putin. It was no doubt with some tribulation that he accepted Russia's demands that Belarus involve itself in Russia's invasion of Ukraine. He accepted – as the authoritarian leader of a pariah state, he could scarcely afford to cross his greatest benefactor.

Lukashenko had encountered Wagner before. Many of Wagner's fighters were Belarusian citizens, a fact that seemed to trouble him little. But in July 2020, in the lead-up to Belarus's contested presidential elections and the largest protest movement yet seen in the country, alleged Wagner mercenaries were arrested by the Belarusian KGB near Minsk.[25] Lukashenko was incensed. He believed that Wagner had been sent to Belarus to organize a disruption of the election – perhaps to force him out of power and forestall the election of a new liberal leader.[26] Belarusian authorities charged the mercenaries with collaborating with Belarus's liberal opposition to overthrow the government. Russian representatives claimed ignorance and Lukashenko accused them of lying.

Russia pushed Lukashenko to hand over the Russian citizens and he eventually relented. The Ukrainians were simultaneously asking Lukashenko to hand the mercenaries over to them so that they could prosecute them for crimes they had committed while fighting with Wagner in the Donbas years earlier. All but one of the mercenaries, a Belarusian citizen, were returned to Russia after a weeks-long diplomatic stand-off.[27]

Lukashenko was wrong. Bellingcat later uncovered evidence of a plot that indicated that it was not Russia behind the mercenaries in Belarus, but Ukraine. According to their Wagnergate investigation, Ukrainian intelligence had organized a sting operation to lure Wagner fighters who had served in eastern Ukraine onto a flight from Belarus to Turkey. They would force the plane to land, arrest the fighters and charge them for their crimes on Ukrainian soil. Different versions of the story blame different parties for its failure, but, whatever the case, Ukrainian authorities hesitated at the last second and the Belarusians torpedoed the whole plan.[28]

Now Lukashenko entered the Wagner story again. At 8.07 p.m. on 24 June Lukashenko's press service announced that he had 'held negotiations with the head of the Wagner PMC, Evgeniy Prigozhin'. Lukashenko's statement said that the negotiations had resulted in agreements by Wagner to stop their advance and by Russia to provide security guarantees for Wagner fighters.[29] At 8.30 p.m., Prigozhin published his first statement in five hours.

> They wanted to disband Wagner. We went on the March of Justice on 23 June. In a day, we came within two hundred kilometres of Moscow. In this time, we didn't spill a single drop of the blood of our fighters. Now the moment has come when blood can be shed. Therefore, understanding the responsibility that Russian blood will be spilled by one of the sides – we are turning around our columns. And we are leaving in the opposite direction according to the plan.[30]

Cheering throngs surrounded Wagner as they departed Rostov, and locals took selfies with Prigozhin as he smiled from the window of his car.[31]

It was a shocking reversal. I landed after my flight to the news that the seemingly unavertable crisis had ended at the drop of a hat. It was clear that a deal had been struck, but it wasn't clear by whom, or what the contours of that arrangement were. Most confounding was the fact that Putin appeared to have allowed a powerful elite to challenge his authority, kill Russian servicemembers and walk away. Many Western observers read this as a sign of the hollowness of Putin's rule, of his inevitable decline, and anticipated that Prigozhin would not be the last to use force to vie for power.

Two days later, the protagonists of the deal each gave their version. Putin gave a speech doubling down on his accusation of betrayal towards the mutiny's leaders: 'the organizers of the rebellion, having betrayed their country and their people, also betrayed those who were dragged into the crime, lied to them, drove them to death, at gunpoint, to shoot at their own people.' He absolved the larger body of Wagner fighters of any crime, saying, 'the vast majority of the fighters and commanders of the Wagner Group are also patriots of Russia, devoted to their people and the state.' He thanked them for stopping 'at the last minute'. He offered three options: they could sign contracts with the Ministry of Defence, return home or go to Belarus.[32]

Putin was clearly furious, which made the last option he offered, exile to Belarus, even more unusual. Lukashenko chimed in with his own message, further muddying the waters. He claimed that Putin had wanted a harsh response to Prigozhin, who wasn't answering calls from the Kremlin – but that he intervened to make a breakthrough.[33]

Prigozhin, not to be outdone, offered his own take. In his telling, he reiterated that Wagner had been willing to surrender its arms on 30 June, but that they had been struck by helicopters and missiles, killing 33 Wagner fighters. In the resulting march to Moscow, he claimed that Defence Ministry personnel had joined them, and that no Wagner fighters were killed. In the end, when more bloodshed seemed inevitable, 'Lukashenko extended his hand and proposed that we find ways to continue the Wagner Group's work within a legal jurisdiction.' He seemed to be unable to help himself and used Wagner's progress towards Moscow as evidence of the failures of Russia's military leadership: 'We gave a master class on what should have happened on 24 February 2022.'[34]

None of these versions of the deal told the full story. Putin was out to save face and didn't want to show all his cards. Lukashenko was milking this opportunity to gain greater international standing and depict himself as the leader who succeeded where Putin could not. Prigozhin was insisting that he could have won if it came to a gunfight and that the abortive mutiny only proved his original point.

There had been more back-channel discussions up to the moment when an agreement was reached and there had been other players in the talks between Prigozhin and Putin. According to Russian journalists citing Kremlin sources, military leadership and government officials tried to negotiate with Prigozhin beginning on the night of 23 June – but he didn't seem able to articulate what he would be satisfied with.[35] He wanted Shoigu out and he wanted more resources and independence for Wagner, but Putin would never be able to bow to these demands and save face, particularly once the rebellion had begun. Prigozhin had simply been too loud in his criticism of Shoigu and Gerasimov, ironically forcing Putin to keep them in place lest he appear weak.

Multiple sources indicate that as the fight escalated around midday, Prigozhin tried to contact the Kremlin, but Putin had no interest in condescending to speak to him. As the military failed to join Wagner's putsch, Prigozhin realized he was in dire straits and unlikely to prevail.

Anonymous sources indicate that several figures within the government intervened: Secretary of the Security Council Nikolai Patrushev, Russia's ambassador to Belarus Boris Gryzlov, Kremlin chief of staff Anton Vaino and governor of the Tula region Aleksey Dyumin.[36] Patrushev was no friend of Prigozhin's but was one of Putin's most influential advisers. Gryzlov seems to have mainly acted as coordinator. The other men had associated with Prigozhin before. Vaino had met him many times in the past according to a leaked copy of Prigozhin's calendar, which he appears to have managed on an antiquated palm pilot.[37]

Of these, Dyumin was perhaps the most significant. A colourful figure who claims he once saved Putin from a bear attack, Dyumin was well positioned to negotiate the stand-off. He had been Putin's bodyguard before becoming the head of Russia's Special Operations Forces and deputy head of the GRU in 2014. He was now serving as governor of the Tula region, a role that some saw as a test of his mettle before being handed a bigger job, such as Minister of Defence.[38] Prigozhin had met Dyumin many times and Dyumin was alleged by some to be the man who connected Utkin and Prigozhin, spurring the formation of the entity that would become Wagner.[39]

It appears most likely that Prigozhin needed a high-level intermediary's involvement to lend legitimacy to the deal, but that Putin himself refused to be involved. Lukashenko offered an alternative as a head of state to whom Putin could pawn off responsibility along with his security elites while keeping himself out of the picture.[40] It wasn't exactly the mark of a strong leader, but it was certainly Putin's style.

Did this deal save Prigozhin, or Wagner, or indeed Putin? It seemed to be a compromise that left everyone in a poor position. Prigozhin would have to settle for a diminished role, which he didn't seem likely to accept. Putin would have to let a traitor who had challenged his power walk free with the knowledge that his friends and foes alike would read it as weakness. Really, only Lukashenko seems to have benefited, using the spotlight to deliver long and grandiose speeches on his role in defusing the situation.

As it happened, neither Prigozhin nor Putin was content to abide by the terms of the deal.

Exile

Over the course of the next week, the implementation of Prigozhin's agreement with the Kremlin and Lukashenko took form. First, the charges against Prigozhin were quietly dropped.[41] Then, on 27 June, Putin made the revelation, already broadly known, that Wagner had been funded from the state budget. This was nonetheless shocking given years of denial. He put the amount of Wagner's payment from May 2022 to June 2023 at around $1 billion. This might have cleared up whether Putin intended to keep up the lie about Wagner's relationship with Moscow, but it didn't answer any of the questions about what would happen to its men, or what the offer to go to Belarus meant.

Less than a week after the mutiny, Putin summoned Wagner's leadership to Moscow. The Council of Commanders – a cast that included Utkin, Ratibor, Brodyaga, Zombie, Lotos, Mekhan and newcomer Dmitriy 'Salem' Podolskiy, who had lost his arm at Bakhmut – were joined in the Kremlin by Prigozhin, Troshev and a few other high-ranking Wagner men. In all, 35 people attended. There, Putin made his offer: join a new structure to be headed by Andrey Troshev or choose exile.[42]

Within a week, Wagner's Council of Commanders elected that Troshev be removed from his role as the head of the Wagner organization the League for the Defence of Veterans of Local Wars and Military Conflicts. He was replaced by Salem. Putin gave an interview to Russian newspaper *Kommersant*, where he described the meeting.

While Prigozhin was silent, pro-Wagner channels posted statements from Wagner commanders on their opinion of Troshev. Kitaev, call sign 'Iceman', the commander who had been present at the killing of Ismail said, 'I saw him only a few times at meetings, where he simply remained silent, not taking any part in the planning.'[43] Wagner artillery chief Aleksandr 'Chips' Palyashchiy said that 'the commander of PMC Wagner is and has always been Ninth

[Utkin]. The fact that Sedoy [Troshev] is positioned as the commander of PMC Wagner is the agony of short-sighted and stupid people, who don't understand why we are strong.'[44] They universally denied that any significant numbers of fighters had opted to go with Troshev. They brought up the case in which he had been found intoxicated with cash and maps of Syria years earlier. He was persona non grata to Wagner.

On the other side, Wagner's former allies in Russia were feeling the heat too. No one had seen Surovikin in days and the Russian and international press were rife with rumours about his arrest or prosecution. Had he really been in on Wagner's plot? Or was association with Prigozhin enough to now tank someone's career? He was relieved of his role in the Defence Ministry, and his information was taken down from its website. When he finally re-emerged months later, he was a free man, but seemed to have an odd new remit. He visited Algeria along with a Defence Ministry delegation, glad-handing with local religious figures. Like the former Minister of Defence Anatoliy Serdyukov, the man who had brought up both Surovikin and Prigozhin, he was being given a comfortable retirement. It was its own form of exile, pushing him out of Moscow and seemingly killing his career trajectory once and for all. It meant that he was viewed as a failure, but not a traitor.

Wagner entered a strange phase of limbo. Its operations in Africa appeared to continue, but it was no longer active in Ukraine. Russian military authorities had already started to shoulder into Syria, compelling the Syrians to cease communication with Wagner soldiers who refused to sign contracts with the Ministry of Defence.[45] A slow but determined takeover of Prigozhin's media empire began.[46] Even while it seemed that the entire Concord empire was being dismantled, Wagner continued recruiting, and Prigozhin's companies even continued to win contracts, whether through conspiracy or oversight.[47] After months of Prigozhin's non-stop announcements, he was oddly quiet.

Incognito

On 24 June 2023, while Wagner advanced up the M4 highway, Russian authorities raided Prigozhin's offices and home. On 5 July, they leaked video and photographs of the raids to Russian media. Masked officers of the Ministry of Internal Affairs went from room to room in his office, brandishing sub-machine guns. They opened door after door marked with the names of different news agencies in Prigozhin's media structures: Nevskiy Novosti, Inforeaktor and RIA FAN. In the parking garage of the offices, police opened a white van filled with boxes, each containing stacks of roubles.

They entered Prigozhin's palatial estate. The interior was decorated garishly, with dark woods, leather, checkerboard marble floors and gold fixtures. The police photographed weapons that they claimed they had seized: automatic rifles, carbines, sniper rifles, handguns and shotguns. They photographed bars of gold and stacks of cash, both U.S. dollars and roubles. They documented Prigozhin's pool, his spa, his prayer room, his helicopter.

The decor became more morbid as they entered Prigozhin's study. It was a museum of Wagner. A giant sledgehammer sat on the ground, engraved with the words 'In case of important negotiations.' On the wall, there was a photograph of severed heads lying in the desert. A suit jacket next to a Wagner flag stored Prigozhin's numerous state awards from Russia and the Luhansk and Donetsk People's Republics, but also Sudan and the CAR.

Images that weren't shared with state media, but that later appeared online, revealed more details. Dozens of Wagner medals were displayed in a glass case: black crests, medals for the taking of Soledar and Popasna, a medal commemorating the Battle of Khasham that showed a soldier standing in front of an American Apache helicopter. Also in that case was a framed document dated 1 May 2014. It appeared to be one of Wagner's founding documents. It was an agreement between a 'Director' and a 'Commander', and it was signed by Prigozhin and 'Wagner', presumably Utkin.[48] It was impossible to verify whether the document was legitimate.

Russia state television broadcast the images. On talk shows, the commentators noted Prigozhin's hypocrisy. 'Let's have a look at the palace built for this campaigner against corruption and crime,' one said.[49] The images that captured the greatest attention weren't the firearms, the medals or even the opulence of Prigozhin's home. Rather, it was a series of photographs of wigs, accompanied by bizarre pictures of Prigozhin appearing to travel in disguise throughout Africa. In one, he wore a Libyan military uniform, sunglasses and a scraggly black beard. In another, he appeared in a brown wig, a beard and a keffiyeh. In some, he appeared to be taking selfies, making faces at the camera. Russian media was undercutting the image that Prigozhin had projected of himself as a populist, a patriot, a hardened criminal mastermind. In these pictures, he looked like a clown. The photographs of Prigozhin gained as much international attention as any of his statements made from the front lines of Bakhmut. Finally, his opponents appeared to be winning the narrative battle – but Prigozhin was nowhere to be found.

Relocation

Tsel is a small village next to an unused military base in central Belarus, near the sleepy town of Asipovichy. It is pine forests and fields, dotted by traditional wooden homes. Residents took note on 26 June when timber trucks hauled in workers to the fields by the village.[50] Later that same week, satellite imagery confirmed the construction of a large camp at Tsel of more than 250 tents.[51] When asked about it, Lukashenko said that he had created this camp and proposed it to Wagner, but Wagner had other ideas about where they wanted to be based.[52]

By early July, the camp sat unoccupied. Prigozhin and Wagner's leadership remained mostly quiet. Lotos gave an interview to a journalist in which he said that 'everyone was on vacation,' but that they were preparing their relocation to Belarus. He acknowledged the negative media coverage of Prigozhin and blamed it on Shoigu and Gerasimov and their plot to take Wagner for themselves. 'Shoigu tried to create his own PMC Redut and other small companies, but nothing worked for him. So, they probably decided it was better to take a PMC that already existed.' Lotos parroted Prigozhin's claims as to why Wagner was inviolable:

> They do not consider that PMC Wagner is not just a structure that unites people, it's an ideology. You've heard the story of King Arthur and the knights of the round table? Like that, all of the commanders of PMC Wagner are the knights and our leader is the director.[53]

Meanwhile, Prigozhin's planes were on the move. Two of his jets had been flying within Russia since the day after the mutiny. On 27 June they started flying back and forth from Belarus as well. It wasn't clear who was aboard – it could have been an elaborate ruse or Prigozhin shuttling back and forth to negotiate the details of Wagner's future.

Within two weeks, Wagner was in Belarus. The Belarusian Ministry of Defence announced that Wagner was training troops near Tsel and published videos of Wagner fighters leading drills for Belarusian troops. They were easy to tell apart. The Wagner fighters were physically imposing and wore the same type of gear they had sported in Ukraine – Western-style multicam-pattern uniforms and modern armour – while the Belarusian soldiers were often older men, wearing dated helmets and mass-issued uniforms. A day later, civil society organizations in Belarus began documenting massive convoys of trucks and armoured vehicles driving from Russia to Tsel. They flew Wagner flags and waved at passing motorists. Over the next month, Belarusian observers estimated that 4,000 to 4,500 Wagner fighters were transferred to Belarus.

Along with their arrival in Belarus, Wagner was being evicted from Russia. Wagner announced that it would officially close its base in Molkino, where it had been since 2014, on 30 July. On 17 July, the group held a ceremony in which the Russian and Wagner flags were lowered at the camp. Wagner officers solemnly folded the flags, which were then to be transferred to Belarus and Wagner's memorial sites in southern Russia.

Prigozhin resurfaced in characteristically dramatic fashion on 19 July. In a video recorded in the dim, dawn light, he stood in a field before a mass of uniformed men.

'Welcome to the Belarusian land!' he boomed. 'Thank you,' they thundered back in unison.

> You fought well. You have done a lot for Russia. What is happening now at the front is a shame that we don't need to take part in. We need to wait until the moment when we are able to fully express ourselves. So, the decision was made that we will stay here in Belarus for some time.

His voice echoed; the arrayed men were silent. 'In that time, I am certain, we will make the Belarusian army the second greatest army in the world.' The ambiguity of who the 'greatest army' might refer to was not lost on the men.

Prigozhin cracked jokes and the men chuckled. He urged them to behave themselves well. He said they would forge new roads to Africa:

> We brought a flag from Molkino, which I give to Sergey 'Pioneer', who will be the senior [commander] here in the Belarus direction. And two ribbons of the Belarusian and Russian flags so that no one can think that we are without a flag or a motherland as they wrote before.[54]

Prigozhin handed the flag to a man, indistinguishable in the darkness, amid raucous cheers. I and others later identified him as Sergey 'Pioneer' Chubko, the same Wagner fighter who had folded the flag at the closing ceremony for Molkino and who had previously served as the head of Wagner's operations department in the CAR in 2019.

Prigozhin, ever the showman, had saved his big reveal. 'And now a word from the commander who gave you the name Wagner.' A tall, hawk-nosed silhouette entered the frame. 'Yes, in case some don't know, I am that very Wagner.' The crowd of men exploded into cheers, waving their hats. Utkin bowed. It was the first time he had been documented publicly in years. He continued, 'This is not the end! This is just the beginning! The biggest work in the world, which will begin very soon' – and he switched to English, 'Welcome to hell!'

This was a defiant announcement of Wagner's continued existence that could not have gone unnoticed in Moscow. In reality, Wagner's role in Belarus would be restricted to training the Belarusian military and menacing its neighbours, especially Poland. Wagner Telegram accounts posted claims that they would stage attacks across the border, and Polish and Lithuanian security officials responded by beefing up their border presence. Two Russians put Wagner Group stickers with the familiar skull and crosshairs in various public areas in Poland, posting the pictures to social media. They were caught in the act and charged with espionage.[55]

This sabre rattling was mostly a series of attempts to stay relevant. Providing training for Belarusian forces in medicine and tactics wasn't exactly headline-grabbing. Belarus was a holding ground, a way station while Wagner found its feet again. The real work to secure its future against a takeover by the Ministry of Defence was happening thousands of miles away in Africa.

Hostile Takeover

It was a strange time to be in the service of the Company, especially if you were based in Africa. The word had come down to corporate managers and mouthpieces from Sudan to Mali – keep your head down. Don't talk to the press. One of the biggest open questions from the truce reached by Putin and Prigozhin was what would become of Wagner's Africa operations, and everyone from the soldiers, to the company directors, to the military leaders of the CAR and Mali seemed to be watching and waiting for what would happen next. Lavrov issued an ambiguous statement after the rebellion that indicated that Russian instructors would 'continue to work in Mali' as well as in the CAR, but it wasn't clear whether that meant Prigozhin would still be the one running the show.[56]

Local partners of Wagner and Russia also had to walk a fine line. The CAR's presidential security adviser, Fidéle Gouandjika, said that the whole affair was a domestic matter for Russia, and that it didn't affect the CAR. He spoke with the *Wall Street Journal* in June and said, 'If Moscow decides to recall them and send us Beethovens or Mozarts, we will have them.'[57] Prigozhin's own RIA FAN outlet subsequently reported that the CAR's Minister of Defence had scolded Gouandjika for his comments, and thanked Wagner for its support.[58] Prigozhin's media network continued to insert this brand of pro-Wagner commentary in spite of reports it had been totally co-opted.

The only statement that the Africa network was making publicly was that they weren't going anywhere. Early reports that Wagner was withdrawing from the CAR were met with rebukes from Prigozhin's Patriot Media Group and Wagner mouthpieces on the ground, insisting that these were just rotations. Prigozhin himself said as much in a July interview with Cameroon's *Afrique Media*, a publication his network had largely taken over. He was also working this angle in Russia. During the Russia–Africa Summit in late

July, Prigozhin was back home in St Petersburg, where he snapped a photograph with one of Touadera's presidential advisers. It might have received some Western media attention, but it was a serious downgrade from meeting with heads of state. According to the *Wall Street Journal*, Putin himself had barred Prigozhin from attending the summit. Instead, other Russians were visible, people like GRU general Andrey Averyanov, who commanded the unit behind the assassinations of Russians abroad, and Viktor Bout, Russia's most famous arms trafficker, now returned from his long stint in U.S. prison to pursue a political career.[59] Prigozhin was not going to be given the space to continue putting himself at the centre of the story of Russia in Africa.

It was harder to keep Wagner out of the picture on the ground in Africa, where their beneficiaries continued to rely on them for support. Wagner wasn't withdrawing from the CAR, but rather reinforcing its troops in advance of a 30 July constitutional referendum. That referendum would eliminate presidential term limits and allow CAR president Touadera to run for office again in 2025.[60] The referendum passed with Wagner providing security, paving the way for the CAR's increasingly authoritarian government to maintain its grip on power.[61]

Prigozhin further fanned the flames by publicly announcing his support for the coup in Niger, one of his few public statements in the period. In the streets of the capital, Niamey, Wagner flags and pictures of Prigozhin were carried by supporters of the new military government.

We may never know the substance of the conversations that took place behind closed doors during this time, and those involved are reluctant to talk about it. What was clear was that there was some kind of disagreement between Prigozhin and the Russian government about what was to happen to Wagner in Africa. His military, commercial and media endeavours on the continent were of great value – financially, but especially politically. Wagner had won political ground for Russia where it would have otherwise remained a secondary player. The Russian military was reticent to send men to fight and die in Sudan, or Libya, or the CAR, or Mali. The political costs back home were simply too great. Likewise, Russia's commercial and information engagement in Africa was constantly hamstrung by a lack of resources and local context. The Russian businesses that did succeed on the continent wanted to stay out of politics, including distancing themselves from Wagner. It was seen as too troublesome, potentially risky and of no benefit to their bottom line.

To kill Wagner and lose this foothold on the continent would be a great loss. Russia, particularly after the invasion of Ukraine, was hard-pressed to find international support, and so pursued the path that the Soviet Union had taken in the twentieth century by courting developing states. Arms sales and occasional shows of humanitarian aid could only go so far. Russia couldn't hope to rival the USA and Europe's massive investments in aid and security in Africa, nor could it counter China's vast commercial engagements. Wagner offered a way to change the rules of the game, to compete in a dimension that other countries couldn't or wouldn't pursue.

Russia's security elites grappled with how to avoid throwing away Wagner and the ground it had gained. What they seemed to have settled on was a peaceful transfer of authority. Wagner's forces in Russia would go to a new directorship under Andrey Troshev, Wagner's former managing director. They would sign with the Defence Ministry, and possibly be placed under the care of other so-called PMCs, but in any case they would no longer pose a threat. Wagner in Africa would similarly move under new management. It was simply too dangerous to allow Prigozhin to continue to hold the reins in Africa and it would demonstrate grave weakness on the part of Putin if he ceded this area of Russia's foreign policy to the man who had marched on Moscow. Wagner could keep their presence in Belarus, which could be dealt with later if need be.

Other PMCs in Russia proposed themselves as alternatives. On 21 August Convoy put on its Telegram channel recruitment posts for pilots for Orion and Sirius combat drones 'in the zone of the Special Military Operation and in Africa'.[62] A Russian journalist contacted Convoy's recruiter, who told them that Convoy had put together a unit for deployment to Africa who would sign contracts with Convoy and the Defence Ministry. Convoy's director, Konstantin 'Mazay' Pikalov, told Russian publication *iStories*, 'The era of bare-arsed Zulus with a Kalashnikov assault rifle is over. We will give African troops new weapons and train them to use them.'[63]

Around the same time, images started appearing on Russian social network VK, usually under posts concerning Wagner or the war in Ukraine, with captions such as 'Forget about Wagner – Come to Redut!' or 'Africa – For real men from Russia – Join Redut.' These posts were difficult to verify, as the phone number they provided did not align with any known contact information for Redut, but they added to the speculation of newcomers shouldering their way onto Wagner's turf.

It's not clear whether Prigozhin was fully aware of these plans for his Africa ventures. It may have been that on 24 June Shoigu, Gerasimov and Putin hadn't yet decided what to do with Wagner in Africa. Either way, Prigozhin was determined to hold on. By July, he was openly saying that times were hard, indicating that there was a disruption to Wagner's business, but that they would not withdraw. He said that he had sold some of his Africa interests to cover the costs of deployment, but it is not possible to confirm his claims.[64]

The competition over Wagner's Africa holdings came to a head in August. Prigozhin set out to visit his local partners and shore up Wagner's commitments – and his own – to stay. On 18 August, he landed in the Central African Republic. He reportedly met President Touadera and Henri Wanzet Linguissar, Touadera's head of intelligence, at the presidential palace to deliver his guarantee that Wagner was a long-term partner. The *Wall Street Journal* claims that he also met representatives of Sudan's Rapid Support Forces (RSF) while visiting.

From the familiar Bangui airport, where Wagner holds its own reserved corner of the tarmac, Prigozhin flew to Mali. As in Bangui, a cordoned area next to the airport belonged to Wagner. It had expanded in the last three months, and Prigozhin would have been able to see the new construction at their base as they made their approach. While in Bamako, Wagner gave him a tour. Dressed in camouflage and his boonie hat, he climbed aboard an armoured vehicle and set off.

He asked one of his travel companions to record him while they were on the road. He responded to the conjecture about whether or not he had been killed. This was a familiar experience for Prigozhin: in 2019, several websites, including those reportedly controlled by him, claimed that he had been killed in a plane crash in Congo.[65] Then, as now, he seemed to relish the reveal that he was, in fact, alive. 'For those discussing whether I'm alive, how I'm doing – it's now the weekend, the second half of August 2023. I'm in Africa. So those who like to discuss my liquidation, intimate life, earnings, or anything else – everything is fine.'

Prigozhin and his men pulled over somewhere in an open field. He put on body armour and collected his weapon, a distinctive East German AKMS-K rifle fixed with a suppressor and aftermarket parts. Armed men and a gun-mounted truck stood in the distance before an expanse of open savanna.

Prigozhin addressed the camera:

On duty. The temperature is plus fifty – just the way we like it. PMC Wagner is conducting reconnaissance and search operations, making Russia even greater on all continents and Africa even more free . . . Justice and happiness for the peoples of Africa, and making life a nightmare for ISIS, al Qaeda, and other bandits.

He hiked the rifle and cradled it against his chest, flashing his favourite Ulysse Nardin watch. 'We hire only real warriors and continue to fulfil the tasks that have been set and that we have promised to fulfil.' The camera panned away to show more Wagner men scattered across the field, on foot or in battered Toyotas. Prigozhin got back into the car, and they returned to Bamako. He flew to Moscow.

Meanwhile, the Ministry of Defence was making the rounds as well. Deputy Minister of Defence Yevkurov, the very same man whom Prigozhin had squabbled with in Rostov two months earlier, touched down in eastern Libya. In Benghazi, he met Wagner's long-time partner, Haftar. Libyan officials said that Yevkurov informed Haftar that Wagner forces would be under new command.[66] The Ministry of Defence declared it the first visit of such a delegation to Libya and said that it was for the purposes of discussing 'prospects for cooperation in combating international terrorism.'[67] To commemorate the meeting, Yevkurov gave Haftar an antique German pistol.

13

THE END AND THE BEGINNING

Death is not the end, it's just the beginning of something else.
Dmitriy 'Ninth' Utkin

It was a clear August day in Moscow. RA-02795 was cleared for take-off. The sleek blue and white Embraer 135 business jet was familiar to many Russia watchers. Until 2019, it had been known by its old registration, M-SAAN. Back then, it was registered to the Isle of Man and owned by a shadowy Seychelles company. I knew it from its previous flights when it carried distinguished passengers like Russian, Central African and Sudanese officials – the commander of the Black Sea Fleet, the CAR's prime minister, Sudan's deputy commander of the Rapid Support Forces – back and forth from Africa. M-SAAN ran these routes for years before it was sanctioned, rechristened and re-registered. Since then, it had mostly kept to Russia. Recently, it had joined the fleet of Prigozhin's private jets travelling back and forth to Belarus.

Now it carried ten people: three crew and seven passengers. The flight attendant aboard, a young woman named Kristina Raspopova, had posted images to social media as she had breakfast in the terminal. Pilots Aleksey Levshin and Rustam Karimov conducted preflight checks.

The other passengers took seats throughout the plane. Among the beige leather seats and wood finishing were Prigozhin, Utkin and four of their men. Valeriy Chekalov, Prigozhin's deputy, was there. He had long served Prigozhin in the Concord companies before becoming the director of Neva, which owned Wagner Group cutout Evro Polis. He was, at least on paper, the corporate head of the structure that paid Wagner's mercenaries. They were accompanied by Wagner members Sergey Propustin, Evgeniy Makaryan, Aleksandr Totmin and Nikolai Matusevich. Makaryan, known by his colleagues as 'Makar' or 'Makarych', had served in the CAR and been injured in Libya. Propustin and Totmin had also served in Africa. Matusevich had been with Wagner since 15 January 2017, including in the 4th Assault Detachment in Syria, before he was recruited to be Prigozhin's personal bodyguard. A portrait of Putin hung in the main cabin behind them.

RA-02975 took off just before 6 p.m. local time, flying northeast on a route towards St Petersburg. It was in the air for less than fifteen minutes.

Locals in the small town of Kuzhenkino, about 100 kilometres (62 mi.) north of Moscow, heard a thunderous boom and rushed outside. One woman began recording with her phone. Against the sky, they could see a trail of smoke. The whine of failing engines became clearer, and the fuselage of the plane fell through the clouds. The woman filming tried to describe what she was seeing: 'Fuck, it's a drone, they shot it down . . . you see, it's falling.' The engine roar subsided, and the plane fell out of view. The woman kept recording as she walked closer to her fence for a better look. She gasped as a tower of smoke came into view. More than 3 kilometres (2 mi.) away, one of the plane's wings and landing gear crashed into woodlands. They tumbled through the canopy onto the forest floor. Most of the plane smashed into a field just north of Kuzhenkino, where it lay burning until an emergency crew arrived to extinguish the fire.

As media began to report on the plane crash, Putin was delivering a speech in front of a new monument commemorating the eightieth anniversary of the Battle of Kursk. The monument stood behind him: a colossal statue of a Russian soldier heaving aside a pair of looming metal walls, illuminated with red lights. Putin presided from the stage, in front of a full orchestra and a line of men in uniform, veterans of the 'special military operation' in Ukraine.

He presented state awards to the personnel of the 127th Motor Rifle Division, members of a T-80 tank crew which had reportedly destroyed a Ukrainian convoy. He declared to his audience, 'Dear comrades! I am now addressing our military. I am grateful to you for your service and I am proud of you!' Putin entered the crowd and shook hands with locals. He posed for photographs, beaming.

Post-Mortem

The smoke had scarcely begun to settle as Russian authorities began preparing an investigation and as observers in Russia and the West speculated about the crash. Was Prigozhin dead, they wondered? Who killed him, and how?

Like many others, at first I wondered whether Prigozhin was in fact gone of if he had staged the whole thing. There was precedent for this: he had reportedly died in a plane crash in Africa in 2019 and later it was claimed he had lost his life at the Wagner base in Popasna in 2022. Prigozhin was known to use body doubles and wear disguises, and was notoriously paranoid about his security. Why, then, had both Prigozhin and Utkin flown together?

The bodies of passengers were too disfigured from the crash to visually identify; Russian authorities collected the remains, loaded them into black vans and carried them to a morgue for testing. Everyone waited for the big reveal that Prigozhin hadn't been aboard. Maybe he would appear in a new video; maybe he was on another plane. But no reveal came.

Prigozhin was dead. So was Utkin; Prigozhin's corporate deputy, Chekalov; and his bodyguards. Russia's aviation authorities publicly released the list of passengers. Wagner channels announced that Prigozhin and Utkin had died and posted memorial videos over the music of Richard Wagner's 'Ride of the Valkyries': 'Evgeniy Viktorovich Prigozhin died as a result of the actions of the enemies of Russia. But even in hell, he will be the best! Glory to Russia!'

Within hours, Wagner fighters and employees of Prigozhin's empire were largely in agreement that the boss was gone for good. As one told Russian journalists, in the case of the previous false reports of his death 'we had concrete protocols about where to post information and how to file it. This time, there was nothing prepared.' There was no statement from the Council of Commanders of Wagner, but Wagner fighters and admirers began to prepare memorials for Prigozhin and Utkin in cities around Russia. The former Wagner Centre in St Petersburg turned on its office lights to form a cross.

At first, Kremlin spokesperson Dmitriy Peskov declined to comment on the events. Putin broke the Kremlin's silence the next day:

> I would like to express my sincere condolences to the families of all those killed. And indeed, if there were people there – and the initial information seems to indicate that there were employees of the Wagner company there – I would like to note that these are people who made a significant contribution to our common cause of fighting the neo-Nazi regime in Ukraine.

He referred to Prigozhin, describing a complicated legacy, using the past tense:

> I knew Prigozhin for a very long time, since the early 1990s. He was a man of difficult fate, and he made serious mistakes in life, and he achieved the results he needed – both for himself and, when I asked him to, for the common cause, as in these last months.[2]

He referred to Wagner's missions abroad: '[Prigozhin] worked not only in our country – and worked with results – but also abroad, in Africa, in particular. He dealt with oil, gas, precious metals and stones there.'

As it became clear that Prigozhin and Utkin were no more, a new set of questions emerged. Who was behind the crash? How did they pull it off? And why now? Putin said that the Russian Investigative Committee would look into the incident, but scarcely anyone expected the results to provide closure.

Immediately after the crash, Wagner accounts expressed the belief that the plane was shot down by a Russian air defence system.[3] This pointed to a state assassination or even the act of a disgruntled soldier, someone with an axe to grind after Wagner had killed thirteen Russian airmen in June. U.S. intelligence announced the day after the crash that they did not believe that the plane was shot down.[4] There was no evidence in the footage of the plane crash or in the remains of the aircraft to suggest a missile had struck the plane. Russian authorities said they were investigating whether it was simply an accident. Given the catastrophic damage to the aircraft, there were realistically two explanations: a bomb or sabotage.[5]

There was a cloud of rumour. Someone had been on the plane prior to the flight and taken a recording that was posted online. It emerged that this was Aleskandra Yulina, chair of the board of the company Rusjet, who was considering buying the plane. Anonymous Telegram channels claimed that Prigozhin's jet manager had provided the plane's upcoming flight times to prospective buyers and that they had been able to bypass airport security to inspect the plane.[6] Maybe this was how a bomb had been placed on it. Others, like nationalist figure Igor Girkin, wondered publicly whether Ukrainian services had rigged the plane – but he conceded that this was unlikely as well.[7]

While the specifics of how the plane was brought down remained elusive, most international observers and Russians believe that the Russian government was behind it.[8] It remains the strongest theory of Prigozhin's death. Putin's language during the mutiny and afterwards had been unambiguous: there would be consequences. The crash itself occurred exactly two months after the attempted mutiny. Prigozhin had continued to prove wilful and to challenge Shoigu and Gerasimov, stubbornly refusing to surrender his Africa holdings, in the months since the deal was struck. Prigozhin's brazenness and incaution made sense when one considered that he hadn't yet faced meaningful repercussions. As one member of his organization told Russian journalists, 'Maybe Zhenya [Prigozhin] decided that Putin got it out of his system: "He didn't kill us right away, so he won't ever kill us"? He considered himself indestructible. He decided that he was immortal.'[9] Prigozhin was gravely mistaken. Russian authorities had motive, the capability and a history of staging spectacular assassinations of political adversaries. His death was a public execution.

Motive and Timing

To analysts in the West, it seemed unusual that Prigozhin had not faced immediate consequences for the mutiny. To some, this pointed to Putin's weakness.[10] This was one way to look at things – at each moment in the Prigozhin drama, Putin might have put a stop to the issue before it became unmanageable – but it also missed the bigger picture, the full scale of the dilemma that Putin had created. There was the practical element of how to deal with Wagner in Russia, Ukraine and Africa, and there was the deeper issue of what Wagner portended for the entire system.

As we've established, the Ministry of Defence and security services were likely in agreement with the Presidential Administration that to throw out Wagner entirely would be not only messy, but a missed opportunity. What they needed was time. And so Wagner was moved to its holding grounds in Belarus while the military and GRU established what to do about Africa. The wheels were already in motion to transfer Wagner responsibilities in Ukraine.

To successfully migrate human capital and relationships, what they needed were defections.

When Putin gathered Wagner commanders to the Kremlin on 29 June, he likely expected a very different outcome. He had a member of their leadership willing to act as a guarantor if they came over to the Ministry of Defence. He was willing to offer amnesty. He was no doubt surprised to find that a significant number of Wagner fighters, and more importantly most of their command staff, preferred exile.

The commanders formed the core of Wagner's human capital and had established relationships of trust, reliance and fear down the chain of authority to their men. They in turn were bound to Prigozhin by personal loyalty, shared experience and the future he had offered them. Wagner's highest-ranking commanders had washed out of the Russian military, having either been convicted of crimes or encountered career roadblocks that prevented their continued ascendance. Many had grown disenchanted with the military during their service or later, as they fought for Wagner in Ukraine, Syria and Africa. But like the Soviet veterans of the war in Afghanistan, they could not find their place in everyday civilian life. Wagner veterans such as Marat Gabidullin attest to the feeling of displacement experienced by veterans in modern Russia – they find identity and purpose in service, but once they leave, they discover that there is no place for them to apply their talents or experience the same camaraderie. Perhaps most fundamentally, there was nowhere they felt they could be useful.

Wagner gave a second chance to men like Ratibor, Utkin, Zombie and Lotos. They were granted community and wealth, and proved their valour, which they never would have had in the armed services or in conventional industries like private security. Prigozhin, through Utkin, was the crux of this guarantee. He had bound Wagner's identity to his own, in Syria, in Africa and in Ukraine. He was the distinguishing factor between Wagner and the Ministry of Defence. As Gabidullin explained to me, 'the commander of an assault detachment is the tsar of his own state.' Wagner's top commanders knew they would be given no such authority in another structure. They had seen at first hand the costs of the Defence Ministry's mismanagement and corruption in Ukraine.

As long as Prigozhin was around, this guarantee was intact. This was the message proclaimed by Prigozhin and Wagner commanders throughout the period immediately before and after the mutiny: we stand as one; defection is betrayal. His campaign to reassure African partners that Wagner, specifically his Wagner, would continue to be the vehicle for partnership with Russia was the other side of this coin. Authorities in the CAR, Mali and Syria weren't going to choose sides without some kind of clear indication of who was going to come out on top, and the reality was that Wagner's men were the ones on the ground.

Whether or not Putin had the intention of assassinating Prigozhin when they came to their agreement on 24 June, Prigozhin had made compromise impossible. He personally stood in the way of the Defence Ministry's designs for life after Wagner in terms of its fighters and its relationships abroad. As long as Prigozhin was alive, he would insist on the organization's survival as an entity distinct from the formal structures of the security services. Wagner could not be peacefully subsumed or destroyed while Prigozhin lived.

There was no evident succession plan. Utkin was the other primary 'father' of Wagner in the organization's mythos and so he would need to be liquidated as well. Chekalov would be inconvenient given his role in logistics, corporate management and his deep knowledge of the network. The bodyguards and flight crew were collateral damage. The other top leadership included Troshev, who had guaranteed his safety by betraying Wagner to join the Defence Ministry, and the assault detachment commanders such as Ratibor and Lotos, who now opted to lie low. No one was left who had a credible claim to leadership.

Why, then, such a spectacular means of assassination? Experience had shown that poison and shootings could just as effectively kill opponents and critics. Russia's leadership had no problem blaming other parties for these killings after the fact either, and Prigozhin had plenty of enemies who could have been blamed.

The destruction of RA-02795 was not only the cleanest way to kill key leadership in one fell swoop with deniability, however implausible – that is, it could be blamed on either a mechanical failure or a Ukrainian plot. It was also symbolically powerful, a display of violence and retribution on par with any of Prigozhin's theatrical statements to date. The burning husk of the jet lying in a field north of Moscow was a warning to any other elite who would dare to challenge not only Putin, but the order he had created.

Changing of the Guard

One by one, Prigozhin and the passengers who died with him were laid to rest. On 29 August journalists scrambled to identify where Prigozhin would be buried in St Petersburg, as authorities had announced multiple possible burial sites and times.[11] They cordoned off a cemetery in the north of the city, leading a swarm of media to descend on it. At around six in the evening, police removed the cordon and revealed that Prigozhin had been buried at a closed ceremony on the other side of town.

Prigozhin's grave is in a leafy cemetery on the outskirts of St Petersburg. On the day of the ceremony, it was ringed by armed security forces and metal barriers. Two flags, one Russian and one Wagner, were planted at his gravesite along with ribbons printed with one of Prigozhin's favourite epithets, 'KIA, we are with you.' He was buried next to the grave of his father, Viktor, and his stepfather, Samuil Zharkoy, who first worked with him to kick-start his food business when he was released from prison. Chekalov was buried in St Petersburg on the same day in a ceremony attended by family and Wagner veterans and reportedly organized by Prigozhin's son Pavel. Kremlin spokesperson Dmitriy Peskov announced that Putin would not be able to make Prigozhin's ceremony due to his busy schedule.

Utkin was subsequently buried outside Moscow at Russia's largest war memorial, the Pantheon of the Defenders of the Fatherland. His medals from Russia, Libya, Mali and the CAR were displayed at his service. Mourners left Wagner patches and bottles of brandy on his grave.

The burials and preceding announcement by the Investigative Committee on 27 August that they had positively identified the bodies of the deceased did not put the legacy of Wagner or Prigozhin to rest. The same week in which Prigozhin, Utkin and Chekalov were buried, the security services accelerated their campaign to establish control in Africa. Yevkurov made another trip, stopping in Mali, the CAR and Burkina Faso, where Wagner had never succeeded in establishing a foothold.

He was joined this time by GRU general Andrey Averyanov, who had appeared at the Russia–Africa forum that Prigozhin was barred from. Averyanov, the commander of GRU's Unit 29155, which was behind the attempted assassinations of Sergey Skripal and Aleksey Navalny, was rumoured to be a frontrunner for the new manager of Wagner's Africa operations.[12] The two men appeared at televised events in Mali and Burkina Faso, before flying to the CAR, where their activities were not made public. They travelled aboard an Il-62 of Russia's 223rd Flight Unit, a state airline that had ferried Wagner for years. In mid-September, the same plane made another series of flights to Mali, Burkina Faso, Libya and Syria, according to flight-tracking data. When devastating floods wracked the Libyan coast in September, the Russian Ministry of Emergency Services sent officers and equipment.

On Telegram, Wagner accounts spread rumours that tensions were rising. A Russian archaeologist in Syria claimed that the Ministry of Defence was commencing a hostile takeover of all Wagner oil and gas enterprises and had ordered the Syrians not to pay them until they were handed over. On 12 September they claimed that the Defence Ministry had prevented a plane carrying Wagner fighters from Libya, including Syrian recruits, from landing at Khmeimim. The anonymous account said that Russian helicopters had been scrambled, threatening to fire on the Wagner plane, but that Wagner representatives on the ground had managed to contact Yevkurov and resolve the issue.[13] These claims were dubious at best, but their spread across Wagner channels was telling of the grievances between established Wagner missions in Syria and Africa and the Defence Ministry interlocutors seeking to seize control.

Wagner's Council of Commanders remained silent, to the chagrin of Wagner fighters and their online followers. Other members of the network were outspoken. Maksim Shugalei wrote that the death of Prigozhin was an indictment of Russian leadership, whether 'internal forces or external forces are to blame'. If internal forces, then 'not a single word given by anyone to anyone at any level can be trusted.' If external forces, 'this demonstrates the insolvency and paralysis of the Russian special services, which cannot protect high-level people at home.'[14]

Wagner remained in Belarus and continued to train forces there. Some veteran former Wagner fighters took part in patriotic education and recruitment drives in Russia. Regardless of how many fighters had defected to the Defence Ministry, the Wagner brand was ripe for the taking. The only people who could make a claim to legitimacy weren't saying anything.

Their quiet was understandable. It wasn't just Prigozhin's death that signalled a change in the climate, but arrests and prosecutions that targeted other 'super-patriot' figures who challenged Putin. Wagner's fellow traveller and long-time critic, the former FSB officer and militant leader Igor Girkin, had been charged with inciting extremism in July.[15] He had spent years criticizing Putin but was widely seen as being protected by his important role as a canary in a coal mine for ultra-nationalist sentiment.[16] The space for opposing the system, even if one supported the war, was closing.

This situation might have been different, and the security services might have found themselves in more dire straits, if Prigozhin had had a viable successor. But like Putin, he led a personalist authoritarian system. Just as it does for Russia, this means that there is little prospect for continuity of command for Wagner after his death. The rumoured successors within Wagner, people like Lotos, are hardly plausible. They are military leaders and do not have the experience, knowledge or connections to manage the element of Wagner that truly belonged to Prigozhin – its corporate infrastructure and relationships. Wagner as we knew it throughout its iterations from 2014 is dead. What remains are its men, their networks and the myth they carry with them. Though they now fall under overlapping and contested control, they are nevertheless dangerous and far-reaching.

Surviving the System

Putin had fostered a system that created men like Prigozhin. It was in many ways feudal. Institutions were hollow and local politicians or businessmen acted as vassals, expected to perform service for the centre. But unlike the medieval feudal system, this one operated in a larger context of globalized capital. That might make Russia vulnerable to sanctions and restrictions from the international financial system, but it also created new opportunities. Global capital empowered the 'vassals' to take on new obligations for the centre around the world: laundering the proceeds of corruption, building political influence and undermining Russia's adversaries financially.

Under this arrangement, for Putin to back actors such as Shoigu or Gerasimov against Prigozhin came with risk. He preferred not

to involve himself in internecine competition, avoiding commitment and relying on the parties to work it out between themselves.
This allowed him to be a mercurial political animal and to avoid
blame for poor decisions, as he had at the onset of the war, when
he had berated his security elites for failing to deliver a successful
invasion.[17] By staying out of the showdown between the Defence
Ministry and Prigozhin, or indeed any elite dispute, he could avoid
having to own a negative outcome.

This style of rule had created Wagner and the other organizations like it in the first place.[18] By creating incentives for elites to
compete in their service to him in exchange for wealth and security,
Putin had given rise to a cast of violent and criminal entrepreneurs.
This arrangement was often very effective. The Russian state didn't
have to be the one to directly orchestrate election interference, prop
up friendly authoritarian governments or even carry out assassinations if it could simply give direction to the right people and count
on them to act. Prigozhin was unique in this rogue's gallery in the
package of services he provided, namely large-scale military force.

The balance of Russia's public–private partnerships had always
relied on some degree of competition, whether it be the security
services trying to outdo each other or entrepreneurs competing for
access to preferential treatment from the state. But when the private turned against the public, when the networks of power within
Putin's system found themselves at odds with the very private networks they had nurtured, there was no effective way to manage the
escalation – not if Putin was unwilling to be decisive and choose
who would come out on top.

The social contract between the state and elites in Russia is
now fundamentally different. Putin made two incompatible promises on 24 June: he promised swift justice for the plotters of the
mutiny, and he promised Prigozhin security. At the end of the day,
his promise of justice was more valuable for the long-term survival of the system. But it does mean that any future challenger will

know that guarantees from Putin cannot be trusted. If one wants to challenge the king, they will have to go all the way; there will be no concessions.

The New Mercenary Marketplace

What Russia is left with are the offspring of the fourth revolution of Russian PMCs: organizations such as Convoy, Redut and Redut's associated Gazprom units. Their handlers are within the state but comprise their own networks as well, as the FSB competes with the GRU, the GRU competes with the Foreign Intelligence Service (SVR), and various cliques within the Ministry of Defence vie for influence.

Some Russian PMCs see an opportunity in Prigozhin's demise and are eager to take Wagner's place, or at least claim to be. Convoy's Vasiliy Yashchikov told the *Wall Street Journal* in early September 2023 that Wagner veterans had joined Convoy, even though they were not being actively recruited. He also claimed that the head of Convoy, Konstantin Pikalov, had recently travelled to African countries with Defence Ministry delegations.[19] Sources attest to Pikalov's presence in Libya, but there is no evidence that he joined Yevkurov on his trip. He would be an odd choice given his apparently lacklustre performance with Wagner in Africa and his generally undistinguished background when compared with the commanders and leadership of the Wagner Group. Then again, the war in Ukraine gave many mediocre people new opportunities in Russia and it's not impossible that Pikalov was at the right place at the right time.

Rumours also circulated about Redut's possible role in Africa. Redut was much larger than Convoy and had strong connections to the Defence Ministry, so this suggestion was not implausible. Pro-Wagner channel Gray Zone claimed that Redut was the basis of a new 'Russian Expeditionary Force', which now had tens of thousands of staff.[20] This was supported by evidence, but Konstantin

Mirzayants, Redut's commander and the former deputy commander of Redut-linked 45th VDV Spetsnaz, visited Burkina Faso along with Yevkurov and Averyanov in September 2023, suggesting that Russia's security services may see a role for Redut in Africa.

The future role of these organizations in Africa is unclear. They are not well suited for the task, lacking the connections and history of Wagner. But they are, however, well positioned to continue their role in Ukraine and remain valuable for the Russian state.

As the war has shown, Russia's military is not purely a paper tiger, but many of the government's institutions are weak and forced to navigate an increasingly intractable balance between the system's social contract with the people and the demands of Putin's revanchist project. The war in Ukraine demands more men, but mass mobilization threatens to be overwhelmingly unpopular. The war in Ukraine demands logistics, training and industry, but corruption has degraded the military and society's ability to deliver outcomes. Public–private partnerships like these PMCs are here to patch the gaps. They are the product of both late-stage state capitalism and a centralized authoritarian system. They are solvent because the global system of capital is poorly equipped to counter them – or in some cases, purpose-built to turn a blind eye. They can hide in secrecy jurisdictions, exploit local corruption and maintain global networks of finance and logistics.

There is demand and opportunity for these arrangements between the Russian state and private businesses. For PMCs, Russia's recent traumatic experiences with Wagner means that they are likely to continue in less spectacular but more sustainable forms. In Ukraine, the distinction between these PMCs, reserve units, volunteer units and other semi-formal structures which have been designed to swell Russia's manpower will become more and more blurred.

These units will not look or fight like Wagner. By the time of the mutiny, the prospects for Wagner to continue to exist or for any future network to attain its level of power were already shrinking. The other entrepreneurs in this space recognized this. Redut, Gazprom's PMCs and Convoy were all limited in their ambitions. They sought to grow influence and wealth by assisting the war effort in ways that didn't have to be battle-changing – they just had to be visible and get more bodies to the front.

For these very same reasons, it is unlikely that any Russian PMC in Africa or Ukraine will achieve the gains that Wagner did. Prigozhin was operating with unique resources and within a unique window of opportunity. No champions in the military or security services will be willing to take the risks that Prigozhin's allies did by so heavily arming and funding an organization, and no private actors will be willing to take the risks that Prigozhin did in competing so directly with the military.

This doesn't mean they won't matter. Ukrainian military officials, while complimentary of Wagner's capabilities in comparison with those of conventional Russian forces, give no impression that they expect an easier fight without Wagner. Nor do they show prejudice against other PMCs. For Ukraine, these other PMCs don't represent a new set of capabilities that Russia will deploy against them or uniquely effective units that they will have to counter. They represent additional forces, some capable, some weak, but all contributing to the immensely challenging task that Ukraine faces.

Wagner's legacy will live on in Russian military doctrine at least as much as it lives on in other PMCs. While Wagner's core unit of assault detachments is not an innovation, drawn as it was from Soviet military doctrine, these units and their application have received more attention in Russian manuals and force structure in 2023 and 2024.[21] The Ukrainian military has noted Russia's use of assault detachments, leveraging tactics similar to those employed by Wagner: the use of artillery to soften enemy fortified positions, small assault teams that seek to claim those positions and better-equipped 'fortification' teams that try to hold ground.[22] Analysts have noted that the application of these techniques differs from their doctrinal definition, but it nonetheless appears to be evidence of learning from Wagner and adaptation to the tactical realities of facing a well-armed, deeply entrenched foe.[23]

Even if Wagner's experience in Popasna, Lysychansk and Bakhmut leads the Russian military to adapt and consider past doctrine that might be better suited to the war than their current approach, they will be missing two key elements of Wagner's success: its commanders and the independence that Wagner gave them.

What Remains of the Orchestra

Whatever structure takes over control of Wagner's resources and infrastructure will have its success determined by its resourcing, its people and its freedom of action. It seems unlikely that, after Prigozhin, any organization will enjoy comparable levels of trust and freedom. It might have better prospects if it can capture Wagner's human capital, the personal element of Wagner's myth: the corporate managers and the top commanders.

With Utkin dead, the highest echelon of Wagner's command is gone. But others, such as Ratibor, Lotos, Zombie and Mekhan are still out there. Some are in Belarus, others in Russia, still others in Africa and Syria. The Council of Commanders, Wagner's most visible veterans such as Salem and Brodyaga, and the litany of mid-level commanders below them formed the identity of Wagner. Some are gifted leaders and strategists, such as Ratibor. Others, such as Iceman, are simply ruthless. They all have the established experience and relationships with their men critical to Wagner's effectiveness as a brand, recruitment tool and fighting force. Yet without Prigozhin, they are just spokes with no wheel; no leader to guarantee their pay and insulation from the fickleness of the state; and no corporate infrastructure to orchestrate their operations.

The fighters of the Wagner Group are still active at the time of writing, in early 2024. They train forces in Belarus. They have people in Libya and Syria. They continue to both fight and die in Mali and in the CAR. The Ministry of Defence and other elements of the security services, from the GRU to Rosgvardiya, have taken over large parts of their operations. The Ministry of Defence has established its own structure, the 'Africa Corps', which inauspiciously shares a name with Nazi Germany's historic North Africa forces, in order to supplant Wagner.[24] Meanwhile in Russia, forces both formal and semi-formal have touted the presence of former Wagner fighters among their ranks.

Wagner will continue as a movement – this much is certain. As a symbol of the potency of Wagner's brand, the Russian state continues to use Wagner's name in training and recruitment. Online recruitment drives tout training by Wagner instructors and advertise that the units recruiting comprise '90 per cent musicians'.[25] Wagner's symbols and lingo are still ubiquitous. From the black flag planted at the site of Prigozhin's crash to the patches worn by Russian fighters in Ukraine, they have become a symbol of a particular brand of Russian militarism.

When Prigozhin insisted that Wagner was 'an army with an ideology', he was correct, but maybe not in the terms that he meant. Despite the large number of white nationalist fighters and *rodnovery* pagan believers in Wagner's command staff, particularly in its early days, this is not what Wagner represents to most. Its core idea is a martial, patriotic and populist twist on late Putinism. More than that, however, it is a particularly ruthless brand of Russian nationalism, anti-elite and pre-occupied with the transformative power of mass violence. The sledgehammer is one of Wagner's most popular symbols for a reason. It represents Wagner's celebration of the very things that the Russian state typically feels the need to deny. The hammer declares *we aren't ashamed to visit horrible violence on our enemies, because they deserve it*. The euphemistic references to 'the orchestra' and 'musicians' were effective precisely because everyone knew what they meant. They succeeded not in hiding anything, but in reinforcing a myth of the 'shadow army', able to go places and do things that the Russian military could not, evading the grasp of Western authorities, and championing the Russian cause far beyond its borders. In this fashion, Wagner's mythos was in many ways an exaggeration of the narrative that Putin himself built of a rogue state reclaiming its historical right, always one step ahead of the established global powers committed to its destruction.

This myth was embodied not just in symbols but in people. As the Battle of Bakhmut ground on, Wagner's established commanders became increasingly public, even giving interviews on state television. Most kept their identities hidden, but some took off the mask and established a legendary status of their own. This has also opened them to being publicly stripped of their titles. Wagner commanders were openly critical of Troshev after he joined the Ministry of Defence, as was the broader set of online communities. When he was reportedly joined by Vadim 'Khrustal' Suvorov, a long-time member of Wagner who had served as the head of their personnel department, both men were condemned. Khrustal was alleged by Wagner commanders such as Artem 'Koldun' Matveenko to be involved in the recruitment of Wagner employees for the Defence Ministry, 'offering them to move to a new PMC to work in Africa', and stealing a database of personnel to bring to Troshev. Kholdun derided Khrustal as having led a unit in Syria that was involved only in guard duties despite claiming that he fought at Palmyra, as acting cowardly in Ukraine, and as being despised as head of the personnel department. Wagner communities called him 'the personification of a traitor and deserter'.[26]

Now, networks within the Russian state compete for control over Wagner's assets in Africa, Syria and Russia. Wagner continues to fight – into 2024 Wagner fighters have been killed in the CAR and in skirmishes in Mali, and are alleged to continue to move fighters between Africa and Syria. There are claims, usually attributed to anonymous U.S. and French intelligence sources, that Wagner is putting its thumb on the scales of Sudan's civil war by arming the RSF. When a CNN team visited Bangui in the CAR in September 2023, they saw that Wagner was still visible, with masked men guarding politicians, protecting the Russian cultural centre and even shopping for groceries. Against the backdrop of Israel's new war against Hamas, unnamed U.S. officials have told journalists that Wagner is arming Hezbollah with air defence systems.[27] It is hard to find a modern conflict where there is not a rumour – either credible or spurious – of Wagner's involvement.

The repurposing of Wagner's assets is most plainly visible in Africa. There, Wagner symbols remain, but the Ministry of Defence has placed its forces under more formalized control through the Africa Corps. The Africa Corps shed the PMC moniker in favour of more clear links to the Russian state, dropping the 'private' element from the original 'public–private partnership'. In spite of this, the Africa Corps and its associated GRU-run influence operation, 'The Africa Initiative', maintain Wagner's image as a globe-trotting clandestine operation and an ally to those spurned by the West.[28]

With Prigozhin out of the way, the Africa transition of Wagner's resources has been a mostly peaceful affair. Wagner fighters appear to have been offered a choice similar to that offered by Putin to their leadership in June 2023: sign on formally with the state or retire. Despite the messaging from Wagner commanders shortly after Prigozhin's death that discouraged defection to the Defence Ministry, many fighters have opted to join their sworn enemy. No doubt the offer to remain in Africa earning competitive pay is preferable to possible service in Ukraine, where compensation is worse and risks are greater. Out of sympathy, compromise or self-preservation, the standard Wagner channels and surviving leadership have not subjected the fighters in Africa to the public castigation of Troshev and Khrustal.

The form of the new enterprise and its relationship to the individual fighters varies by country. While the CNN team that visited Bangui in 2023 reported that men had been rotated back to Russia to sign contracts with the Ministry of Defence, other experts on Wagner and the CAR report that these fighters have not signed on.[29] They are instead subject to more or less informal control by the Ministry, who places relatively less strategic significance on the CAR than Prigozhin did. They maintain the Wagner brand and continue to enjoy the benefit of Ministry resources and logistics, an arrangement likely contingent on their cooperation.

Mali holds greater strategic value for Russia, as the lynchpin for its growing influence in the Sahel. Here, the picture is different. Russian security services maintained a strong presence before and during Wagner's arrival, allowing the Defence Ministry's Africa Corps to more conclusively subsume the pre-existing operation and sign its fighters on formally. Subsequently, Wagner fighters under the banner of the Africa Corps have taken part in significant campaigns, including a successful assault that drove Tuareg separatists out of the northern town of Kidal in November 2023.[30]

Kidal had been outside of Bamako's control for nearly a decade, making its capture a major victory for the military government of Mali, and a poignant signal to regional governments that the Africa Corps was no less of a formidable force than Wagner.[31] The fighters themselves, however, maintain their traditions and identities: when they seized Kidal, they flew Wagner's black flag from the tower of the town's old French colonial fort.[32]

These gains and the new, less overtly commercial character of the enterprise have opened new opportunities for Russia in Africa. Wagner struggled to gain purchase in Burkina Faso, in no small part due to the Burkinabe government's scepticism of Prigozhin and his resource-led ventures in the region.[33] The Africa Corps, on the other hand, with its more formal links to the Russian state, has cast itself as a more trustworthy and predictable partner. In late January

2024, the Africa Corps achieved what Wagner had failed to do and deployed more than a hundred Africa Corps fighters to the capital of Ouagadougou on the invitation of the government.[34] The Africa Corps' growing footprint in Burkina Faso is a sign of the limitations of the PMC approach, the advantages of the new model, and the Russian state's continued ambitions for expansion in the Sahel.

Back in Russia, other parts of the Russian state were claiming what Wagner had left behind. Wagner's prison recruits who had survived Bakhmut had received pardons or were languishing in hotels in southern Russia awaiting amnesty.[35] Some of these men were recruited by the Russian National Guard, one of the winners of Wagner's mutiny. Headed by Viktor Zolotov, Putin's former bodyguard, whom Prigozhin had joked with in his restaurateur days in St Petersburg, Russia's National Guard, or Rosgvardiya, is a pillar of the Putin regime's security and an instrument for foreign military intervention that has been deployed abroad in Syria and Ukraine. After the mutiny attempt, Rosgvardiya won the right to operate heavy vehicles and tanks and was given responsibility for elite units previously under the Ministry of Internal Affairs.[36] In August 2023, Rosgvardiya began recruiting from Wagner's former convicts, placing them in roles that ranged from protecting Moscow to guarding territory in occupied Ukraine.[37]

Rosgvardiya was also rumoured to be working towards incorporating more of Wagner into its structure, including talks with Pavel Prigozhin and Lotos – though there was no evidence to support this. Several channels indicated that elements of Wagner's 1st Assault Detachment's 3rd Platoon had arranged with Rosgvardiya to return to Bakhmut as an 'independent unit', but it was unclear how this was organized or with whom members of this unit were contracted.[38] They took photographs with their family members outside the bus station in Rostov holding a Wagner flag. Rosgvardiya under Zolotov perhaps bears less of the taint of the Defence Ministry under Shoigu and Gerasimov; Wagner fighters may consider it less treacherous to work under the National Guard than to join 'the internal enemy'.

Late in October 2023, pro-Wagner channels claimed to confirm this version of events. Aleksey 'Brest' Bergovin, a Wagner instructor in Belarus, had established a Telegram channel where he celebrated Wagner's continuing work, even after Prigozhin's death. He claimed that 'the Wagner Group officially became a unit of the Russian National Guard', retaining its structure and establishing a new base in Russian's Northern Military District.[39] Soon, Russian media began claiming that Wagner had resumed recruitment in places such as Perm. They cited claims from Wagner recruiters that the PMC was now run by Prigozhin's closest thing to an heir apparent, his 25-year-old son Pavel.[40] The claims were supported mostly by the statements of alleged Wagner associates but were at least partly plausible – the State Duma was considering a new law that would allow Rosgvardiya to hire 'volunteers', legalizing their expansion into the realm of semi-formal recruitment.[41]

On 5 February 2024, Anton 'Lotos' Elizarov became the first and only one of the Council of Commanders to publicly bless one of Wagner's new incarnations. He recorded a video in Rostov, in southern Russia, making light of the rumours of his arrest and disappearance. He showed off a meagre cluster of tents and spoke glowingly of Wagner's integration into Rosgvardiya's Volunteer Corps.[42] He has said little since, while Telegram channels allege that under his mismanagement, particularly his failure to attract a large number of fighters, former Wagner fighters have been dispersed from the Volunteer Corps elements that he represents.[43] Wagner veterans were appearing in other areas as well. On 29 October Ramzan Kadyrov said that 170 former Wagner fighters would be joining his Akhmat unit, a claim supported by a Russian television segment that showed fighters bearing Akhmat and Wagner patches training in small-unit tactics.[44] Forces ranging from Shoigu's Defence Ministry to Zolotov's Rosgvardiya and Kadyrov's Akhmat have realized the value of recruiting former Wagner fighters, both for their experience and the branding opportunity. Wagner as a recruitment tool is here to stay, and it will be exploited by Russian networks inside and outside the state for years to come.

Yet aside from their condemnation of the Defence Ministry traitors, and Lotos' tepid celebration of Rosgvardiya's newly formed Volunteer Units, as I write this in the spring of 2024, Wagner's top commanders are mostly silent. Their subordinates are intentional in their comments to the press. No one wants to concede that the group has lost and that Shoigu and Gerasimov, Wagner's chief antagonists, have won.

The most skilled of Wagner's commanders will likely find it hard to retire for the same reason that they joined Wagner in the first place. In the words of Wagner veteran Marat Gabidullin, 'It will be a movement based on inertia by people who can't live another way. Who have forgotten how to live a different life.'[45] The bulk of Wagner's men are likely to continue to fight, whether within other paramilitary units, the Defence Ministry, Rosgvardiya, Redut or some new structure. The same is true of Wagner's top commanders. They bear years of experience that are unique among Russia's armed forces. More importantly, they are indelibly marked with the Wagner brand and myth. They might seek to cash in, recruiting for other forces, but they are bound by a culture of loyalty that, at least for now, persists after Prigozhin's death. Men like Ratibor, Zombie, Lotos and Mekhan, and the litany of Wagner men scattered across Ukraine and the Sahel, will almost certainly find another fight, where each will bring a small part of Wagner with them.

The Global Market for Force

Almost everywhere Wagner went, it shared ground with other mercenaries and foreign interlopers. Wagner was prolific because it was opportunistic and operated in a world full of opportunity.

Authoritarian governments across the developing world demanded both force and politics for hire, and Wagner provided. The future will see more opportunists, and the state's monopoly on violence will continue to slip.

In Mozambique, Wagner competed in a liberalized security market with established South African PMSCs. In Sudan, it entered a political and security sphere already inundated by outside powers such as the UAE, Saudi Arabia and Egypt. In the CAR, Wagner's arrival heralded an uncomfortable partnership with the UN in peace enforcement. In Mali, Wagner replaced a more conventional model of foreign security assistance, allowing the new military government to swap France's Operation Barkhane for Wagner's ruthless counterinsurgency. In Syria, Wagner fought in a war rife with local and foreign mercenaries, national militaries ranging from Turkey to the United States and armed groups from Lebanon, Iran and beyond. In Libya, Wagner was just one of an exceptionally diverse and often confounding cast of mercenaries and outside powers – it coordinated with the UAE and was joined in support for Haftar by the former head of Blackwater, that most famous of Western PMSCs, via the short-lived Project Opus.

Since the end of the Cold War, many scholars and analysts have forecast the end of interstate war.[46] It seemed that conflicts between national armies were a thing of the past, replaced by long-burning civil wars, insurgencies and proxy conflicts. The modern PMSC model was born in the crucible of this post-Cold War order, where it was no longer only states who needed firepower to turn the tide and claim resources or legitimacy. Embattled governments could call on PMSCs, but so could rebel groups and even companies.

Russia's invasion of Ukraine challenged this belief. Politicians, military leaders, scholars and journalists were shocked to see a major territorial war between two developed countries. It looked like a return to the twentieth century – two states arraying tanks, artillery, airpower, missiles and their navies against one another.

The appearance of trench warfare seemed to turn the clock back even further.

A closer look at Russia's war effort revealed that what we were really seeing was the same layered model of war that was on display in places such as Syria and Libya – countries where insurgents formed shifting alliances and governments worked with private actors and paramilitaries to wage war.

This was guided by Russia's need to balance the war effort with domestic political sensitivities, the challenges Russia faced and the tools it had to solve them. Russia had fostered a range of paramilitary organizations to wage a deniable war against Ukraine since 2014. They could now be leveraged to draw in additional fighters. Regional politicians and corporations such as Gazprom were beholden to the desires of the government. They could be tapped to use their resources to create and field new units in exchange for favourable treatment. Ukraine has also leveraged unusual forces in this fight, from armed civil defence units in Kyiv, to Chechen volunteer units, to the Freedom of Russia Legion and the Russian Volunteer Corps, who have carried out attacks even in Russian territory.[47] And, of course, there was Wagner.

Armed with resources far surpassing any other irregular unit and the mandate to draw fighters from Russia's prison population, Wagner was battle-changing. It wasn't a silver bullet; Wagner would not make or break the war for Russia. But it would play an important role for Russia in wearing down the Ukrainian military in Bakhmut, giving breathing room to Russia's military on other fronts and improving their prospects as the war went on. It would leverage the flexibility and freedom conferred by its position, one foot in the state and one foot out, to fight more adaptably and effectively than the Russian military.[48]

During the war, some Russian forces, from individual military units to semi-state networks such as Ramzan Kadyrov's Akhmat, would express grievances directed at Russia's military leadership.

Wagner would take this a step further, to challenge them with force. In the process, the Russian state was exposed not as a single entity driven by Putin's personal desires, but as a competing mass of networks both inside and outside government, which Putin and his inner circle manipulated and directed with incentives and coercion. The individual components fight for survival, resources, legitimacy and the favour of Putin, who could guarantee all the above.

Prigozhin clocked this system for what it was. Putin still held primary legitimacy but other players, even state officials, were only as powerful as the networks behind them. He believed that if he increased the temperature enough, he could cause a reaction that would fundamentally change the system in his favour. His own network, most of all the Company, could secure long-term wealth and influence. He appears to have genuinely believed this was the best thing for Russia. Maybe he fancied himself as a future contender for the top spot, earned through the criminal empire. Maybe, like Putin, he wanted to be a great man of Russian history.

Russia's semi-state networks were not independent, however. They were parasitic. They fed off the state that they had hollowed out, turning it from an agent to an instrument, a pool of resources to be looted.

Ultimately, Prigozhin controlled a powerful network, but it could not bend the power of the state itself, the superstructure that ultimately determined which networks would succeed or fail. Prigozhin had been exceptionally talented when it came to serving the state, but he was less well versed in how to wield it for his own ends. Shoigu, Gerasimov and the security elites around them were talented politicians who were closer to the centre and who had the better pitch for Putin: stability.

We can be nearly certain that Putin himself ordered Prigozhin's assassination. In doing so, he made a compromise that will challenge him for the rest of his rule – he made good on his public word for justice and reneged on his private word for amnesty. He signalled that the state has one primary means to resolve conflict: violence. Prigozhin's mutiny and death marked a turning point in Russia's acceleration down a path of internal violence and strife, a return to the 'wild '90s', when disputes between networks were resolved outside the law and might made right. It won't lead to civil war, not immediately, but it is a lesson for anyone seeking to negotiate with Putin in the future, best summarized by Zelenskyy when he told the UN, 'Ask Prigozhin if one bets on Putin's promises.'[49]

Wagner was a harbinger not just for Russia's future, but for the future of global conflict. Wagner and the other networks Russia has deployed against its adversaries represent not only Russia's reliance on these networks, but their growing primacy globally. Some have termed this brand of conflict 'irregular warfare', or 'grey-zone competition', implying that it is somehow anomalous and foreign, occupying a space outside the 'black and white' of politics, commerce and war. As others have pointed out, this pattern is far from new.[50] War has always been fought beyond the battlefield, to include information operations and economic competition. States and the myriad networks they contain – corporations, political parties, religious movements, militaries, intelligence agencies – have always competed with one another using means beyond simple violence and by leveraging proxies to do work on their behalf, from Italian condottieri to modern mercenaries.

What is novel about these networks and the way they compete is their context. They occupy a world of global capital where networks, including those violent and criminal, can move money and goods over greater distances at greater speeds than ever before. This gives them advantages over the slower, politically constrained leviathan of the state. The state needs them because they can do things it cannot or accomplish them faster and more cheaply – particularly when they are politically costly, like fighting wars. The state isn't going away; it still holds unparalleled resources through the right to tax and confer legitimacy, but it will be increasingly reliant on the sub-state networks it fosters to compete on the global stage.

We might assume that authoritarian states, less constrained by democratic politics, would be less reliant on such networks. They can undertake policies and wage war whether their people want to or not. Yet most authoritarian states are at least semi-competitive and, like Russia, must maintain legitimacy, if not among their people, then among powerful patrons who would challenge unscrupulous leadership. Even the most totalitarian regimes, countries such as North Korea, must engage internationally to keep powerful cliques satisfied with wealth and their militaries and security apparatus armed against enemies foreign and domestic. For this, they must turn to the outside world. This makes them vulnerable to instruments like sanctions that the international community can apply against the worst pariahs, but it leaves windows of opportunity. North Korea has run successful sanctions evasions operations the world over to give its leadership access to everything from luxury goods to nuclear technology. The liberal world order of trade and commerce is simply too sprawling, too accommodating of secrecy and inequality, to prevent criminal actors, even the most violent and abhorrent, from exploiting it.

As states, particularly authoritarian states, become more reliant on sub-state networks to engage in competition, we will see more Wagners. It is unlikely that they will look exactly like Wagner in their scale or operations. But states, both weak and strong, will increasingly need to privatize force. Violence, perhaps the sole realm in which the state has traditionally maintained a monopoly in the liberal world order, is simply too inviting. It is the most politically costly and, as Wagner and other PMCs have shown, it is an arena in which semi-state networks can perform exceptionally well.

Even as PMCs proliferate, particularly those like Wagner which act at the behest of authoritarian states, it does not have to mean that we face a more violent future. We can change the context of global capital that permits violent and criminal networks to flourish. If we are willing to sacrifice secrecy and expend political capital to compel the world's havens for dirty money to become transparent or suffer economic and diplomatic costs, we can create a less welcoming environment for actors like Wagner.

Perhaps more boldly, we can even learn to leverage these tools ourselves – not to protect authoritarian governments as Wagner has, but to more decisively and effectively defend nascent democracies and the world's most vulnerable populations. The rise of 'peace enforcement' operations demonstrates a global acknowledgement that security, backed by force, is a prerequisite for peace in many of the world's most protracted conflicts. The right actors, governed by the right laws and subject to accountability in their home jurisdictions, could turn the tide for governments seeking to protect their people from extremists and insurgents. As we saw in Chapter Three, these actors can often be held to even greater standards than conventional militaries. Given incentives based on conflict resolution and paired with coordinated and committed diplomatic efforts, we may find that these networks can be leveraged in the interests of peace as much as war. We must consider whether, in the years since Kofi Annan invoked the concept in 1994, we are 'ready to privatize peace'.

To defeat networks like Wagner itself, we will need to think beyond force and coercion. Wagner is both the product of a global economy that permits secrecy and tolerates crime and a failure of Western policies in the developing world. Corruption, lack of human development and authoritarian governments in the global South have created conditions in which actors like Wagner find fertile ground.

During Sudan's democratic transition, grass-roots civil society had for years sounded the alarm about the grip that the military and paramilitary organizations such as the RSF held over the economy and their relationship with actors such as Wagner. Western policy sought a middle ground and continued to engage with authoritarian actors such as the RSF in the hopes that they would reform given the right incentives. Had we listened more closely to the diagnoses of the civilians who had opened the path for democratic transition in the 2019 revolution, we might have been able to enact more decisive policy that would have further empowered civilian leadership, created a less inviting environment for Wagner, and, most importantly, averted Sudan's current civil war.

Similarly, Ukraine has fought Wagner and its fellow violent entrepreneurs for years and in ways that no other country has. It has alerted its Western partners to the gravity of the threat posed not just by Russia, but by its criminal networks, since 2014. For Ukraine, the fight is existential. Even if Wagner as we knew it is gone, this war is a testing ground for both Russia's approach to interstate war that leverages these groups and the international community's resolve in countering them. Support for Ukraine's fight for survival is vital to stem the rise of global networks such as the Wagner Group. Investment in Ukraine's defence is a statement that both wars of conquest and the use of unaccountable violent organizations like Wagner will be met with a committed, collective response that no revanchist authoritarian government can overcome. Wagner will cast a long shadow into the future, one that extends beyond the death of Prigozhin. The steps that our governments take in the months and years to come will determine how far that shadow stretches.

REFERENCES

1 ATROCITY EXHIBITION

1 Candace Rondeaux, 'Building the Wagner Group Brand: How Yevgeny Prigozhin Sold a Battlefield Rumor to the World', *New America Foundation*, www.newamerica.org, 16 February 2023.
2 Alec Bertina, 'FSB Alpha Group: Russia's Elite A Team', *Grey Dynamics*, https://greydynamics.com, 22 September 2023.

2 SOUS CHEF

1 Fyodor Dostoyevsky, *Demons* [1872], trans. Constance Garnett (New York, 1913), p. 216.
2 Evgeniy Vyshenkov, 'С каждого ларька платил по 100 долларов бандитам', Gorod-812, https://online812.ru, 28 February 2011.
3 Anastasiya Kirilenko, 'Tambovskaya Gang Calling: How Mafia Keeps in Touch with Putin's Entourage (Intercepted Conversations)', *The Insider*, https://theins.ru, 15 November 2018.
4 'Кто такой Пригожин', *Novaya Gazeta*, https://novayagazeta.ru, 2 September 2011.
5 Anastasiya Kirilenko, 'Владимир Путин и казино: кто остался в выигрыше', *Radio Svoboda*, www.svoboda.org, 28 February 2012.
6 Karen Dawisha, *Putin's Kleptocracy* (New York, 2014), pp. 127–8.
7 Michael Lewis, 'Has Anyone Seen the President?', *Bloomberg*, www.bloomberg.com, 9 February 2018.
8 Mikhail Komin, 'Как кувалда в масло: Кто в российской элите может поддерживать Пригожина', *Carnegie Politika*, https://carnegieendowment.org, 26 June 2023.
9 The Alliance for Securing Democracy and C4ADS, 'Illicit Influence. Part One: A Case Study of the First Czech Russian Bank', https://securingdemocracy.gmfus.org, 28 December 2018.

3 ORIGINS

1 Anton Stepanenko, dir., *Солдаты напрокат*, Channel 1, 2013.
2 Sean McFate, *The Modern Mercenary: Private Armies and What They Mean for World Order* (New York, 2014), pp. 26–40.

3 P. W. Singer, *Corporate Warriors: The Rise of the Privatized Military Industry* (New York, 2003), pp. 19–39.

4 Kofi Annan, 'Secretary-General Reflects on "Intervention" in Thirty-Fifth Annual Ditchley Foundation Lecture', United Nations press release, https://press.un.org, 26 June 1998.

5 Stepanenko, dir., *Солдаты напрокат.*

6 Denis Korotkov, 'Заложники Нигерии ждут коммандос от президента', *Fontanka*, https://fontanka.ru, 25 February 2013.

7 Claudia Rosett, 'Russia's Chariot Calls at Iran', *Forbes*, www.forbes.com, 6 March 2012.

8 Ibid.

9 Kirill Metelev, 'Русские в Сирии', *Versiya*, https://neva.versia.ru, 7 November 2013.

10 Denis Korotkov, 'Последний бой "Славянского корпуса"', *Fontanka*, https://fontanka.ru, 14 November 2013.

11 'Putin Chef's Kisses of Death: Russia's Shadow Army's State-Run Structure Exposed', *Bellingcat*, www.bellingcat.com, 14 August 2020.

4 UKRAINE, 2014–15: THE FIRST CAMPAIGNS

1 Irek Murtazin, 'Задачи ставили генералы', *Novaya Gazeta*, https://novayagazeta.ru, 29 June 2023.

2 Telegram post, @NeoficialniyBeZsonoV, 9 July 2023.

3 'Wagner Mercenaries with GRU-Issued Passports: Validating SBU's Allegation', *Bellingcat*, www.bellingcat.com, 30 January 2019.

4 Nadana Fridrichson, 'Bakhmut', Fridrih_Show, https://m.dzen.ru/fridrihshow, 21 June 2023.

5 Sergey Khazov-Kassiya, 'Проект "Мясорубка": Рассказывают три командира "ЧВК Вагнера"', *Radio Svoboda*, www.svoboda.org, 7 March 2018.

6 Denis Korotkov, '"Хайль Петрович" История Дмитрия Уткина – человека, который подарил группе "Вагнера" название', *Dossier Center*, https://dossier.center, 10 April 2023.

7 Marat Gabidullin, *Io, Commandante di Wagner* (Milan, 2022), p. 56.

8 'PMC "Wagner" Commander Utkin Conversation with Deputy Troshev', *Euromaidan Press*, www.youtube.com, 3 November 2017.

9 'MH17 – Russian GRU Commander "Orion" Identified as Oleg Ivannikov', *Bellingcat*, www.bellingcat.com, 25 May 2018.

10 'PMC "Wagner" commander Utkin Conversation with Deputy Troshev'.

11 Dmitriy Cheretun, 'Как вагнеровцы подбитую под Дебальцево технику РФ вывозили: аудио', *Liga*, https://liga.net, 19 May 2018.

5 SYRIA: BLOOD AND TREASURE

1 Pjotr Sauer, '"Mercenaries Have Skills Armies Lack": Former Wagner Operative Opens Up', *The Guardian*, www.theguardian.com, 10 February 2022.

2 Denis Korotkov, 'Кого Россия потеряла в Сирии', *Fontanka*, www.fontanka.ru, 21 August 2017.

3 Marat Gabidullin, *В Одну Реку Дважды* (Ekaterinburg, 2022), p. 54.

4 John Sparks, 'Revealed: Russia's "Secret Syria Mercenaries"', *Sky News*, https://news.sky.com, 10 August 2016. *Soldiers for Hire*, dir. Anton Stepanenko, Channel 1, 2013.

5 Telegram post, @concordgroup_official, 12 June 2023. Denis Korotkov, 'Заложники Нигерии ждут коммандос от президента', *Fontanka*, https://fontanka.ru, 25 February 2013.

6 Amy Mackinnon, 'Putin's Shadow Warriors Stake Claim to Syria's Oil', *Foreign Policy*, https://foreignpolicy.com, 17 May 2021.

7 'Жаба и Минобороны: Как поссорились Евгений Викторович с Сергеем Кужугетовичем', *The Insider*, https://theins.ru, 12 May 2023.

8 Sarah Rainsford and Kathryn Armstrong, 'Wagner Mutiny: Group Fully Funded by Russia, Says Putin', *BBC*, www.bbc.co.uk, 27 June 2023.

9 'Illicit Influence – Part Two: The Energy Weapon', *German Marshall Fund*, https://securingdemocracy.gmfus.org, 25 April 2019.

10 Denis Korotkov, 'Без "Щита"', *Novaya Gazeta*, https://novayagazeta.ru, 29 July 2019.

11 Candace Rondeaux, 'Decoding the Wagner Group: Analyzing the Role of Private Military Security Contractors in Russian Proxy Warfare', www.newamerica.org, 17 November 2019.

12 'Россия заявила о завершении операции по разгрому боевиков в районе Акербата', *RIA Novosti*, https://ria.ru, 25 August 2017.

13 '"Ребята, вы предназначены для войны"', *Meduza*, https://meduza.io, 1 December 2020.

14 Kevin Maurer, 'Special Forces Soldiers Reveal First Details of Battle with Russian Mercenaries in Syria', *The War Horse*, https://thewarhorse.org, 11 May 2023.

15 'Евгений Пригожин о трагедии 8 февраля 2018 в Хшаме', https://telegra.ph, 12 June 2023.

16 'Частная армия для президента: история самого деликатного поручения Евгения Пригожина', *The Bell*, https://thebell.io, 29 January 2019.

17 Ellen Nakashima, Karen DeYoung and Liz Sly, 'Putin Ally Said to Be in Touch with Kremlin, Assad before His Mercenaries Attacked U.S. Troops', *Washington Post*, www.washingtonpost.com, 22 February 2018.

6 SUDAN AND THE CAR: THE NEXT FRONTIER

1 Wasil Ali, 'Russia Says Fighter Pilot Shot Down in Sudan Was an Ex-Military Officer', *Sudan Tribune*, https://sudantribune.com, 29 May 2008.

2 See the document filed as 'United States of America v. Internet Research Agency LLC et al.', announced by the U.S. Department of Justice, www.justice.gov, 16 February 2018.

3 Khadija Sharife, Lara Dihmis and Erin Klazar, 'Documents Reveal Wagner's Golden Ties to Sudanese Military Companies', *Organized Crime and Corruption Reporting Project*, www.occrp.org, 2 November 2022.

4 Janean Davis, 'Great Power Competition Implications in Africa: The Chinese Communist Party', written statement to the U.S. House of Representatives Foreign Affairs Committee, https://foreignaffairs.house.gov, 18 April 2023.

5 Michelle D. Gavin, 'Major Power Rivalry in Africa', *Council on Foreign Relations*, www.cfr.org, May 2021.

6 Candace Rondeaux, 'How a Man Linked to Prigozhin, "Putin's Chef," Infiltrated the United Nations', *Daily Beast*, www.thedailybeast.com, 27 November 2020.

7 Roman Popkov, '"Публичные казни мародеров и другие зрелищные мероприятия": советы людей Пригожина свергнутому диктатору', *MBKh Media*, https://mbk-news.appspot.com, 25 April 2019.

8 Ibid.

9 Tim Lister, Sebastian Shukla and Nima Elbagir, 'Fake News and Public Executions: Documents Show a Russian Company's Plan for Quelling Protests in Sudan', *CNN*, www.cnn.com, 25 April 2019.

10 'Убийство журналистов было только началом', *Dossier Center*, https://dossier.center, 18 June 2023.

11 'Russia Provides Free Military Aid to Central African Republic – Foreign Ministry', *TASS*, https://tass.com, 22 March 2018.

12 'Убийство журналистов было только началом', *Dossier Center*, https://dossier.center, 18 June 2023.

13 'Survivors Describe Massacre in Bangui', *New York Times*, www.nytimes.com, 30 September 1979.

14 David Smith, '"Cannibal" Dictator Bokassa Given Posthumous Pardon', *The Guardian*, www.theguardian.com, 3 December 2010.

15 Ruth Maclean, Elian Peltier and Anatoly Kurmanaev, 'Russian Official in Africa Wounded by Package Bomb, Moscow Says', *New York Times*, www.nytimes.com, 16 December 2022.

16 Benoit Faucon and Gabriele Steinhauser, 'The Elusive Figure Running Wagner's Embattled Empire of Gold and Diamonds', *Wall Street Journal*, www.wsj.com, 21 September 2023.

17 'Wagner Mercenaries with GRU-Issued Passports: Validating SBU's Allegation', *Bellingcat*, www.bellingcat.com, 30 January 2019.

18 Nathalia Dukhan, 'Dangerous Divisions: The Central African Republic Faces the Threat of Secession', *Enough Project*, https://enoughproject.org, 15 February 2017.

19 Paula Dear and Samuel Hauenstein Swan, 'Displaced and Forgotten in Central African Republic', *Al Jazeera*, www.aljazeera.com, 27 July 2016.

20 'Making the Central African Republic's Latest Peace Agreement Stick', *International Crisis Group*, www.crisisgroup.org, 18 June 2019.

21 Ibid.
22 Adrienne Surprenant, 'Central African Troops and Russian Mercenaries Accused of Abuses in Anti-Rebel Offensive', *New Humanitarian*, www.thenewhumanitarian.org, 29 April 2021.
23 'Rapport d'enquete sur l'attaque de Boyo, préfecture de la Ouaka', *Office of the United Nations High Commissioner for Human Rights*, www.ohchr.org, 25 July 2022.
24 Ibid.
25 'Architects of Terror', *The Sentry*, https://thesentry.org, June 2023.
26 'Letter Dated 25 June 2021 from the Panel of Experts on the Central African Republic Extended Pursuant to Resolution 2536 (2020) Addressed to the President of the Security Council', *United Nations Security Council*, https://digitallibrary.un.org, 25 June 2021.
27 Ibid.
28 Ibid.

7 LIBYA: BLUEPRINT FOR CONTEMPORARY WAR

1 'Libya: Violations Related to Mercenary Activities Must Be Investigated', *Office of the United Nations High Commissioner for Human Rights*, www.ohchr.org, 17 June 2020.
2 Isabel Ivanescu and Eva Kahan, 'Syria's Wretched Foreign Legion', *New Lines Magazine*, https://newlinesmag.com, 1 June 2021.
3 Jack Margolin, 'Paper Trails', *C4ADS*, https://c4ads.org, 13 June 2019.
4 Irina Dolinina and Alesya Marokhovskaya, 'Спецы и специи', *Novaya Gazeta*, https://novayagazeta.ru, 4 February 2019.
5 Ilya Barabanov and Nader Ibrahim, 'The Lost Tablet and the Secret Documents: Clues Pointing to a Shadowy Russian Army', *BBC*, www.bbc.co.uk, 11 August 2021.
6 'Washington's Secret War against Wagner's Planes', *Africa Intelligence*, www.africaintelligence.com, 3 May 2022.
7 Gerjon, 'From Russia to Libya and the Central African Republic: Russia's Paramilitary Ilyushin Fleet', *Gerjon's Aircraft Finds*, https://gerjon.substack.com, 2 July 2022.
8 Benjamin Roger, 'La Mystérieuse Compagnie aérienne de Wagner au Mali', *Jeune Afrique*, www.jeuneafrique.com, 27 January 2023.
9 'Letter Dated 3 February 2023 from the Panel of Experts on the Central African Republic Extended Pursuant to Resolution 2648 (2022) Addressed to the President of the Security Council', *United Nations Security Council*, https://digitallibrary.un.org, 10 February 2023.
10 'Letter Dated 24 May 2022 from the Panel of Experts on Libya Established Pursuant to Resolution 1973 (2011) Addressed to the President of the Security Council', *United Nations Security Council*, https://digitallibrary.un.org, 27 May 2022.
11 Peter Kirechu, 'Assets in Flight: Libya's Flying Armories', *C4ADS*, https://c4ads.org, 2 January 2020.

12 Candace Rondeaux, Oliver Imhof and Jack Margolin, 'The Abu Dhabi Express: Analyzing the Wagner Group's Libya Logistics Pipeline & Operations', *New America Foundation*, www.newamerica.org, 3 November 2021.

13 'Letter Dated 24 May 2022 from the Panel of Experts on Libya Established Pursuant to Resolution 1973 (2011)'.

14 Samer al-Atrush, 'Russian Missile System Spirited Out of Libya by U.S.', *Sunday Times*, www.thetimes.co.uk, 28 January 2021.

15 Matthew Agius, 'Investigators Uncover Roles of Mercenaries in UAE-Backed Libya Helicopter Gunship Plan', *Malta Today*, www.maltatoday. com.mt, 26 May 2020.

16 'Letter Dated 8 March 2021 from the Panel of Experts on Libya Established Pursuant to Resolution 1973 (2011) Addressed to the President of the Security Council', *United Nations Security Council*, https:// digitallibrary.un.org, 8 March 2021, p. 31.

17 Declan Walsh, 'Erik Prince, Trump Ally, Violated Libya Arms Embargo, UN Report Says', *New York Times*, www.nytimes.com, 19 February 2021.

18 'Letter Dated 8 March 2021 from the Panel of Experts on Libya Established Pursuant to Resolution 1973 (2011)', pp. 310–29.

19 Ibid.

20 Ibid.

21 Benoit Faucon, 'Russian Fighters Help Tighten Rebel Control of Libya's Largest Oil Field', *Wall Street Journal*, www.wsj.com, 26 June 2020.

22 Ilya Barabanov and Nader Ibrahim, 'Wagner: Scale of Russian Mercenary Mission in Libya Exposed', BBC, www.bbc.com, 11 August 2021.

23 Marc Bennetts, 'Airstrike Kills "Kremlin Mercenaries" Backing Libyan Strongman Khalifa Haftar', *Sunday Times*, www.thetimes.co.uk, 4 October 2019.

24 Maria Tsvetkova, 'Exclusive: Russian Clinic Treated Mercenaries Injured in Secret Wars', *Reuters*, www.reuters.com, 7 January 2020.

25 Alton A. Ozler, 'Libya: A Catastrophe for Russia's Pantsir S1 Air Defense System', *RealClear Defense*, www.realcleardefense.com, 19 June 2020.

26 Tsvetkova, 'Exclusive: Russian Clinic Treated Mercenaries Injured in Secret Wars'.

27 Nick Paton Walsh and Sarah El Sirgany, 'Foreign Fighters Were Meant to Leave Libya This Week. A Huge Trench Being Dug by Russian-Backed Mercenaries Indicates They Plan to Stay', CNN, www.cnn.com, 22 January 2021.

8 THE SAHEL: CRISIS AND OPPORTUNITY

1 Working Group on the Use of Mercenaries et al., 'Letter to the High Commissioner for Human Rights', *Office of the United Nations High Commissioner for Human Rights*, www.ohchr.org, 30 December 2022.

2 Alexandra Reza, 'Why Are French Soldiers in the Sahel? Protesters Have an Answer', *The Guardian*, www.theguardian.com, 20 February 2020.

3 John Irish and David Lewis, 'EXCLUSIVE Deal Allowing Russian Mercenaries into Mali Is Close – Sources', *Reuters*, www.reuters.com, 13 September 2021.

4 Jack Margolin, https://twitter.com, post dated 27 November 2021.

5 Aude Dejaifve and Poline Tchoubar, 'Des Mercenaires Wagner entraînant (déjà) des soldats maliens: deux photos et des doutes', *Observateurs France 24*, https://observers.france24.com, 26 November 2021.

6 'Treasury Targets Malian Officials Facilitating Wagner Group', *U.S. Department of the Treasury*, https://home.treasury.gov, 24 July 2023.

7 'Congratulations on the Graduation of the Class of 2019!', *National Defense University*, https://ismo.ndu.edu, 25 July 2019.

8 Fred Muvunyi, 'Was Russia behind the Coup in Mali?', *DW*, www.dw.com, 26 August 2020.

9 'Treasury Sanctions the Head of the Wagner Group in Mali', *U.S. Department of the Treasury*, https://home.treasury.gov, 25 May 2023.

10 Irish and Lewis, 'EXCLUSIVE Deal'.

11 Cyril Bensimon and Morgane Le Cam, 'Malian State Security Suspected of Financing Russian Wagner Mercenaries', *Le Monde*, www.lemonde.fr, 4 February 2023.

12 Benoit Faucson and Joe Parkinson, 'Russian Mercenaries Project the Kremlin's Power Far from Its Troubles in Ukraine', *Wall Street Journal*, www.wsj.com, 21 August 2022.

13 @Gerjon_, https://twitter.com, post dated 19 December 2021.

14 Wassim Nasr, 'How the Wagner Group Is Aggravating the Jihadi Threat in the Sahel', *CTC Sentinel*, xv/11 (November/December 2022), pp. 21–31.

15 Tanguy Berthement, 'Au Mali, premiers accrochages entre Wagner et djihadistes', *Le Figaro*, www.lefigaro.fr, 5 January 2022.

16 Nasr, 'How the Wagner Group Is Aggravating the Jihadi Threat in the Sahel', p. 23.

17 'François Hollande's African Adventures', *The Economist*, www.economist.com, 21 July 2014.

18 Eyder Peralta, 'France Kills Top West Africa ISIS Leader in Drone Strike', *NPR*, www.npr.org, 16 September 2021.

19 Nasr, 'How the Wagner Group Is Aggravating the Jihadi Threat in the Sahel', pp. 25–6.

20 'Letter Dated 3 August 2022 from the Panel of Experts on Mali Established Pursuant to Resolution 2374 (2017) Addressed to the President of the Security Council', *United Nations Security Council*, https://digitallibrary.un.org, 3 August 2022.

21 Nasr, 'How the Wagner Group Is Aggravating the Jihadi Threat in the Sahel', pp. 24–5.

22 Jason Burke, 'Russian Mercenaries Accused of Civilian Massacre in Mali', *The Guardian*, www.theguardian.com, 1 November 2022.

23 'Mali: New Atrocities by Malian Army, Apparent Wagner Fighters', *Human Rights Watch*, www.hrw.org, 24 July 2023.

24 Hamza Mohamed, 'Analysis: What's Next for Mali after MINUSMA Withdrawal?', *Al Jazeera*, www.aljazeera.com, 3 July 2023.

25 'Mali Must Allow UN Peacekeeping Mission to Fulfill Its Mandate', *Voice of America*, https://editorials.voa.gov, 28 April 2023.

26 'Ivory Coast to Withdraw from Mali Peacekeeping Force – Letter', *Reuters*, www.reuters.com, 15 November 2022.

27 Sylvie Corbet and Samuel Petrequin, 'France and EU to Withdraw Troops from Mali, Remain in Region', AP, https://apnews.com, 17 February 2022. Michael Schwirtz, 'Wagner's Influence Extends Far beyond Ukraine, Leaked Documents Show', *New York Times*, www.nytimes.com, 8 April 2023.

28 Mathieu Olivier and Benjamin Roger, 'Wagner in Mali: An Exclusive Investigation into Putin's Mercenaries', *Africa Report*, www.theafricareport.com, 18 February 2022.

29 Ladd Serwat, Heni Nsaibia and Nichita Gurcov, 'Moving Out of the Shadows: Shifts in Wagner Group Operations around the World', ACLED, https://acleddata.com, 2 August 2023.

30 'Mali: Barkhane mène des opérations anti-terroristes dans la région de Gao', RFI, www.rfi.fr, 23 February 2018.

31 'Mali: Dan Nam Ambassagou refuse sa dissolution demandée par les autorités', RFI, www.rfi.fr, 28 March 2019.

32 Andrew Lebovich, 'Stabilising Mali – Why Europe Must Look beyond Technicalities', *European Council on Foreign Relations*, https://ecfr.eu, 24 May 2017.

33 Nasr, 'How the Wagner Group Is Aggravating the Jihadi Threat in the Sahel', p. 23.

34 Working Group on the Use of Mercenaries et al., 'Letter to the High Commissioner for Human Rights'.

35 'Mali's Army Launches Probe into Alleged Killings of Civilians', *Barron's*, www.barrons.com, 8 October 2022 (originally published by Agence France-Presse).

36 Benjamin Roger, 'Mali: In Nia Ouro, Wagner's Men "Tore Off Women's Clothes and Raped Them"', *Africa Report*, www.theafricareport.com, 9 September 2022.

37 Nick Turse, 'Wagner Group Disappeared and Executed Civilians in Mali', *The Intercept*, https://theintercept.com, 24 July 2023.

38 David Baché, 'Mali: Soldats maliens, russes et chasseurs dozos accusés de vols massifs de bétail', RFI, www.rfi.fr, 24 November 2022.

39 Wassim Nasr, https://twitter.com, post dated 31 October 2022.

40 Serwat, Nsaibia and Gurcov, 'Moving Out of the Shadows'; 'Islamic State Sahel Province Releases Photos Documenting Execution of Two Alleged Spies of Russian Wagner Group in Mali', MEMRI *Jihad and Terrorism Threat Monitor*, www.memri.org, 9 August 2023.

41 Kathryn Armstrong, 'Niger Coup: Wagner Taking Advantage of Instability – Antony Blinken', *BBC*, www.bbc.com, 8 August 2023.

42 Janean Davis, 'Great Power Competition Implications in Africa: The Chinese Communist Party', written statement to the U.S. House of Representatives Foreign Affairs Committee, https://foreignaffairs.house.gov, 18 April 2023.

43 Rinaldo Depagne and Mathieu Pellerin, 'An Initial Assessment of Burkina Faso's Transitional Leadership', *International Crisis Group*, www.crisisgroup.org, 14 September 2022.

44 Jack Margolin, https://twitter.com, post dated 7 August 2023.

45 Morgane Le Cam, 'How the Russian Propaganda Machine Works in Africa', *Le Monde*, www.lemonde.fr, 31 July 2023.

46 Elliot Smith, 'Niger Coup Draws Condemnation from Russia and the West as Regional Body Threatens Force', *CNBC*, www.cnbc.com, 31 July 2023.

47 'Coup d'État au Burkina Faso: Le parrain du groupe Wagner salue une "nouvelle ère de décolonisation"', *Le Monde*, www.lemonde.fr, 26 January 2022.

48 Sam Mednick, 'After Burkina Faso Ousts French, Russia's Wagner May Arrive', *AP*, https://apnews.com, 7 April 2023.

49 Philip Obaji Jr, 'African President Was Ousted Just Weeks after Refusing to Pay Russian Paramilitaries', *Daily Beast*, www.thedailybeast.com, 25 January 2022.

50 Aleksandr Ivanov, post dated 25 January 2022, *Officers Union for International Security*, https://officersunion.org.

51 Jeff Seldin, 'U.S. Aware of Allegations of Russian Links to Burkinabe Coup', *Voice of America*, www.voanews.com, 27 January 2022.

52 Edward Mcallister, 'Who Is Ibrahim Traore, the Soldier behind Burkina Faso's Latest Coup?', *Reuters*, www.reuters.com, 4 October 2022.

53 Telegram post, @prigozhin_hat, 1 October 2022.

54 Elian Peltier, 'In Burkina Faso, the Man Who Once Led a Coup Is Ousted by One', *New York Times*, www.nytimes.com, 2 October 2022.

55 Telegram post, @orchestra_w, 27 July 2023.

56 Jack Margolin, https://twitter.com, post dated 12 August 2023.

57 Armstrong, 'Niger Coup: Wagner Taking Advantage of Instability'.

58 Sam Mednick, 'Niger's Junta Asks for Help from Russian Group Wagner as It Faces Military Intervention Threat', *AP*, https://apnews.com, 5 August 2023.

59 'Acting Deputy Secretary of State Victoria Nuland on the Situation in Niger', *U.S. Department of State*, www.state.gov, 7 August 2023.

60 Nicholas Bariyo and Benoit Faucon, 'A U.S. Ally Promised to Send Aid to Sudan. It Sent Weapons Instead', *Wall Street Journal*, www.wsj.com, 10 August 2023.

61 Jared Malsin and Benoit Faucon, 'Russia's Wagner Offered Arms to Sudanese General Battling Army', *Wall Street Journal*, www.wsj.com, 21 April 2023.

62 Dan De Luce, 'u.s. Accuses Russia's Wagner Group Mercenaries of Fueling War in Sudan', NBC, www.nbcnews.com, 26 May 2023.

63 Nima Elbagir et al., 'Exclusive: Evidence Emerges of Russia's Wagner Arming Militia Leader Battling Sudan's Army', CNN, www.cnn.com, 21 April 2023.

64 Jason Burke, 'A War for Our Age: How the Battle for Sudan Is Being Fuelled by Forces Far beyond Its Borders', The Guardian, www.theguardian.com, 30 April 2023.

65 Benoit Faucon, 'u.s. Intelligence Points to Wagner Plot against Key Western Ally in Africa', Wall Street Journal, www.wsj.com, 23 February 2023.

66 Edouard Takadji, 'Thousands Demonstrate in Chad against Military Transition', AP, https://apnews.com, 27 April 2021.

67 Mat Nashed, 'The Soft-Power Campaign of Sudan's RSF Leader "Hemedti"', Al Jazeera, www.aljazeera.com, 20 April 2023.

68 'The Future of Sudan's Resistance Committees', The Horn, www.crisisgroup.org, 26 July 2023.

69 'Sudan Opposition Welcome u.s. Sanctions against Central Reserve Police', Dabanga Sudan, www.dabangasudan.org, 23 March 2023.

70 Abdelmagid Elfeky, 'Recovery of Stolen Assets Amassed from Corruption Crimes. Egypt–Nigeria Case Studies', MA thesis, International Anti-Corruption Academy, 25 September 2022.

71 'Treasury Sanctions Three Individuals for Their Roles in the Conflict in South Sudan', u.s. Department of the Treasury, press release, https://home.treasury.gov, 14 December 2018.

72 See 'Seiden Law, Led the Successful Effort from the Start to Remove General Israel Ziv from the u.s. Treasury OFAC Sanctions List', www.seidenlaw.com, 28 February 2020.

73 'Treasury Targets Corruption Linked to Dan Gertler in the Democratic Republic of Congo', u.s. Department of the Treasury, press release, https://home.treasury.gov, 6 December 2021.

74 Saleha Mohsin, Nick Wadhams and Michael J. Kavanagh, 'Israeli Billionaire Loses Trump-Granted Sanction Reprieve', Bloomberg, www.bloomberg.com, 8 March 2021.

75 Aram Roston, 'A Middle East Monarchy Hired American Ex-Soldiers to Kill Its Political Enemies: This Could Be the Future of War', Buzzfeed, www.buzzfeednews.com, 16 October 2018.

9 PILLAGE

1 'Architects of Terror', The Sentry, https://thesentry.org, June 2023.

2 Nima Elbagir et al., 'Russia Is Plundering Gold in Sudan to Boost Putin's War Effort in Ukraine', CNN, https://edition.cnn.com, 29 July 2022.

3 Simon Marks and Stephanie Baker, 'What Wagner's Mutiny Means for Its Sprawling Business Empire', Bloomberg, www.bloomberg.com, 27 June 2023.

4 Ibid.

5 'Лучшие друзья Пригожина', *Dossier Center*, https://dossier.center, 2 December 2022.

6 'Artisanal Mining and Property Rights under the Strengthening Tenure and Resource Rights II (STARR II) IDIQ, Quarterly Progress report, April 1–June 30, 2022', *USAID*, www.land-links.org, July 2022.

7 Marks and Baker, 'What Wagner's Mutiny Means for Its Sprawling Business Empire'.

8 Erin Banco, Sarah Anne Aarup and Anastasiia Carrier, 'Inside the Stunning Growth of Russia's Wagner Group', *Politico*, www.politico.com, 18 February 2023.

9 Elbagir et al., 'Russia Is Plundering Gold in Sudan to Boost Putin's War Effort in Ukraine'.

10 Eeben Barlow, 'Russian PMC Wagner's Set-Backs in Mozambique', https://eebenbarlowsmilitaryandsecurityblog.blogspot.com, 2 December 2019.

11 Michael Weiss and Pierre Vaux, 'The Company You Keep: Yevgeny Prigozhin's Influence Operations in Africa', *Free Russia Foundation*, www.4freerussia.org, 29 September 2020.

12 Robyn Dixon, 'Russian Political Action Man Sets Up Shop in Kabul in Bid to Win Deals for Moscow', *Washington Post*, www.washingtonpost.com, 10 January 2022.

13 Thomas Moller-Nielson, 'Russian Mercenary Group Wagner Allegedly Exporting Diamonds to Belgium', *Brussels Times*, www.brusselstimes.com, 2 December 2022.

14 AXMIN INC., consolidated financial statements, years ending 31 December 2018 and 2019, 9 June 2020.

15 Jenne Jan Holtland, 'Wagners bloedgeld wordt witgewassen in de blinkende wolkenkrabbers van Dubai', *de Volkskrant*, www.volkskrant.nl, 19 July 2023.

16 Candace Rondeaux, 'The Tangled, Mercenary Network of "Putin's Chef" Is Starting to Unravel', *World Politics Review*, www.worldpoliticsreview.com, 4 October 2019.

17 Miles Johnson, 'Wagner Inc: A Russian Warlord and His Lawyers', *Financial Times*, www.ft.com, 24 January 2023.

18 'ACF Investigation: Yevgeny Prigozhin Owns Assets Worth Trillions of Rubles', https://acf.international, 7 July 2023.

19 David D. Kirkpatrick, Mona El-Naggar and Michael Forsythe, 'How a Playground for the Rich Could Undermine Sanctions on Oligarchs', *New York Times*, www.nytimes.com, 9 March 2022.

10 CRY HAVOC

1 '"We Need to Take a Page from North Korea's Book": Evgeny Prigozhin Speaks Even More Frankly Than Usual in New 77-Minute Interview', *Meduza*, https://meduza.io, 24 May 2023.

2 Vladimir Putin, 'Article by Vladimir Putin "On the Historical Unity of Russians and Ukrainians"', http://en.kremlin.ru, 12 July 2021.

3 'Прошлое и будущее Пригожина', *Dossier Center*, https://dossier.center, 6 July 2023.

4 Mark Galeotti, *Putin's Wars* (Oxford, 2022), pp. 113–20.

5 Andrey Guselnikov, 'Признание бойца ЧВК Вагнера: "Шойгу приказал отобрать у нас оружие"', *Ura*, https://ura.news, 22 October 2018.

6 Denis Korotkov, 'Список Вагнера', *Fontanka*, www.fontanka.ru, 21 August 2017.

7 'Частная армия для президента: история самого деликатного поручения Евгения Пригожина', *The Bell*, https://thebell.io, 29 January 2019.

8 'Евгений Пригожин о трагедии 8 февраля 2018 в Хшаме', https://telegra.ph, 12 June 2023.

9 Telegram post, @concordgroup_official, 12 June 2023.

10 Denis Korotkov, 'Охотники за паролями', *Novaya Gazeta*, https://novayagazeta.ru, 29 July 2021.

11 'Wagner's Parallel Diplomacy Embarrasses Moscow', *Africa Intelligence*, www.africaintelligence.com, 28 October 2021.

12 Evgeniy Antonov, 'Кто помогает Беглову стать следующим губернатором Петербурга и что будет, если он победит', *Bumaga*, https://paperpaper.ru, 17 July 2019.

13 Andrey Pertsev, '"He Wants His Own Deputies": Meduza's Sources Say Evgeny Prigozhin Hopes to Take Control of the Party A Just Russia in a Quid-pro-Quo with Its Leader', trans. Sam Breazeale, *Meduza*, https://meduza.io, 11 April 2023.

14 'Жаба и Минобороны. Как поссорились Евгений Викторович с Сергеем Кужугетовичем', *The Insider*, https://theins.ru, 12 May 2023.

15 Mark Krutov and Sergey Dobrynin, 'Лаборатории смерти: "Частные" армии России будущего', *Radio Svoboda*, www.svoboda.org, 19 May 2023.

16 Viktoriya Dovgan, 'Контрразведка "слила" компромат на ГРУшника в Луганске, – журналист', *Obozrevatel*, https://incident.obozrevatel.com, 16 December 2020.

17 Jack Margolin, https://twitter.com, post dated 29 June 2023.

18 Telegram post, @vchkogpu, 25 February 2023.

19 'Best of Enemies: Wagner Chief Prigozhin's Feud with Defense Minister to Blow Up in His Face', *The Insider*, https://theins.ru, 12 May 2023.

20 Krutov and Dobrynin, 'Лаборатории смерти: "Частные" армии России будущего'.

21 Lilia Yapparova, Andrey Pertsev and Alexey Slavin, 'A Mercenaries' War: How Russia's Invasion of Ukraine Led to a "Secret Mobilization" that Allowed Oligarch Evgeny Prigozhin to Win Back Putin's Favor', trans. Kevin Rothrock, *Meduza*, https://meduza.io, 14 July 2022.

22 'Best of Enemies: Wagner chief Prigozhin's Feud with Defense Minister to Blow Up in His Face'.

23 'British Intelligence Says Russia's Wagner Group Deployed to Eastern Ukraine', *Reuters*, www.reuters.com, 28 March 2023.

24 Philip Obaji Jr, 'Notorious Russian Mercenaries Pulled Out of Africa Ready for Ukraine', *Daily Beast*, www.thedailybeast.com, 31 January 2022.

25 Samer Al-Atrush and Laura Pitel, 'Russia Reduces Number of Syrian and Wagner Troops in Libya', *Financial Times*, www.ft.com, 27 April 2022.

26 Melanie Amann, Matthias Gebauer and Fidelius Schmid, 'German Intelligence Intercepts Radio Traffic Discussing the Murder of Civilians', *Der Spiegel*, www.spiegel.de, 7 April 2022.

27 Lilia Yapparova, Andrey Pertsev and Alexey Slavin, 'Грубо говоря, мы начали войну: Как отправка ЧВК Вагнера на фронт помогла Пригожину наладить отношения с Путиным – и что такое "собянинский полк"', *Meduza*, https://meduza.io, 13 July 2022.

28 Ibid.

29 David Axe, 'The Russians Are Throwing Everything They've Got at One Ukrainian Garrison', *Forbes*, www.forbes.com, 19 May 2022.

30 Telegram post, @grey_zone, 6 May 2022.

31 Oleg Chernysh, 'Кровавое наследие, которое оставили в Украине Пригожин и ЧВК "Вагнер"', *BBC*, www.bbc.com, 25 August 2023.

32 Telegram post, @grey_zone, 3 May 2022.

33 Telegram post, @grey_zone, 23 April 2023.

34 Telegram post, @dossiercenter, 16 March 2023.

35 Elena Senina, 'Евгений Пригожин заявил, что ЧВК "Вагнер" не потеряла ни одного метра освобожденной территории', *Vremya Press*, https://vremya.press, 16 March 2023.

36 'Герой России, командир ЧВК "Вагнер" Ратибор вспоминает, как с отрядом вступали в спецоперацию', https://deda14.livejournal.com, 24 June 2023.

37 Mason Clark, George Barros and Karolina Hird, 'Russian Offensive Campaign Assessment, April 20', *Institute for the Study of War*, www.understandingwar.org, 20 April 2022.

38 Jack Margolin, https://twitter.com, post dated 13 July 2023.

39 Yapparova, Pertsev and Slavin, 'Грубо говоря'.

40 Jack Margolin, https://twitter.com, post dated 3 June 2023.

41 Yaroslav Trofimov, 'Nearly Encircled, Ukraine's Last Stronghold in Luhansk Resists Russian Onslaught', *Wall Street Journal*, www.wsj.com, 10 May 2022.

42 Tatyana Katrichenko, 'Стратегическая высота: Что происходит в Лисичанске и чем важна его оборона', *Focus UA*, https://focus.ua, 16 June 2022.

43 Ivana Kottasova et al., 'Ukrainian Forces Withdraw from Lysychansk, Their Last Holdout in Key Region', *CNN*, www.cnn.com, 3 July 2022.

44 Alona Mazurenko, 'In Lysychansk, 150 People Are Buried in a Mass Grave – Haidai', *Ukrainska Pravda*, www.pravda.com.ua, 25 May 2022.

11 THE MEAT GRINDER

1 '"We Need to Take a Page from North Korea's Book": Evgeny Prigozhin Speaks Even More Frankly Than Usual in New 77-Minute Interview', *Meduza*, https://meduza.io, 24 May 2023

2 Telegram post, @netgulagu, 2 July 2022.

3 Anna Pavlova and Elizaveta Nesterova, '"В первую очередь интересуют убийцы и разбойники – вам у нас понравится". Похоже, Евгений Пригожин лично вербует наемников в колониях', *Media Zona*, https://zona.media, 6 August 2022.

4 Alex Statiev, 'Penal Units in the Red Army', *Europe Asia Studies*, LXII/5 (2010), pp. 721–47 (pp. 721–2).

5 Sergey Goryashko et al., '"Из них такое поперло, что никто не ожидал": Как заключенные реагируют на призывы вступить в "ЧВК Вагнера"', BBC, www.bbc.com, 17 September 2022.

6 Sergey Satanovskiy, 'Ольга Романова: Заключенных россиян бросают в бой первыми', DW, www.dw.com, 12 August 2022.

7 Aric Toler, 'How Wagner Gave Three Russian Crime Bosses from the 90s a New Lease of Death', *Bellingcat*, www.bellingcat.com, 13 February 2023.

8 'ЧВК "Вагнер" вербует в ростовских колониях заключенных для участия в войне в Украине', *Kavkaz Realii*, www.kavkazr.com, 1 September 2022.

9 Jack Margolin, https://twitter.com, post dated 16 August 2023.

10 Marc Santora, Eric Schmitt and Michael Levenson, 'Ukrainian Strikes May Be Slowing Russia's Advance', *New York Times*, www.nytimes.com, 19 August 2022.

11 Julian E. Barnes and Eric Schmitt, 'Russia's Shortfalls Create an Opportunity for Ukraine, Western Officials Say', *New York Times*, www.nytimes.com, 4 August 2022.

12 'Указ "Об объявлении частичной мобилизации в Российской Федерации"', http://kremlin.ru, 21 September 2022.

13 concordgroup_official, https://vk, post dated 30 September 2023.

14 Telegram post, @RKadyrov_95, 1 October 2022.

15 David Axe, 'The Ukrainian Army Reportedly Destroyed Another Russian Division', *Forbes*, www.forbes.com, 26 September 2022.

16 Tristan Fiedler and Sergei Kuznetsov, 'Russian Troops Retreat from Kherson in New Blow to Putin', *Politico*, www.politico.eu, 9 November 2022.

17 Charles Bartles, 'The Composition and Tactics of Wagner Assault Detachments', U.S. *Foreign Military Studies Office: OE Watch Commentary*, https://community.apan.org, 1 May 2023.

18 'The "Cannon Fodder" Advantage: Why Wagner Group Is More Effective on the Battlefield than the Russian Military', trans. Sam Breazeale, *Meduza*, https://meduza.io, 22 March 2023.

19 @Tatarigami_UA, https://twitter.com, post dated 22 February 2023.

20 Guy Faulconbridge, 'Video Shows Sledgehammer Execution of Russian Mercenary', *Reuters*, www.reuters.com, 13 November 2022.

21 Murtaza Hussain, 'The Grisly Cult of the Wagner Group's Sledgehammer', *The Intercept*, https://theintercept.com, 2 February 2023.

22 Telegram post, @SolovievLive, 15 January 2023.

23 Telegram post, @concordgroup_official, 10 January 2023.

24 concordgroup_official, https://vk, post dated 13 January 2023.

25 Telegram post, @mod_russia, 13 January 2023.

26 Ibid.

27 Jack Margolin, https://twitter.com, post dated 29 June 2023.

28 Telegram post, @concordgroup_official, 9 February 2023.

29 Telegram post, @concordgroup_official, 15 February 2023.

30 Telegram post, @concordgroup_official, 21 February 2023.

31 Vladimir Mikhailov, '"Вагнеровцы" на Донбассе просят у Минобороны РФ оружие и не получают его: Эксперт объясняет, как военные "показывают конкуренту, кто хозяин"', *Current Time*, www.currenttime.tv, 17 February 2023.

32 Telegram post, @concordgroup_official, 16 February 2023.

33 Olga Ivshina, Anastasia Lotareva and Sergey Goryashko, 'Убойная сила: как Минобороны России вербует заключенных из колоний', *BBC*, www.bbc.com, 3 May 2023.

34 Jack Margolin, https://twitter.com, post dated 23 February 2023.

35 John Hardie, 'Moscow Shakes Up Command of Its Forces in Ukraine (Again)', *FDD Long War Journal*, www.longwarjournal.org, 12 January 2023.

36 Matt Murphy, 'Wagner, Prigozhin, Putin and Shoigu: Bitter Rivalries that Led to a Rebellion', *BBC*, www.bbc.com, 25 June 2023.

37 'Wagner Chief Urges Russians to Press Army to Give Fighters Ammo', *Moscow Times*, www.themoscowtimes.com, 22 February 2023.

38 Murphy, 'Wagner, Prigozhin, Putin and Shoigu.

39 Telegram post, @concordgroup_official, 22 February 2023.

40 Telegram post, @concordgroup_official, 5 March 2023.

41 Telegram post, @concordgroup_official, 9 March 2023.

42 Jack Margolin, https://twitter.com, post dated 29 August 2023.

43 Tara Law, 'Gazprom Is Launching a "Private Military": Could It Be the Next Wagner Group?', *Time*, https://time.com, 14 February 2023.

44 'Госдума рекомендовала бизнесу закупать ПВО', *Moscow Times*, www.moscowtimes.ru, 4 March 2023.

45 Elizaveta Fokht and Ilya Barabanov, '"Поток" под Бахмутом: Что известно о ЧВК, связанных с "Газпромом"', *BBC*, www.bbc.com, 16 May 2023.

46 Telegram post, @evgeniylinin_official, 23 April 2023.

47 Tatyana Kozak, 'Не только "Вагнер": Троих бойцов российской ЧВК "Редут" осудили за наемничество и военные преступления', *Graty*, https://graty.me, 1 February 2023.

48 Polina Ivanova, Christopher Miller and Max Seddon, '"Stream" and "Torch": The Gazprom-Backed Militias Fighting in Ukraine', *Financial Times*, www.ft.com, 1 June 2023.

49 Mark Krutov and Sergey Dobrynin, 'Лаборатории смерти: "Частные" армии России будущего', *Radio Svoboda*, www.svoboda.org, 19 May 2023.

50 Ivanova, Miller and Seddon, '"Stream" and "Torch"'.

51 Anastasia Chumakova, 'Нас продали в ЧВК: Будем держать дорогу в Бахмуте. Что делать, не знаю', *ASTRA*, https://telegra.ph, 11 April 2023, archived at https://web.archive.org.

52 Telegram post, @brussinf, 21 April 2023.

53 Denis Korotkov, 'Казаки, эльф и Аркадий Ротенберг', *Dossier Center*, https://dossier.center, 14 August 2023.

54 Jack Margolin, https://twitter.com, post dated 4 April 2023.

55 Korotkov, 'Казаки, эльф и Аркадий Ротенберг'.

56 Ibid.

57 'География культурной станицы', *Fontanka*, www.fontanka.ru, 18 February 2023.

58 'Putin Chef's Kisses of Death: Russia's Shadow Army's State-Run Structure Exposed', *Bellingcat*, www.bellingcat.com, 14 August 2020.

59 Korotkov, 'Казаки, эльф и Аркадий Ротенберг'.

60 Maria Zholobova, 'Глава Крыма создал собственную ЧВК: Она связана с Евгением Пригожиным', *iStories*, https://istories.media, 23 March 2023.

61 Ann M. Simmons and Isabel Coles, 'Wagner Says 20,000 of Its Troops Have Died Taking Ukraine's Bakhmut', *Wall Street Journal*, www.wsj.com, 24 May 2023.

62 David Rising, 'Russia's Wagner Boss Threatens Bakhmut Pullout in Ukraine', *AP*, https://apnews.com, 5 May 2023.

63 Telegram post, @concordgroup_official, 3 May 2023.

64 Telegram post, @concordgroup_official, 4 May 2023.

65 Telegram post, @concordgroup_official, 5 May 2023.

66 'Wagner Group to Get More Ammo after Bakhmut Pull-Out Threat', *Moscow Times*, www.themoscowtimes.com, 7 May 2023.

67 Mikhail Komin, 'Как кувалда в масло: Кто в российской элите может поддерживать Пригожина', *Carnegie Politika*, https://carnegieendowment.org, 26 June 2023.

68 Telegram post, @concordgroup_official, 21 May 2023.

69 Katherine Tangalakis-Lippert, 'Putin Praises Wagner Mercenaries for Bakhmut Claims of Victory, His First Time Directly Crediting the For-Hire Army for Their Military Efforts', *Business Insider*, www.businessinsider.com, 21 May 2023.

70 Andrey Pertsev, '"They Thought the Risk Was Nil": Prigozhin's Armed Insurrection Caught Kremlin Officials Off Guard. Meduza's Sources Say that by All Appearances, Attempts to Negotiate Have Failed', trans. Anna Razumnaya, *Meduza*, https://meduza.io, 24 June 2023.

71 Telegram post, @astrapress, 27 May 2023.

72 Alya Ponomareva, '"Армия разрушена": Блогеры о признаниях Романа Веневитина', *Radio Svoboda*, www.svoboda.org, 9 June 2023.

73 Telegram post, @concordgroup_official, 31 May 2023.

74 Jack Margolin, https://twitter.com, post dated 11 June 2023.

12 MUTINY

1 Telegram post, @concordgroup_official, 12 June 2023.

2 Lilia Yapparova, Svetlana Reiter and Andrey Pertsev, '"There's Nobody on Earth Who Can Stop Them": What Wagner Group Veterans Have to Say about Yevgeny Prigozhin's Armed Rebellion', trans. Sam Breazeale, *Meduza*, https://meduza.io, 24 June 2023.

3 Bojan Pancevski, 'Wagner's Prigozhin Planned to Capture Russian Military Leaders', *Wall Street Journal*, www.wsj.com, 28 June 2023.

4 Telegram post, @NetGulagu, 1 July 2023.

5 Shane Harris and Isabelle Khurshudyan, 'Wagner Chief Offered to Give Russian Troop Locations to Ukraine, Leak Says', *Washington Post*, www.washingtonpost.com, 15 May 2023.

6 Andrey Pertsev, '"They Thought the Risk Was Nil": Prigozhin's Armed Insurrection Caught Kremlin Officials Off Guard. Meduza's Sources Say That by All Appearances, Attempts to Negotiate Have Failed', trans. Anna Razumnaya, *Meduza*, https://meduza.io, 24 June 2023.

7 'Wagner Chief Says Russia's Invasion of Ukraine Unjustified', *Moscow Times*, www.themoscowtimes.com, 23 June 2023.

8 Telegram post, @concordgroup_official, 23 June 2023.

9 Telegram post, @razgruzka_vagnera, 23 June 2023.

10 'Пригожин начал свой "мятеж" после того, как российская армия якобы нанесла удар по лагерю его наемников "Медуза" внимательно посмотрела видео с "последствиями удара" и уверена: это наверняка фейк', *Meduza*, https://meduza.io, 23 June 2023.

11 Yapparova, Reiter and Pertsev, 'There's Nobody on Earth Who Can Stop Them'.

12 Pertsev, 'They Thought the Risk Was Nil'.

13 Telegram post, @genprocrf, 23 June 2023.

14 'На Первом канале показали экстренный выпуск новостей о "мятеже" Евгения Пригожина: Екатерина Андреева процитировала ФСБ, которая назвала его приказы "преступными и предательскими"', *Meduza*, https://meduza.io, 23 June 2023.

15 'Силовики начали рейды по домам бойцов ЧВК "Вагнера": им угрожают "госизменой" за "присягу" Пригожину. Некоторых задержала ФСБ, сообщили "Важным историям" родные', *iStories*, https://istories.media, 24 June 2023.

16 '"Пока не поздно, нужно остановить колонны и подчиниться воле президента": Генерал Суровикин призвал бойцов ЧВК Вагнера

"решить вопросы мирным путем", *Meduza*, https://meduza.io, 23 June 2023.

17 'Пригожин объяснил высшим чинам российской армии, что с ним надо говорить на вы Презрительные переговоры основателя ЧВК с замминистра обороны Евкуровым и замначальника Генштаба Алексеевым. Расшифровка беседы', *Meduza*, https://meduza.io, 24 June 2023.

18 'В Москве, Подмосковье и Воронежской области введен режим "контртеррористической операции"', *Meduza*, https://meduza.io, 23 June 2023.

19 'Минобороны РФ обратилось к бойцам ЧВК Вагнера: "Вас обманом втянули в преступную авантюру Пригожина"', *Meduza*, https://meduza.io, 24 June 2023.

20 'В Воронежской области повреждены 19 домов из-за перестрелки во время прохождения колонны ЧВК Вагнера: Baza сообщила, что наемники сбили два вертолета и самолет', *Meduza*, https://meduza.io, 25 June 2023.

21 Stijn Mitzer and Jakub Janovsky, 'Chef's Special: Documenting Equipment Losses During the 2023 Wagner Group Mutiny', *Oryx*, www.oryxspioenkop.com, 24 June 2023.

22 Vladimir Putin, 'Обращение к гражданам России', https://kremlin.ru, 24 June 2023.

23 Sebastien Roblin, 'The Wagner Mutiny Hit Russia's Air Force Hard. Really Hard', *Popular Mechanics*, www.popularmechanics.com, 27 June 2023.

24 Kateryna Stepanenko et al., 'Russian Offensive Campaign Assessment, June 24, 2023', www.understandingwar.org, 24 June 2023.

25 'Под Минском задержаны 32 боевика иностранной частной военной компании (подробности)', *Belta*, www.belta.by, 29 July 2020.

26 'Belarus Ruler Lukashenko Says Russia Lying over "Mercenaries"', *BBC*, www.bbc.com, 4 August 2020.

27 'Inside Wagnergate: Ukraine's Brazen Sting Operation to Snare Russian Mercenaries', *Bellingcat*, www.bellingcat.com, 17 November 2021.

28 Ibid.

29 Telegram post, @pul_1, 24 June 2023.

30 'Пригожин: "Мы разворачиваем колонны и уходим обратно"', *Radio Svoboda*, www.svoboda.org, 24 June 2023.

31 'Prigozhin, Wagner Troops Cheered as They Leave Rostov-on-Don as March on Moscow Ends', *Radio Free Europe*, www.rferl.org, 25 June 2023.

32 '"We Know the Vast Majority of Wagner Fighters Are Patriots": In Another Short Speech, Putin Condemned Prigozhin's Rebellion While Letting Participants off the Hook', *Meduza*, https://meduza.io, 26 June 2023.

33 Valerie Hopkins, 'One Big Winner of Kremlin–Wagner Clash? The Dictator Next Door', *New York Times*, www.nytimes.com, 25 June 2023.

34 '"We Gave a Master Class": Prigozhin's First Public Statement since Wagner Group's 24-Hour Rebellion', *Meduza*, https://meduza.io, 26 June 2023.

35 Andrey Pertsev, '"Putin Was Nowhere to Be Found": An Inside Look into the Kremlin's Attempted Negotiations with Prigozhin and Why It Took Lukashenko to Put an End to the Rebellion', *Meduza*, https://meduza.io, 25 June 2023.

36 Andrey Pertsev, 'Is Prigozhin's Mutiny the Nail in the Coffin for Putin's Golden Boy, Dyumin?', *Carnegie Politika*, https://carnegieendowment.org, 7 July 2023.

37 Mattathias Schwartz, 'Exclusive: The Secret Calendar of Russian Rebel Warlord Yevgeny Prigozhin Revealed', *Business Insider*, www.businessinsider.com, 7 July 2023.

38 Pertsev, 'Is Prigozhin's Mutiny the Nail in the Coffin for Putin's Golden Boy, Dyumin?'.

39 Irek Murtazin, 'Задачи ставили генералы', *Novaya Gazeta*, https://novayagazeta.ru, 29 June 2023.

40 Pertsev, 'Putin Was Nowhere to Be Found'.

41 'Prigozhin Has Moved to Belarus, and Russia Won't Press Charges for Mutiny, *AP*, https://apnews.com, 27 June 2023.

42 Aleksey Kolesnikov, 'Путин рассказал "Ъ" подробности встречи с бойцами ЧВК "Вагнер"', *Kommersant*, www.kommersant.ru, 13 July 2023.

43 Telegram post, @grey_zone, 15 July 2023.

44 Telegram post, @orchestra_w, 16 July 2023.

45 Suleiman Al-Khalidi and Maya Gebeily, 'Syria Brought Wagner Fighters to Heel as Mutiny Unfolded in Russia', *Reuters*, www.reuters.com, 7 July 2023.

46 'Prigozhin-Controlled Russian Media Group Shuts after Mutiny', *Reuters*, www.reuters.com, 2 July 2023.

47 'Компании Пригожина за месяц после мятежа заключили госконтрактов не менее чем на 2 млрд рублей', *Agentstvo*, www.agents.media, 3 August 2023.

48 Jack Margolin, https://twitter.com, post dated 9 July 2023.

49 Vitaly Shevchenko, 'Wagner Group: Russian State Media Takes Aim at Prigozhin', *BBC*, www.bbc.com, 6 July 2023.

50 Telegram post, @belamova, 26 June 2023.

51 Sarah Cahlan and Meg Kelly, 'Satellite Imagery Shows What Could Be Wagner's Future Camp in Belarus', *Washington Post*, www.washingtonpost.com, 30 June 2023.

52 'Inside a Camp in Tsel, Belarus, which Has Been Offered to the Russian Mercenary Group Wagner', *Sky News*, https://news.sky.com, 7 July 2023.

53 Timofey Ermakov, 'Эксклюзивное интервью с Лотосом: что ждет ЧВК "Вагнер"', https://telegra.ph, 7 July 2023.

54 Telegram post, @razgruzka_vagnera, 19 July 2023.

55 'Poland Detains Russians Spreading Wagner Group Propaganda', *DW*, www.dw.com, 14 August 2023.

56 'Wagner Will Continue Mali, C. Africa Operations – Lavrov', *Moscow Times*, www.themoscowtimes.com, 26 June 2023.

57 Benoit Faucon, Joe Parkinson and Drew Hinshaw, 'Putin Moves to Seize Control of Wagner's Global Empire', *Wall Street Journal*, www.wsj.com, 28 June 2023.

58 Telegram post, @riafan_everywhere, 28 June 2023.

59 Benoit Faucon et al., 'The Last Days of Wagner's Prigozhin', *Wall Street Journal*, www.wsj.com, 24 August 2023.

60 'Wagner Forces Arrive in CAR before Referendum', *Al Jazeera*, www.aljazeera.com, 17 July 2023.

61 John Lechner and Vianney Ingasso, 'Wagner Woes and a Rebel Crackdown: A Briefing on the Central African Republic's Shifting Conflict', *New Humanitarian*, www.thenewhumanitarian.org, 7 September 2023.

62 Telegram post, @convoywe, 21 August 2023.

63 Nikita Kondratev, Anastasia Korotkova and Maria Zholobova, 'Накануне гибели Пригожина Минобороны начало набор бойцов в Африку через свои ЧВК, выяснили "Важные истории"', *iStories*, https://istories.media, 23 August 2023.

64 Telegram post, @dnobangui, 19 July 2023.

65 Irina Pankratova, 'В интернете пять дней обсуждали гибель Евгения Пригожина: Кто запустил этот слух', *The Bell*, https://thebell.io, 16 October 2019.

66 'Yevkurov's Visit to Libya Signals Continued Russian Role after Prigozhin's Demise', *Arab Weekly*, https://thearabweekly.com, 25 August 2023.

67 'Russian Army Officials Visit Libya after Haftar Invite', *Moscow Times*, www.themoscowtimes.com, 22 August 2023.

13 THE END AND THE BEGINNING

1 Lilia Yapparova and Svetlana Reiter, '"He Considered Himself Indestructible": Meduza Spoke to Wagner Mercenaries about the Plane Crash that Killed Yevgeny Prigozhin', trans. Emily Laskin, *Meduza*, https://meduza.io, 24 August 2023.

2 '"Это был человек сложной судьбы. Талантливый человек": Путин впервые прокомментировал крушение самолета Пригожина', *Meduza*, https://meduza.io, 24 August 2023.

3 Tuqa Khalid, 'Wagner Affiliated Channel Claims Prigozhin's Plane Was Shot Down by Defense Ministry', *Al Arabiya*, https://english.alarabiya.net, 23 August 2023.

4 Michael R. Gordon et al., 'Early Intelligence Suggests Prigozhin Was Assassinated, U.S. Officials Say', *Wall Street Journal*, www.wsj.com, 24 August 2023.

5 Riley Mellen, Muyi Xiao and Robin Stein, 'Flight Data and Video Analysis Point to a Catastrophic Midair Event in the Russian Plane Crash', *New York Times*, www.nytimes.com, 24 August 2023.

6 Telegram post, @vchkogpu, 24 August 2023.

7 Telegram post, @strelkovii, 24 August 2023.

8 Andrew Roth, 'Is Yevgeny Prigozhin Really Dead? Not Everyone Is Convinced', *The Guardian*, www.theguardian.com, 24 August 2023.

9 Liliya Yapparova, '"Он считал себя неприкасаемым. Решил, что бессмертный" "Медуза" выяснила, что о крушении самолета Пригожина думают сами наемники из ЧВК Вагнера', *Meduza*, https://meduza.io, 24 August 2023.

10 'Experts React: What the Prigozhin Plane Crash Reveals about Putin, the Wagner Group's Future, and the War in Ukraine', Atlantic Council, www.atlanticcouncil.org, 23 August 2023.

11 Nina Petlyanova, 'Частное военное кладбище "Вагнера"', *Novaya Gazeta*, https://novayagazeta.ru, 30 August 2023.

12 Anton Troianovski et al., 'After Prigozhin's Death, a High-Stakes Scramble for His Empire', *New York Times*, www.nytimes.com, 8 September 2023.

13 Telegram post, @grey_zone, 13 September 2023.

14 Telegram post, @max_shugaley, 7 September 2023.

15 Andrew Osborn, 'Pro-War Nationalist Putin Critic Girkin Charged with Inciting Extremism', *Reuters*, www.reuters.com, 22 July 2023.

16 Pjotr Sauer, '"We Have Already Lost": Far-Right Russian Bloggers Slam Military Failures', *The Guardian*, www.theguardian.com, 8 September 2022.

17 Shaun Walker, 'Putin's Absurd, Angry Spectacle Will Be a Turning Point in His Long Reign', *The Guardian*, www.theguardian.com, 21 February 2022.

18 Allen Maggard, 'Russia's Wagner Group Is a Feature Not a Bug of the Putin Regime', *Atlantic Council*, www.atlanticcouncil.org, 4 April 2023.

19 Matthew Luxmoore and Benoit Faucon, 'Russian Private Military Companies Move to Take Over Wagner Fighters', *Wall Street Journal*, www.wsj.com, 5 September 2023.

20 Telegram post, @grey_zone, 16 September 2023.

21 Jack Watling and Nick Reynolds, 'Meatgrinder: Russian Tactics in the Second Year of Its Invasion of Ukraine', Royal United Services Institute, www.rusi.org, 19 May 2023, pp. 5–6.

22 Charles Bartles, 'The Composition and Tactics of Wagner Assault Detachments', u.s. Foreign Military Studies Office: oe Watch Commentary, https://community.apan.org, 1 May 2023.

23 Watling and Reynolds, 'Meatgrinder', pp. 5–6.

24 Frédéric Bobin and Morgane Le Cam, 'Africa Corps, le nouveau label de la présence russe au Sahel', *Le Monde*, www.lemonde.fr, 15 December 2023.

25 Telegram post, @ordenbat, 17 August 2023.

26 Telegram post, @grey_zone, 19 August 2023.

27 Michael R. Gordon and Vivian Salama, 'Russia's Wagner Group Plans to Send Air Defenses to Hezbollah, U.S. Says', *Wall Street Journal*, www.wsj.com, 2 November 2023.

28 'Fact Sheet: The Kremlin's Efforts to Spread Deadly Disinformation in Africa', U.S. Department of State, www.state.gov, 12 February 2024.

29 John Lechner and Sergey Eledinov, 'Is Africa Corps a Rebranded Wagner Group?', *Foreign Policy*, https://foreignpolicy.com, 7 February 2024.

30 Frédéric Bobin and Morgane Le Cam, '"Africa Corps": Russia's Sahel Presence Rebranded', *Le Monde*, www.lemonde.fr, 17 December 2023.

31 'Mali Junta Seizes Strategic Northern Stronghold of Kidal', *France24*, https://france24.com, 14 November 2023.

32 Telegram post, @rsotmdivision, 22 November 2023.

33 Lechner and Eledinov, 'Is Africa Corps a Rebranded Wagner Group?'.

34 Rachel Chason and Michael Birnbaum, 'U.S Struggles for Influence in West Africa as Military Juntas Rise', *Washington Post*, www.washingtonpost.com, 25 February 2024.

35 '"Проект К закрылся": ЧВК "Вагнер" после мятежа распустила всех бывших заключенных по домам', *iStories*, https://istories.media, 19 July 2023.

36 John Hardie, 'Russia's National Guard to Get Tanks Following Wagner Mutiny', *FDD's Long War Journal*, www.longwarjournal.org, 29 June 2023.

37 Nikita Kondratev, 'Росгвардия начала принимать на службу наемников ЧВК из числа помилованных заключенных', *iStories*, https://istories.media, 11 September 2023.

38 Telegram post, @wagnernew, 16 September 2023.

39 Telegram post, @otechestvo_by, 28 October 2023.

40 Anna Skok, '"Вагнер" в Новосибирске вновь начал набирать бойцов на СВО – с судимыми контракты заключать не будут', *Novosibirsk Online*, https://ngs.ru, 1 November 2023.

41 'State Duma Legislators Set Out to Expand Russia's Riot Police with "Volunteer" Units, While Also Protecting It from Public Criticism', *Meduza*, https://meduza.io, 22 September 2023.

42 Telegram post, @razgruzka_vagnera, 5 February 2024.

43 Telegram post, @vchkogpu, 16 March 2024.

44 Sergey Gusarov, 'Контракт с Родиной: бывшие сотрудники ЧВК "Вагнер" создали отряд "Камертон" в составе спецназа "Ахмат"', *RT*, https://russian.rt.com, 2 November 2023.

45 Yapparova and Reiter, 'He Considered Himself Indestructible'.

46 John Mueller, 'War Is on the Rocks', *War on the Rocks*, https://warontherocks.com, 1 July 2020.

47 'Who Are the Freedom of Russia Legion and Russian Volunteer Corps?', *Reuters*, www.reuters.com, 5 June 2022.

48 'The "Cannon Fodder" Advantage: Why Wagner Group Is More Effective on the Battlefield than the Russian Military', trans. Sam Breazeale, *Meduza*, https://meduza.io, 22 March 2023.

49 J. D. Capelouto, 'Zelenskyy Tells UN Assembly: "Evil Cannot Be Trusted – Ask Prigozhin", *Semafor*, www.semafor.com, 19 September 2023.

50 Sean McFate, *Mercenaries and War: Understanding Private Armies Today* (Washington, DC, 2019), available at https://ndupress.ndu.edu.

ACKNOWLEDGEMENTS

There are many people, more than I can name, whom I am deeply indebted to for their contributions of time and knowledge. Their support was essential to the process of researching and writing this book and my work on Wagner over the last seven years. They include John Lechner, Candace Rondeaux, Amy Mackinnon, Sorcha Macleod, Stella Cooper, Brian Castner, Sean McFate, Eva Kahan, Daria Kaleniuk, Ethan Krauss, Alec Bertina, Kimberly Marten, Christiaan Triebert, Julia Steers, Amel Guettatfi, Lilia Yapparova, Isaac Zukin, Eiliv Flydal, Erin Banco, Varun Vira, Alice Speri and Jade McGlynn.

This book would not have been possible without the courageous efforts of Ukrainian, Russian and Sudanese journalists and activists. They have illuminated much of what we know about the Wagner Group at great personal risk and are cited frequently in these pages. To those I have known personally and to those who I've only encountered through their fearless writing, thank you.

INDEX

Abramovich, Roman 39
Afghanistan 48, 50, 59, 65, 181
AFRIC (Association for Free Research
 and International Cooperation)
 165–6
Africa
 countering criminal networks
 158–9
 Sahel region *see* Burkina Faso;
 Chad; Mali; Niger; Sudan
 Ukraine invasion (2022), Wagner
 Rebellion 257–62, 268, 270, 272,
 276, 282–4
 Wagner expansion prevention
 156–7, 159–60
 Wagner Group expansion
 102–3
 Western governments and
 partnerships and objectives
 157–60
 see also individual countries
Alekseev, Vladimir 88, 180, 184–6,
 189, 220, 239–40, 241, 242
Alliance for Mining 167–8
Alrosa diamonds 168
Angola 46, 47, 151, 165, 168, 226
Apachev, Akim (rapper) 20
al-Assad, Bashar 17, 56, 60, 80–84,
 92, 94, 96, 132
Assault Detachments (shos) 69, 70,
 78, 82–3, 84, 106, 113, 117–21, 124,
 194
Aurum 21, 196

Averyanov, Andrey 258, 272, 276
Azzam, Mansour 86, 96–7

Bakhmut *see* Ukraine invasion
 (2022), Bakhmut
Barlow, Eeben 45–6, 47, 66, 98, 165
al-Bashir, Omar 98–9, 100, 101, 107,
 108, 110, 154, 156, 162, 166
battalion tactical group (BTG) 74, 82
Bednov, Aleksandr 'Batman' 71–2, 73
Beglov, Aleksandr 31, 183, 218
Belarus exile, Wagner Rebellion
 245–6, 247, 250–51, 253–6, 259,
 268–9, 273, 279
Bellingcat 69, 74–5, 119–20, 171–2,
 200, 246
'Bes' (Budko) 120–21, 194
The Best in Hell (film) 21, 194, 196, 205
Blackwater 43, 48–9, 134, 287
Bogatov, Andrey 'Brodyaga' 22, 84,
 93, 206, 217, 250, 279
Bondarenko, Aleksander 'Granit' 21,
 104–5, 120
Bout, Viktor 131, 159, 258
branding, effective 15–16, 19–20, 192,
 202, 224, 273, 279, 280, 283, 286
breweries 162
'Brodyaga' (Bogatov) 22, 84, 206,
 250, 279
Broker Expert 100, 163, 170
Budko, Nikolai 'Bes' 120–21, 194
Burkina Faso 146, 150, 151–2, 272,
 283–4

Bush, George 24, 30
Bychkov, Petr 109, 116

Capital Legal Services 171–2
catering business (Prigozhin) 24–5,
    28, 29–34, 170, 181, 183, 218–19
Central African Republic (CAR) 8,
    19–20, 21, 103, 110–25, 143, 166,
    279, 287
  armed forces (FACA) 114, 116, 118,
    121, 123, 124, 125
  arms trafficking and corruption
    111–12
  Assault Detachments 113, 117–21,
    124, 194
  Bush War 121–5
  Coalition of Patriots for Change
    (CPC) 114
  Cross of Military Valour 183
  Diamville 162, 163, 168
  French peacekeeping force 122
  Fulani ethnic group 123, 125
  human rights violations 123–4
  journalistic investigations into
    Wagner 115–16
  Libya, CAR-registered aircraft
    130–31
  Lobaye Invest company 113
  Ndasimma gold mine 162, 164, 167
  security work and training 112–13,
    114, 118–19, 120, 121
  Ukraine and Wagner Rebellion
    effects 257–8, 260–61, 270, 272,
    283
  UN arms embargo 112
  UN mission (MINUSCA) 114, 115,
    118, 123
  Wood International Group SARLU
    162
Chad 122, 146, 155–6
Chechnya 8, 52, 59, 65, 192
  Akhmat unit 196, 215, 229, 285,
    288
Chekalov, Valeriy 263–4, 265, 270,
    272

'Chief' (Shevchuk) 210, 211
commercial activities 161–75
  commercial industry and influence
    165–9
  as financial lifeline 166–7
  network of companies 169–74
  opaque market operations and
    income estimates 163–5
  Russian state as funding source
    165, 166–7
  and sanctions 171–3
  see also individual companies
Concord 30, 31–3, 85, 99, 100, 169,
    251, 263
Conoco Fields (Khasham) Battle,
    Syria 80, 93–7, 120, 182, 211
Convoy Security, Ukraine invasion
    (2022) 223–7, 260, 276, 277–8
Cossacks 50–51, 58–9, 73, 75, 120, 225
Crimea 39–40, 72, 79, 185
cryptocurrency use 173

Dagalo, Mohamed Hamdan
    'Hemedti' 98, 100, 101, 154, 156
Debaltseve Battle 75–8
'Ded' (Gabidullin) 70, 73, 80, 81–2,
    92, 95, 223, 269–70, 286
Degtyarev, Sergey 59, 61, 62, 69
Diamville 162, 163, 168
Dobronravin, Nikolai 107, 110–11
Donbas 40, 72–3, 186, 196, 245
Donetsk 40, 76, 178, 196, 202
Dossier Centre, London 66, 100–101,
    111, 180
Dyumin, Aleksey 67, 248, 249

Elizarov, Anton 'Lotos' 120–21, 191,
    210, 217, 236, 250, 253–4, 269–70,
    274, 279, 284–6
Emelyanov, Aleksander 97, 120, 124
Epishkin, Sergey 41–2, 53
Evro Polis 85–7, 96–7, 107, 111, 169,
    170, 195, 263
Executive Outcomes EO 45–7, 66, 165

fascist and neo-pagan imagery 16,
17–18, 70–71
films 21, 170, 194, 196, 205
flag 23
Fomin, Maksim 'Vladlen Tatarskiy'
215, 218, 219–20
Foundation for the Defence of
National Values 21, 166
France, Mali involvement 139, 142,
146, 147, 148
future of global conflict 290–93
'peace enforcement' operations
292–3

Gabidullin, Marat 'Ded' 70, 73, 80,
81–2, 92, 95, 223, 269–70, 286
Gaddafi, Muammar 21, 127
Gazprom Security 51–2, 53, 220–23,
226, 276, 277–8, 288
see also Ukraine invasion (2022)
Geneva Conventions 44, 188
Gerasimov, Valeriy 215, 231, 233,
235–6, 239, 248, 254, 260, 268,
274–5, 286, 289
Girkin, Igor 'Strelkov' 214, 267, 273–4
Goita, Assimi 139, 142, 144, 147, 149
Gorbenko, Igor 28, 29, 31
'Granit' (Bondarenko) 21, 104–5, 120
Gusev, Vadim 41–2, 53–5, 59–61, 225

Haftar, Khalifa 126, 127, 129, 130,
131–2, 133, 134, 135–6, 155, 262
'Hemedti' (Dagalo) 98, 100, 101, 154,
156

'Iceman' (Kitaev) 120, 121, 250, 279
Insider 119, 184–5, 186
Internet Research Agency (IRA) 35–7,
99, 107, 108
see also online media use
Iraq 41–2, 50
Nisour Square massacre 48–9
ISIS Hunters, Syria 19, 23, 126–7
Islamic State 60, 61, 83, 104, 142, 146,
148–9

Ismail al-Abdallah, Muhammed Taha
execution 18–19, 20, 22, 90, 121
Israel 107–8, 158–9, 282
Ivanov, Mikhail 187, 188

Kadyrov, Ramzan 175, 192, 196,
204–5, 213, 215, 229, 233, 285, 288
Kalashnikov, Vyacheslav 59
Karaziy, Anatoliy 184–5, 186
Kherson 189, 204, 207, 226
'Khrustal' (Suvorov) 281, 282
Kitaev, Vladimir 'Iceman' 120, 121,
250, 279
Kurchenko, Sergey 179
Kuznetsov, Aleksandr 'Ratibor' 8, 22,
70, 269, 270, 279, 286
in Libya 137
in Sudan 106, 107
in Syria 84, 85, 93
in Ukraine 194–5, 230
and Wagner Rebellion 235, 236,
250

Lakhta project 36–7
Lavrov, Sergey 112, 143, 183, 257
Le Pen, Marine 39
Lebedev, Andrey 65, 210, 211
Libya 8, 21, 103, 126–38, 158, 166, 194,
262, 272, 279
Al Jufra Airbase 126–7, 128, 132,
136, 144, 155
CAR-registered aircraft 130–31
ceasefire negotiations 137
Government of National Accord
(GNA) 127–8, 137
Libyan National Army (LNA)
127–8, 133, 136, 137
oil fields 136
Prigozhin in 129, 130, 136
Project Opus 134–6, 159, 287
Syrian mercenaries in 126–7, 128,
133, 137
Tripoli advance 136–7
Turkey involvement 128, 131, 133,
135, 136, 137

UAE involvement 130, 131–3, 134,
    135, 159
UN arms embargo 128, 130, 133
U.S. sanctions 133
Wagner air operation bases 126–7,
    128–31, 132, 136, 137–8, 144, 155
Wagner Assault Detachments
    126–7, 128–9, 137
Lobaye Invest 113
'Lotos' (Elizarov) 120–21, 191, 210,
    217, 236, 250, 253–4, 269–70, 274,
    279, 284–6
Luhansk 40, 64–5, 68, 71, 72, 73, 75,
    78, 178, 185, 196–7, 211
Lukashenko, Aleksandr 175, 245–6,
    247–8, 250, 253
Lysychansk 23, 192, 196–7

M Invest 99–101, 107, 111, 118–19, 130,
    144, 163, 170
Madagascar 101, 104, 120, 162, 164–5,
    224, 225
Main Line 57, 58, 170
Mali 103, 139–60, 166, 261–2, 270,
    272, 279, 283, 287
    cattle raiding 149
    Dogon village self-defence groups
      148
    French involvement 139, 142, 146,
      147, 148
    human rights abuses 139–40,
      146–7, 149
    insurgents, treatment of 140–42
    Islamic State Sahel Province (ISSP)
      146, 148–9
    Jama'at Nusrat ul-Islam wa al-
      Muslimin (JNIM) militants
      145–6, 148–9
    Malian Armed Forces (FAMA)
      143, 145, 146, 147, 149
    Moura massacre 140–41
    Movement for the Salvation of
      Azawad (MSA) 148
    Robinet El Ataye massacre 146
    and Sahel region 142–5, 283

and Sahel region, Western
    engagement failures 143–4
Tuareg Self-Defence Group and
    Allies (GATIA) 148
UN MINUSMA mission 147, 152
Wagner's airlift bases 145, 147–8
Wagner's fee 144–5
Wagner's social media and fake
    posts 142–3
Malyshev crime syndicate 28
Maslov, Ivan 'Miron' 144–5
'Mazay' (Pikalov) 119–20, 223–5,
    226–7, 260, 276
Medvedev, Dmitry 31, 99, 183
'Mekhan' (Titov) 59, 61, 62, 69, 217,
    236, 250, 279, 286
mercenaries
    modern, rise of 44–7
    origins 43–4
    see also individual countries;
      private military and security
      companies (PMSCS)
Meroe Gold 99–101, 107, 110, 162, 163,
    167–8
Meroe Gold company 99–101, 107,
    110, 162, 163, 167–8
Midas Resources 161–2
Milonov, Vitaliy 192, 195
Mirilashvili, Mikhail 28, 30–31
'Miron' (Maslov) 144–5
Mizintsev, Mikhail 181, 229, 231
Moran Security 54–9, 61, 67, 170,
    184, 225
    Syrian Express/Odesa Network
      companies 55–8, 67
Mozambique 21, 104–5, 120, 151, 164,
    194, 226, 287

Nagin, Aleksey 'Terek' 13, 21, 194, 195,
    196, 206, 217
Navalny, Aleksey 33, 38, 174, 175, 243,
    272
Ndasimma gold mine 162, 164, 167
neo-pagan imagery 16, 17–18, 70–71
Neva-Shans company (Putin) 29

New Island restaurant 24, 30
Niger 142, 146, 150, 152–3, 258
Nigeria 54–5, 58, 142, 158
'Ninth' *see* Utkin, Dmitry
Nizhevenok, Boris 'Zombie' 78, 106,
    120–21, 124, 217, 250, 269, 279, 286
North Korea 291

Obshchepit 170
Odesa Network *see* Syrian Express/
    Odesa Network companies
Officer Corps origins 66–71
online media use 16, 17, 18, 22–3, 114,
    142, 191, 218, 224, 252, 280
    Internet Research Agency (IRA)
        35–7, 99, 107, 108
    Telegram social network *see*
        Telegram social network
    Vkontakte (VK) social network 16,
        17, 217–18
'orchestra' references 16–19, 191, 195,
    210, 280

Palmyra 22, 83–5, 86, 93, 182, 281
Paritet Film 170
passports 68–9, 115–16, 121
Patriot Media Group 239, 257
Patrushev, Nikolai 25, 248
Perfilev, Vitaliy 119
Pikalov, Konstantin 'Mazay' 119–20,
    223–5, 226–7, 260, 276
Podolskiy, Dmitriy 'Salem' 250, 279
Popasna 23, 191–6, 205, 252, 265
Potepkin, Mikhail 99, 107, 109
Prigozhin, Evgeniy 8, 13–15, 21, 23,
    64, 89
    Bakhmut and ultimatum 227–30
    catering business 24–5, 28, 29–34,
        170, 181, 183, 218–19
    Concord 30, 31–3, 85, 99, 100, 169,
        251, 263
    early life 26–8
    Evro Polis 85–7, 96–7, 107, 111, 169,
        170, 195, 263
    in gambling industry 28–9

Hero of Russia medal 195, 199
M Invest 99–101, 107, 111, 118–19,
    130, 144, 163, 170
Main Line 57, 58, 170
Patriot Media Group 239, 257
power and state influence
    aspirations 38–40, 289
professional cross-country skier
    ambitions 26
Project Shakespeare 171, 173
as Putin's chef 30
Russia, Ministry of Defence,
    message to 57, 89, 237–8
social media exploitation 35–8
Syrian Express 55–8
Ukraine invasion (2022), feud with
    Russia 180–84
Ukraine invasion (2022), self-
    promotion and domestic
    information campaign 216–18,
    227–31, 232
Wagner connection admission
    198–9, 202–4
Wagner Group creation 66–8
Wagner Rebellion *see* Ukraine
    invasion (2022), Wagner
    Rebellion
see also individual countries;
    Wagner Group
Prigozhin, Evgeniy, family
    Lyubov (wife) 32, 175
    Pavel (son) 174, 271, 284, 285
    Polina and Veronika (daughters)
        174, 175, 232–3
    Violetta (mother) 172, 174
    Zharkoy, Samuil (step-father) 27,
        28, 271
Prigozhin, Evgeniy, plane crash and
    death 8, 263–93
    Kremlin on legacy 266
    memorials 266
    motive and timing analysis 268–71
    new mercenary market place,
        emergence of 276–9
    post-mortem 265–8

Russian government involvement
    speculation 267–8, 289–90
Russia's changed social contract
    between state and elites 275–9
St Petersburg burial 271–2
succession plan, lack of 270, 274
Wagner's resources and
    infrastructure, remains of
    279–86
Prince, Erik 134, 135, 136
prison recruitment (Project K),
    Ukraine invasion (2022)
    198–202, 203, 207–10, 211, 212,
    228, 284
private military and security
    companies (PMSCS) 41–2, 43, 44,
    45–50
    human rights abuses 48–9
    maritime security companies 50
    and War on Terror 47–8, 50, 62
    see also individual companies and
        countries; mercenaries
Project Opus, Libya 134–6, 159, 287
Project Shakespeare 171, 173
Putin, Vladimir 8, 9–10, 14, 22, 24,
    28, 31, 33–4, 92, 93
    Neva-Shans company 29
    and New Island restaurant 24, 30
    Presidential Administration 31, 35,
        66–7, 183, 268
    and Ukraine see Ukraine headings
    vertical of power (absolute
        governance) 15
    Wagner Rebellion, televised
        address and treason suggestion
        242–3
    see also Russia

'Ratibor' see Kuznetsov, Aleksander
Redut Security 61, 90–92, 184–7,
    212, 220–23, 226, 260, 276,
    277–8
    see also Ukraine invasion (2022)
Romanovsky, Kirill 115, 202
Rostec arms manufacture 41, 181

Rostov plan, Wagner Rebellion 236,
    237–41
Rotenberg, Arkady 224, 226
RSB Group 53, 69
Russia
    Alrosa diamonds 168
    Capital Legal Services 171–2
    Charter Green Light Moscow
        aircraft 130
    Federal Security Services (FSB) 17,
        52, 58–60, 61, 67–8, 187, 237, 239,
        276
    Hero of Russia medals 22, 84, 97,
        195, 199, 206
    Internet Research Agency (IRA)
        35–7, 99, 107, 108
    National Guard (Rosgvardiya) 30,
        241–2, 284–6
    New Island restaurant, St
        Petersburg 24–5, 30
    Order of Courage 97
    Presidential Administration 31, 35,
        66–7, 183, 268
    Rostec arms manufacture 41, 181
    Southern Military District 68
    spetsnaz special operations units
        52, 58, 59, 61, 67, 69, 70
    Telegram social network see
        Telegram social network
    see also Putin, Vladimir
Russia, Main Directorate of Military
    Intelligence (GRU) 52, 61, 66–9,
    75, 81, 88, 92, 121, 180, 220, 268,
    276, 279
    Military Unit 29155 272
    and Redut 184–6
    RLSPI Military Unit 35555 185, 212
Russia, Ministry of Defence 32, 38,
    58, 66, 80–81, 85, 204, 229–30,
    262, 278–80
    Africa Corps 280, 282, 283–4
    contracts with 32, 87–8, 99, 118,
        129, 236, 247
    Prigozhin's messages to 57, 89,
        237–8

and Redut 186, 187, 222
Ukraine invasion (2022), contract mandate 233–4, 235, 247, 251, 268–9
Ukraine invasion (2022), 'direct obstruction' claim (shell hunger) 213–17, 228–9, 233
Wagner's distrust of 212, 213, 214, 217, 221, 226, 228, 232, 233
see also Shoigu, Sergey
Russia Today 203
Russia–Africa Summit 257–8, 272

'Salem' (Podolskiy) 250, 279
'Sedoy' (Troshev) 22, 67, 75–6, 86, 93, 231, 236, 250–51, 259, 270, 281, 282
Serdyukov, Anatoliy 32, 181, 251
Seychelles companies 170
Shevchuk, Viktor 'Chief' 210, 211
Shoigu, Sergey 25, 57, 89, 180–84, 197, 231, 236, 241, 248, 254, 274–5, 285–6, 289
Prigozhin meetings with 129, 130, 215
Ukraine invasion (2022), contract mandate 233–4, 235, 247, 251, 268–9
see also Russia, Ministry of Defence
Shugalei, Maksim 21, 139, 151, 152, 166, 195, 273
Sidorov, Evgeniy 59, 61, 91, 184
Sierra Leone 46, 47, 165
Skripal, Sergey 69, 243, 272
Slavonic Corps 59–62, 65, 67, 81, 184, 211, 217, 220
sledgehammer symbol 19, 23, 210, 213, 252, 280
social media *see* online media use
Soledar 206, 210–12, 221, 243, 252
South Africa 50, 102, 104, 105
Executive Outcomes EO 45–7, 66, 165
Spektor, Boris 28, 29, 31

'Strelkov' (Girkin) 214, 267, 273–4
StroyTransGaz 91, 184
Sudan 7–8, 98–102, 106–10, 153–8, 166, 287, 292–3
Alliance for Mining 167–8
Aswar Multi-Activities 100–101
civil war 153–60, 281–2
civilian influence and transparency and rule of law 157–8
international arms embargo 158
Meroe Gold company 99–101, 107, 110, 162, 163, 167–8
political interference 107–9, 110
protestors, dealing with 109–10
Rapid Support Forces (RSF) 98, 101, 106–7, 109–10, 154–5, 156, 261, 282, 292–3
Russian Port Sudan naval base 101, 106, 110
Russia's military exports to 100–101
Sudanese Armed Forces (SAF) 101, 110, 154–5, 156, 168–9
Transitional Military Council (TMC) 109–10
Wagner Assault Detachments 106, 154
Sunlight (film) 21, 194
Surovikin, Sergey 93, 181, 207, 214–15, 229, 231, 233, 236–7, 239, 251
Suvorov, Vadim 'Khrustal' 281, 282
Syria 8, 17–19, 22, 59–61, 80–97, 251, 264, 270, 279, 287
Conoco Fields (Khasham) Battle 80, 93–7, 120, 182, 211
Fourth and Fifth Campaigns 80–85
ISIS Hunters' unit 19, 23, 126–7
Islamic State (ISIS) 60, 61, 83, 84, 86, 93–4, 182
Ismail al-Abdallah execution 18–19, 20, 22, 90, 121
Latakia and Homs 81, 82
mercenaries in Libya 126–7, 128, 133, 137
Palmyra 22, 83–5, 86, 93, 182, 281

Prigozhin input 80–81, 182
Redut Security and oil and gas
    sites' protection 90–92
Rusich paramilitary group 17
Slavonic Corps 59–62, 81, 91
Syrian oil and Wagner
    involvement 86–7, 90, 92, 96–7,
    272–3
U.S. Operation Inherent Resolve
    93–5
Wagner losses 81–2, 84–5
Syrian Express/Odesa Network
    companies 55–8
    see also Moran Security
Sytiy, Dmitriy 119, 162

Tambov crime syndicate 28
'Tatarskiy' (Fomin) 215, 218, 219
Telegram social network 16, 17,
    20, 192, 198, 202, 205, 208, 267,
    272–3, 285
    Prigozhin family videos 175, 232–3
    Prigozhin press service use 212–13,
    217–18
    and Wagner Rebellion 236, 238,
    239, 256, 260
    see also online media use
'Terek' (Nagin) 13, 21, 194, 195, 196,
    206, 217
Timchenko, Gennady 39, 91, 92,
    184
Titov, Vladimir 'Mekhan' 59, 61, 62,
    69, 217, 236, 250, 279, 286
Touadera, Faustin-Archange 111, 112,
    114, 116, 122, 123, 125, 162, 183,
    258, 260
Tourist (film) 21
troll farms 35–6, 99, 107
Troshev, Andrei 'Sedoy' 22, 67, 75–6,
    86, 93, 231, 236, 250–51, 259, 270,
    281, 282
Trump, Donald 37, 49, 158–9
Turkey 57–8, 128, 131, 133, 135, 136,
    137

UAE 130, 131–3, 134, 135, 159, 167
Ukraine campaign (2014–15) 14, 16,
    21, 64–79, 293
    and Crimea 39–40, 72, 79, 185
    Debaltseve Battle 75–8
    Debaltseve Battle, regular Russian
    units' involvement 77–8
    Donbas 40, 72–3, 186, 196, 245
    Donetsk 40, 76, 178, 196, 202
    Luhansk 40, 64–5, 68, 71, 72, 73,
    75, 78, 178, 185, 196–7, 211
    Wagner Group creation 66–71
    Wagner Group growth 74–5
Ukraine invasion (2022) 8, 12–13, 172,
    174, 175, 178–234, 287–9
    competition from other groups
    220–23
    and Convoy Security 223–7, 260,
    276, 277–8
    'direct obstruction' by MOD claim
    (shell hunger) 213–17, 228–9, 233
    Fomin death 219–20
    and Gazprom Security 51–2, 53,
    220–23, 226, 276, 277–8, 288
    'K' designation combatant 201
    Kherson 189, 204, 207, 226
    Lysychansk 23, 192, 196–7
    'M' designation Wagner fighter
    193, 200
    Mariupol 191
    Ministry of Defence contract
    mandate 233–4, 235, 247, 251,
    268–9
    partial conscription 204–5
    Popasna 23, 191–6, 205, 252, 265
    Prigozhin self-promotion and
    domestic information campaign
    216–18, 227–31, 232
    Prigozhin and Wagner connection
    admission 198–9, 202–4
    Prigozhin/Wagner feud with
    Russia 180–84
    prison recruitment (Project K)
    198–202, 203, 207–10, 211, 212,
    228, 284

and Redut Security 61, 90–92, 184–7, 212, 220–23, 226, 260, 276, 277–8

Russian public–private partnerships and effects on sovereignty 179–80

Soledar 206, 210–12, 221, 243, 252

Wagner recruitment adverts 191–2

Wagner's territorial defence role 232

Ukraine invasion (2022), Bakhmut 23, 192, 204–10, 212–13, 216–17, 219, 221, 223, 226, 243, 281, 284, 288

assault strategies 208–10

deserters 210

Prigozhin's ultimatum 227–30

victory 230–31, 233

Ukraine invasion (2022), Wagner Rebellion 235–62, 268

and Africa operations 257–62, 268, 270, 272, 276, 282–4

and Africa operations, authority transfer 259–60

bargain struck 245–9, 250

Belarus exile 247, 250–51, 253–6, 259, 268–9, 273, 279

Channel One emergency broadcast 239

Defence Ministry, unprovoked attack claim 237–8, 239

March for Justice 241–4

pleas to halt 239–40

Prigozhin's audio statements 237–8, 239

Prigozhin's offices and home, raids on 252–3

Putin and Wagner budget revelation 250

Putin's televised address and treason suggestion 242–3

Rostov plan 236, 237–41

Rostov plan, troop withdrawal declined 241

Voronezh attack 243–4

UN arms embargo, Libya 128, 130, 133

UN MINUSMA mission, Mali 147, 152

USA

and Lakhta project 36–7

Operation Inherent Resolve, Syria 93–5

presidential election, Russian interference 21

private military and security companies (PMSCS) 48–9

sanctions, Libya 133

Utkin, Dmitry 'Ninth' 17, 22, 59, 84, 91, 93, 129, 236, 249, 250, 256

plane crash and death 263, 265, 266, 269, 270, 272, 279

Ukraine campaign (2014–15) 65, 67, 69, 70–71, 74–6, 77, 78

Ukraine invasion (2022) 194, 200, 227, 229

Wagner Rebellion 236, 249, 250, 256

Vkontakte (VK) social network 16, 17, 217–18

see also online media use

Wagner Group

Assault Detachments (SHOS) 69, 70, 78, 82–3, 84, 106, 113, 117–21, 124, 194

as battalion tactical group (BTG) 74, 82

branding, effective 15–16, 19–20, 192, 202, 224, 273, 279, 280, 283, 286

commercial activities *see* commercial activities

Company and funding 85–90, 102–3

fascist and neo-pagan imagery 16, 17–18, 70

flag 23

online media use *see* online media use

'orchestra' references 16–19, 191,
    195, 210, 280
origins 8–10, 16, 50–53
origins, Officer Corps 66–71
sledgehammer symbol 19, 23, 210,
    213, 252, 280
see also individual countries;
    Prigozhin, Evgeniy
Wagner Rebellion *see* Ukraine
    invasion (2022), Wagner
    Rebellion
Wood International Group
    SARLU 162, 163–4

Yashchikov, Vasiliy 224, 276
Yevkurov, Yunus-Bek 187, 240–41,
    262, 272

Zakharov, Valeriy 116, 118–19, 122
Zelenskyy, Volodymyr 186, 231, 290
Zharkoy, Samuil (stepfather of
    Prigozhin) 27, 28, 271
Ziminov, Kirill 29–30, 31
Zolotov, Viktor 30, 284, 285
'Zombie' (Nizhevenok) 78, 106,
    120–21, 124, 217, 250, 269, 279,
    286